Theatre, Communication, Critical Realism

WHAT IS THEATRE?

Series Editor: Ann C. Hall

Given the changing nature of audiences, entertainment, and media, the role of theatre in twenty-first century culture is changing. The **WHAT IS THEATRE?** series brings new and innovative work in literary, cultural, and dramatic criticism into conversation with established theatre texts and trends, in order to offer fresh interpretation and highlight new or undervalued artists, works, and trends.

ANN C. HALL has published widely in the area of theatre and film studies, is president of the Harold Pinter Society, and is an active member in the Modern Language Association. In addition to her book *A Kind of Alaska: Women in the Plays of O'Neill, Pinter, and Shepard*, she has edited a collection of essays, *Making the Stage: Essays on Theatre, Drama, and Performance* and a book on the various stage, film, print, and television versions of *Gaston Leroux's Phantom of the Opera*.

Published titles:

Theatre, Communication, Critical Realism by Tobin Nellhaus

THEATRE, COMMUNICATION, CRITICAL REALISM

TOBIN NELLHAUS

THEATRE, COMMUNICATION, CRITICAL REALISM
Copyright © Tobin Nellhaus, 2010.

All rights reserved.

Portions of this book derive from the following articles and are used here, in revised form, by permission of the original publishers: "Signs, Social Ontology, and Critical Realism," *Journal for the Theory of Social Behaviour* 28.1 (1998): 1–24; "Literacy, Tyranny, and the Invention of Greek Tragedy," *Journal of Dramatic Theory and Criticism* 3.2 (1989): 53–71; "Performance Strategies, Image Schemas, and Communication Frameworks," *Performance and Cognition: Theatre Studies and the Cognitive Turn*, ed. Bruce McConachie and F. Elizabeth Hart (London: Routledge, 2006): 76–94; "Critical Realism and Performance Strategies," *Staging Philosophy: New Approaches to Theater and Performance*, ed. David Krasner and David Saltz (Ann Arbor: University of Michigan Press, 2006): 57–84; "Social Ontology and (Meta) theatricality: Reflexions on Performance and Communication in History," *Journal of Dramatic Theory and Criticism* 14.2 (2000): 3–39. Additional portions draw upon ideas first explored in "Science, History, Theater: Theorizing in Two Alternatives to Positivism," *Theatre Journal* 45.4 (1993): 505–27; "Mementos of Things to Come: Orality, Literacy and Typology in the *Biblia Pauperum*," *Printing the Written Word: The Social History of Books, c. 1450–1520*, ed. Sandra Hindman (Ithaca: Cornell University Press, 1991): 292–321; "From Embodiment to Agency: Cognitive Science, Critical Realism, the Framework of Communication," *Journal of Critical Realism* 3.1 (2004): 103–32.

Cover photo: *Bartholomew Fair* by Ben Jonson. Stratford Shakespeare Festival, 2009. Cliff Saunders as Lantern Leatherhead (center) with members of the company. Photo by David Hou. Courtesy of the Stratford Shakespeare Festival Archives.

First published in 2010 by
PALGRAVE MACMILLAN®
in the United States—a division of St. Martin's Press LLC,
175 Fifth Avenue, New York, NY 10010.

Where this book is distributed in the UK, Europe and the rest of the world, this is by Palgrave Macmillan, a division of Macmillan Publishers Limited, registered in England, company number 785998, of Houndmills, Basingstoke, Hampshire RG21 6XS.

Palgrave Macmillan is the global academic imprint of the above companies and has companies and representatives throughout the world.

Palgrave® and Macmillan® are registered trademarks in the United States, the United Kingdom, Europe and other countries.

ISBN: 978–0–230–62363–7

Library of Congress Cataloging-in-Publication Data is available from the Library of Congress.

A catalogue record of the book is available from the British Library.

Design by Newgen Imaging Systems (P) Ltd., Chennai, India.

First edition: June 2010

10 9 8 7 6 5 4 3 2 1

Printed in the United States of America.

Transferred to Digital Printing in 2011

Contents

List of Illustrations — vii
Acknowledgments — ix

Introduction — 1
1 Philosophy, History, Theatre — 19
2 Orality, Literacy, and Early Theatre — 57
3 Embodiment, Agency, and Performance Strategies — 95
4 Social Ontology, (Meta)theatricality, and the History of Communication — 143
Conclusion: New Media, Old Problems — 183

Notes — 199
Bibliography — 211
Index — 227

Illustrations

Figures

1.1	Bhaskar's Semiotic Triangle	36
1.2	The Peircean Sign (basic version)	37
1.3	The Peircean Sign (elaborated version)	38
4.1	Theatrical Doubling	154
4.2	The Ontological Shift	154
4.3	Theatrical Doubling as Semiosis	158

Table

1.1	The Ontological and Phenomenological Dimensions of Social Activity	46

Acknowledgments

My thanks first go to Bruce McConachie. Without his urging, I would never have sought one more time to turn my ideas into a book, and he kindly read an early draft. I began exploring the ideas developed here in a dissertation written under the guidance of Joe Roach, with Leonard Barkan, Sandra Hindman, and Stephen Toulmin. Howard Engelskirchen, Ruth Groff, and other members of the critical realism email discussion list debated some key issues with me. I received invaluable advice and encouragement from Talia Rodgers and LeAnn Fields. Brigitte Shull and Lee Norton shepherded the book at Palgrave Macmillan. Ellen Charendoff of the Stratford Shakespeare Festival Archives made the cover photo possible. My friendships with Susan Haedicke and E. J. Westlake have sustained me perhaps more than they know.

I conducted some of my research and writing with the support of a fellowship from the American Council of Learned Societies, and a Fulbright lectureship at the University of Helsinki. I am deeply grateful to both organizations.

One of the advantages of critical realism is its commitment to fallibilism. Indeed, one of the few unshakable truths in human possession is that error is always possible. And this is a good thing: we don't improve our understanding unless we first learn where we were mistaken. The errors in the following pages are mine alone; but at least my errors support part of my argument.

This book is written in memory of my parents, Gerhard and Arlynn.

Introduction

> Bad as it may sound, I have to admit that I cannot get along as an artist without the use of one or two sciences.
>
> Bertolt Brecht (73)

THEATRE HISTORY CONSISTS OF LONG PERIODS OF STABILITY PUNCTUATED by rapid shifts. Classical Greeks and Romans built amphitheatres; in the Middle Ages theatre used various *locus* and *platea* arrangements, which were followed by a move indoors. The allegorical figures of medieval drama were replaced by the more person-like characters of the Renaissance. House lights across Europe were darkened in the late nineteenth century, when they could just as well have stayed bright.

The existence of long periods with little alteration is as interesting as the transformations. The basic fault of the "swings of fashion" and similar theories of culture—a fault shared by positivism and social constructionism—is that they lack a viable theory of historical change. Depending on the account, the reason why a style alters at a specific time in a specific manner is either wholly arbitrary (the whim of trendsetters or Power), or meets some sort of mechanistic law like the motions of a pendulum. These are not ways to explain change, merely ways to explain it away.

An obvious analogue to theatre's history of stability and sea change is the succession of economic systems (classical slavery, medieval serfdom, modern capitalism). Marxism explains this as changes in the dominant mode of production. Methodologically, that argument is promising, because it grounds the historical shifts in fundamental social relationships and material practices. But the chronology doesn't match theatre's: sometimes transformations in theatre have preceded changes in economic systems, and sometimes they have occurred while no major economic transition was afoot. Without question, economics plays important roles in theatre history, but it doesn't seem to play the decisive one. However, there is no inherent reason why marxism shouldn't be just one example of an approach to social analysis belonging to a broader analytic and historiographic philosophy, valid for many fields of research.

Theatre, Communication, Critical Realism resulted from this line of thinking. I argue that communication as an embodied activity generates the fundamental strategies of thought and performance underlying theatre and its historical transformations. By "communication" I do not mean an "exchange of meanings" as some type of signal transmission: I am referring to practices through which we produce meaning materially, in particular the social use and development of speech, handwriting, printing, and electronic media. In order to make this argument I draw on the broader philosophy I alluded to, critical realism, which helps me place theatre firmly within its social and historical matrix. But the analysis flows in several directions: critical realism illuminates history and theatre in part by providing a differentiated and dynamic concept of society, but historiography forces us toward philosophical subtlety, and theatre turns out to identify and fill one or two gaps in critical realist philosophy. Ultimately I posit a definition of theatre based not on formal grounds but on social ontology. Thus as the title of the first chapter puts it, this is a book about philosophy, history and theatre—not just yoked together, but intertwined.

1

My argument arises within a larger scholarly context, one that reveals some of the stakes involved. This introduction will concentrate on the philosophies behind the theories of communication that have been adopted for the analysis of theatre and performance. Given the current upheaval in modes of communication, not surprisingly the topic has attracted broad interest. The study of print is becoming an established field in its own right. Interest in the relationship between theatre and writing—in most cases, specifically printing—has begun to grow. The most impressive recent work on the subject is Julie Stone Peters's *Theatre of the Book, 1480–1880*. Her ambitious volume "offer[s] an account of the entangled histories of print and the modern stage, addressing the meaning of this relationship for the theatre itself and for the broader understanding of text and performance between the sixteenth and nineteenth centuries" (2). With enormous, indeed humbling erudition, Peters pursues her topic in a variety of areas, such as issues of ownership, changes in the relative importance of voice and image, and the mutual reflection between staging and book illustration.

There is a general similarity between Peters's subject and mine, although I pay greater attention to performance than does she. However, our goals and approaches could scarcely be more different, in ways that are central to this book's project. The chief contrast pertains to the issues of historiography I mentioned above. Peters describes the interactions between print and performance with rich detail, but other than establishing that their relationship is an interaction rather than a one-way impact, she does not attempt to establish a larger case. An example is her discussion of the tableaux, the painterly scenic descriptions, and the pictorial tropes in the productions and playtexts of the eighteenth century:

> such pictorialism was driven not just by the demands of an audience raised on pictures, or the market-sense of managers using the technical improvements of the industrial revolution, but by dramatists who were, like managers, envisioning the scene in pictorial terms and, at the same time, approximating the descriptive specificity of the novel. (270)

Peters's point is true, as far as it goes, but I don't think it goes very far. It is of the same order as assertions that plays of the late twentieth century sometimes seem indebted to the conventions and characters of television. Whatever the accuracy of those claims, the problem is the focus on a single ontological level (observables like people, pictures, perceptions and interpersonal interactions) and a simple type of causality. What are the underlying conditions of possibility, the driving social forces, and the emergent meanings? What is the theory behind her analysis?

"Theory" has somewhat deservedly gotten a bad reputation lately, sometimes pronounced dead or declared anathema (see for example the quick survey in Saltz). Post-structuralism has indeed run aground. But I hope I can redeem "theory" a bit. I have in mind two senses of the term: on the one hand, a theory about a particular thing, in this case the nature of theatrical performance, its relationship with print and other modes of communication, and their location and functioning within social structures (this is theory proper); and on the other hand, a more general theory about the aims of critical investigation, its objects and how to define them, and its best analytic methodology (theory as grounding philosophy—specifically, ontology and epistemology). The two senses are connected, since one develops theories about particular things by using ideas and methods derived from the overarching philosophy, and corrects the philosophy with knowledge gleaned about specifics. Peters is certainly familiar with a host of theories: she mentions drawing from phenomenology, hermeneutics, and semiotics, and a few of her early endnotes reveal her acquaintance with arguments for and against deconstruction and technological determinism (2, 313–15n4–6). However, she explicitly declines to apply them:

> I have...left out further discussion of the theoretical and methodological concerns that have informed my study.... My eclectic, multiplicitous (often *ad hoc*) methodology, eschewing a driving theoretical position and suggested

as much as possible by the sources on which I draw, is meant to reflect the multiplicity and contrariness of the materials themselves—the contentious dialogue among and between texts. (3)

But the history of writing raises urgent questions about the writing of history. If one is to avoid implying that "history is just one damn thing after another," one needs a much more coherent historiographical philosophy than Peters applies. Ultimately such noncommittal viewpoints shortchange the study of both theatre and history. If we want to understand why theatre changes historically, we need to delve into the conditions and relationships that push certain matters to the fore. If we hope to grasp the nature of an audience's enjoyment of a performance, we must go past aesthetics to the concrete and cognitive dynamics through which it experiences what happens on stage. Most of all, we must connect the two—historical processes and cognitive dynamics. Without truly *causal* explanations of what happens in the world and in the theatre, one is left with mere descriptions and speculations.

That is not to say that the absence of a chapter on theory is itself a flaw: to the extent that the value of any historiographic philosophy lies not in its pronouncements but in its product, an author can quite legitimately spend not even a page expressing her philosophical commitments. My concern, rather, is with the nature of the commitments, if there are any.

It is tempting, especially for humanities scholars, to adopt an eclectic, instrumentalist, or "pragmatic" approach to theories. Eclectic scholars choose more or less opportunistically among theories for whatever seems to produce useful insights into the question at hand (whatever "useful" might mean). Peters exercises her eclecticism by submerging theory under the evidence; in most cases, however, eclecticism means piecemealing a bit of Derrida here, some Foucault there, a dash of Marx, a dollop of Lacan, without any regard for the compatibility of their ideas. The approach often evinces a pluralism reluctant to adopt a hard line toward theory lest other views of (presumed) equal observational, analytical or explanatory merit be suppressed, without even proving they *have* equal merit, as though one can view stars equally well by using a telescope as by opening the refrigerator. It is telling that eclectic scholars often describe theories as "tools." Attach your theory-wrench, crank it around, see what you get and then apply something else, say the theory-pliers, until you finally get to the theory-screwdriver.

Now, there definitely are circumstances in which such instrumentalism is acceptable, and some in which having an express theory isn't especially necessary. For example, we do not always know in a detailed way how some things operate or whether certain dynamics might be connected, and in the absence of that type of explanatory theory, some sort of eclecticism may be unavoidable. Trying various models may then serve a largely heuristic purpose. It can lead to the discovery that a certain model works exceptionally well, thereby paving the way to a genuinely explanatory analysis.[1] And sometimes it's enough to trace in a provisional way the parameters of a historical or analytical problem, and not even attempt an explanation, a strategy which strives to bracket out one's underlying theories because hasty theorizing may interfere with identifying the issue, even as theories lurk behind many of the questions one asks. Moreover, theories should be understood as provisional, fallible, open to the possibility of later disproof, and for that matter able in principle to stipulate some possible forms of disproof. Thus the pre-theorized nature of perception is not inherently a barrier to subsequent retheorization.

At issue now, however, is whether instrumentalism is coherent and cogent as an intellectual position. It is one thing to take a multidisciplinary approach that invokes various subject-specific theories which have (or could readily be given) a consistent philosophical basis, quite another to mix ideas with wildly disparate philosophical underpinnings. If one considers eclecticism an intelligible methodology, its intelligibility hangs on two assumptions: (1) theories need only correctly or "usefully" describe behavior, the meaning of some text, et cetera; and (2) there are no underlying structures of reality or logic justifying the choice of one theory over another. The first assumption accepts the notion of regularities or tendencies in behavior, or the related focus on repeated behavior, but is at best ambivalent about the idea that there are real causal structures (not just in people's minds). These are empiricist motifs. Setting theoretical concerns aside as Peters does effectively lands one in the same philosophical place, in which things interact but not through underlying forces, structures, or conditions. The second assumption purports that all theories are equally valid, equally valuable, and there is no rational or for that matter ethical way to adjudicate among them; to the contrary, judging people's theories is thoroughly an act of power. The "truth" of a theory is wholly relative to its social context or origin; one's choice of theory is just a personal preference or at most a hand-me-down of history, and in the end even the connection between history and theory is arbitrary and dubious. In short, in its very effort to avoid privileging one view over another, eclecticism sells the farm to the positivist/relativist problematic.

In the absence of causal explanations about historical events, one plumps for either the sort of positivism that contents itself with description; or else the sort of positivism which represents theatre history as just one event or style after another, in which case either change lacks any particular significance, or (as Peters asserts under the banner of an "eclectic" methodology) the evidence supposedly speaks for itself and directs its own methodology. The alternative is a realist concept of theory, which sees instrumental uses of theories as an unsatisfactory but with luck temporary situation. Ultimately the stopgap should be replaced through the development of properly causal explanations, some of which may prove better than others. Therein lies the principal difference between Peters's project and mine: my goal in analyzing the relationship between theatrical performance and modes of communication is to develop causal and structural explanations.

2

Within the study of communication, the denial of causal explanations constitutes the widespread "conduit" theory, according to which "communications media" are totally neutral pipelines for ideas that in no way affect meaning itself—communication is purely a technical matter, a delivery system that can be subtracted without loss from the process of transporting information or the information itself. Causal explanations reject such notions of neutrality.

However, there are causal explanations, and there are causal explanations. It is easy to fall into a technological determinism in which writing or printing directly establishes certain ways of thinking, or else a social constructionism which claims that communication technologies possess only the significance that a society imparts to them. Technologically determinist theories, which today appear in countless mass market discussions of computerization and the Internet, were popularized by Walter Ong and especially Marshall McLuhan, whose aphorism "the medium is the message" epitomizes the position. Their theories were among the first to hold that the means of communication affect thought. But they claim that the means of communications *directly* determine the content of thought, and that it does so automatically and immediately, regardless of context or usage.

Something along these lines affects another recent foray into the relationship between print and theatre, W. B. Worthen's *Print and the Poetics of Modern Drama*, which repeatedly attributes historical developments and interpretive patterns to "the iterative logic of print" (6), "the properties and proprieties of print" (9), "the shaping force of print on the interface between literary and performance culture" (158) and so forth, as though society had no role in configuring such logics, properties and forces. Granted, Worthen's interest is not history (despite the loosely chronological organization of the book) but rather the hermeneutics or semiology of the printed page as a compromised representation of drama, an interest that puts causal and social questions in the background. But that doesn't legitimize his excision of social dynamics from his concept of print and its powers. Thus his seemingly materialist attention to the details of the printed page (arguing it is a deeply flawed "delivery system" for drama) ends up becoming reductive and technologistic. Worthen also treats us to a history of drama that has more to do with authors and publications than playscripts and performances.

At a crucial juncture in *Liveness: Performance in a Mediatized Culture*, Philip Auslander too relies on a technologically determinist argument as a way to challenge the notion that a key distinction between live performance and television is that the former is evanescent, the latter not. Images, he observes, appear on the TV screen because an electron beam makes a phosphor illuminate for a fraction of a second, after which it fades and must be re-lit by another scan of the electron beam. Consequently, for Auslander, "disappearance may be even more fundamental to television than it is to live performance—the televisual image is always simultaneously coming into being and vanishing" (48), as though that has the slightest effect on audience experience. Auslander's tactic is particularly dismaying because he seems to recognize the failings of technological determinism (50n34). But he avails himself of technological determinism once more when he writes that "Although digital *technologies* are based on binary logic, they have had the ironic effect of dismantling *cultural* binaries" (119; my emphasis). Technologies do have cultural effects, but people experience electronic devices through what the technology does for them, not through transistors' binary logic, knowledge of which is neither necessary nor relevant. As I will show later, Auslander's technologically determinist assumptions undermine his analysis of how theatre and television (or related media) are different or similar.

More typically, technological determinism's claims concentrate on rationality. Since writing lacks the overtones of voice or gesture, technological determinists presume that it is free from the demands of a shared place and time, and from the qualifications of intersubjectivity. Writing consequently cultivates logic and objectivity, and promotes critical thought and abstraction. Thus writing is sociologically neutral, but not cognitively neutral: literacy affects cognition. For some writers, that implies that it also provides a neutral anthropological distinction between "advanced" and "primitive" cultures, so that the presence or absence of literacy becomes a mask for legitimating Western superiority (see the critique in Street 19–65). The determinist model also tends to present cultures as either pre-literate or fully literate. In actuality, of course, speech and writing are "mixed" in most societies—and in most theatre, for that matter.

Written language is no more context-free, autonomous, or fixed in meaning than speech. Research instead shows that *all* language involves abstraction and contextual interpretation; the concepts of rationality and objectivity are socially constructed and ideologically motivated. Oral cultures do employ logic and analysis, although not always in forms familiar to Europeans and

Americans. When deterministic theorists examine non-literate people's reasoning, they usually test the impact of schooling and a particular rhetorical tradition, not the effects of literacy (Street 3–4, 41–42; Simons and Murphy; Rader; McCarty).

While technological determinism asserts that the materiality of communication affects ideation, it ignores the social conditions and relations underlying communication practices. Consequently its findings must be handled cautiously: sometimes it does correctly identify effects that a mode of communication has on discourse, but because it fails to account for the social dynamics in which the mode is used, it assumes that these effects are due solely to the technology and arise universally.

Paradoxically, while some anthropologists claim that writing stimulated the efflorescence of reason and logic, some philosophers have disparaged writing as a supplement to speech, contending that voice guarantees authenticity and the stable presence of meaning—a tradition Jacques Derrida calls "phonocentrism" (see *Of Grammatology*). For him, speech itself is a form of writing, consisting of signs of signs and the incessant displacement and deferral of meaning associated with metaphoricity. Derrida's deconstruction appears anti-determinist, yet his approach to speech and writing shares much with the determinist model and is subject to similar criticisms. He isolates writing from its social and historical contexts, ignores changes in literate practices, and assumes that phonocentrism occurring today, when texts dominate education and philosophy, has the same basis as in antiquity, when manuscripts were rare and silent reading virtually unknown. Derrida writes that phonocentrism descends from the nature of writing itself; he sees writing as continuing unchanged since Plato ("Plato's Pharmacy"). His concept of writing remains decontextualizing, which makes it problematic for analyzing theatre and society, in which speech and writing interact within a definitively social context.

Many scholars will agree that communication technology must be placed in its social context. But it makes considerable difference how one understands "social." In many cases it is undifferentiated and vague, which is evident in social constructionism. There are two main sorts. The "strong" form of social constructionism is exemplified by the relativism advocated by David Bloor and Barry Barnes, which (as Margaret Archer puts it) "asserts the *social* character and *social* causation of *all* knowledge" (*Culture and Agency* 112; her emphases). On this view the effects of a communications medium would be *entirely* socially determined. That would appear to be a claim that technologies are not socially neutral, and indeed are thoroughly imbued with the force of social power. But actually it implies that if the effects of a technology stem entirely from society, then the technology *per se* possesses nothing that leans this way or that. It is utterly malleable, easily fitting whatever uses ideology and political interests might assign it, and what is utterly malleable is socially neutral. Consequently "strong" social constructionism leans toward functionalism.

In contrast, "weak" social constructionism in communication theory maintains that communication practices arise in a social context and are not neutral, but it does not assume social forces determine everything. The general position conceptualizes literacy "as socially and historically situated, fluid, multiple, and power-linked.... This orientation does not ignore the psycholinguistic, cognitive, or technical aspects of literacy, but rather embeds them within sociocultural settings and the discursive practices and power relations of everyday life" (McCarty xvii–xviii). The means of communication, and technology in general, remain sociologically non-neutral since it is shaped by and sometimes a direct instrument of forms of power.

I support this conclusion. But the analysis is incomplete. While "weak" social constructionists do not deny the other aspects of literacy, neither do they typically pay them much attention. For example, when Brian Street writes that "Technology...is a cultural form, a social product whose shape and influence depend upon prior political and ideological factors" (96), the material aspects of reading and writing seem to disappear into ideology and social determinations. If technology isn't neutral, then to some extent it *does* somehow influence consciousness due to its own inherent characteristics, as implemented in practice. But social constructionists avoid investigating this matter, for fear of falling into technological determinism. Social constructionism, then, recognizes the social conditions and relations involved in communication, but even if it acknowledges the materiality of communication, it gives it no weight within its analysis and leaves it little more than a hedge.

Technological determinism and "strong" social constructionism are both reductive, because they assume that the effects of communication practices derive exclusively from *either* materiality *or* social relations. "Weak" social constructionism leans this way too (in effect, if not in theory) when it neglects the materialities that enable, condition and limit technology's use and can even contradict the uses to which social powers may wish to put it. But recognizing technology's social dependence does not entail collapsing into relativism, nor is any assertion whatsoever of technology's influence on culture tantamount to determinism. Technological determinism is certainly attractive, but its weaknesses are readily identified. Social constructionists rightly critique technological determinism's lack of social analysis and consequent claims that literacy leads to more or less quantifiable degrees of rationality, objectivity, and truth. However, the story doesn't end there. The effects of communication practices might not be differing *degrees* of rationality: the *strategies* of reasoning—especially its organizational methods and generative metaphors—could be affected instead. And strategies of reasoning, I will argue, are closely related to the pragmatics of communication.

Communication is not simply a technology, nor is it purely a set of social relations: it's both. It is vital to recognize that communication technologies, like all other material entities, possess various powers, susceptibilities, and dispositions. Technologies are developed in order to achieve certain results, that is, to produce particular material effects. Significantly, however, technologies may also have effects that are unforeseen (perhaps even abhorred) by the technology's makers and users. Technology's unforeseeable consequences are often crucial ones. This too is a reason to acknowledge gaps in the social constructionist account of technology. The unforeseeable consequences of communication structures, upon theatre in particular, comprise the focus of this book.

However, *which* of a technology's powers are actually exercised, to what extent, and in what manner, depends on the social conditions and methods of the technology's use. Technology is usually shaped by social interests—which is necessary partly *because* technologies possess their own powers and dispositions. And if communication technologies do affect rationality in some manner, their effect must be assessed not according to scales ranging from subjectivity to objectivity or from bad to good logic, but in terms of the different strategies of reasoning which emerge at least in part according to the way cultures use and organize the available modes of communication. Thus if there is an association between printing and (a particular form of) rationality, it is a sociohistorical outcome, not a natural or ineluctable bond. Modes of communication derive their significance neither solely from their technical natures nor strictly from their social relations, but from the historically conditioned conjunction of the two.

3

The "bothness" that I am proposing returns us to the recent tendency toward philosophical eclecticism. By the late 1990s, social constructionism of one sort or another had become de rigueur for humanities scholars in the United States, but even as they pay it the necessary obeisance, many have begun to back away from its most extreme versions, and for some it has hit a dead end. Yet at another level they take its lessons unwaveringly to heart. There are many reasons for the current situation, among them probably the sheer number of competing theories, with varying degrees of intellectual insight, political acceptability, cultural cachet, institutional hegemony, sex appeal, and fetishized authority, making it hard for one to decide what to believe—if, that is, one dares admit to believing anything. For the most profound impact of social constructionism has been to drill an almost instinctual relativism into the humanities, then pouring in fears that any and all assertions of truth or falsity (or adjudication among truth claims) impose power and subjugate other peoples. I am not here speaking of relativism toward faiths and aesthetic values, but rather toward statements such as "The theory of evolution is disproved by the Bible," "People X are inferior creatures," and "Saddam Hussein possessed weapons of mass destruction"—statements which are or were somebody's "truths" but nevertheless can be supported or disproved by evidence and analysis. I hope most readers have strong opinions about these claims and would hesitate to say all such "truths" are valid. As these examples show, it's vital to have the ability to assert truth and falsity; but like objectivism, relativism about truth forces one to choose *either* to respect other views and experiences *or* to insist on the ethical legitimacy of adjudicating truth claims, but not both. (As others have shown, this is a false dichotomy: on a realist basis one can indeed achieve both, partly because one can and should differentiate types of ideas.) A sad result is that scholars consign themselves to irrelevance. Moreover, adherence to the idea that because we have no unmediated access to reality, we therefore have no ascertainable access to reality, leaves one unable to propound existence at all. There is a skepticism that speaks of the limits to one's own knowledge and certainty, and the possibility of limits to what humans can ever know; but this is a skepticism that treats the act of making knowledge claims as *inherently* suspect, and ultimately doubts whether knowledge is possible at all because there is no absolute certainty. Between theory overload, cognitive and moral dissonance, and skepticism about knowledge as such, the upshot is often eclecticism.

Although I maintain that one can accept certain insights of technological determinism and social constructionism, one cannot simply pop these pieces together: they must be reconceptualized within a coherent philosophical framework. It is possible to agree with particular ideas associated with a range of theories, without abandoning rigorous analysis or unwittingly acceding to a merely more temperate sort of positivism. However, achieving that coherence requires taking seriously what some in the humanities dismiss as uninteresting, naive, self-contradictory or even absurd, and others secretly believe is true yet don't believe can be successfully argued: there's a real world independent of our ideas about it, and we can have genuine knowledge about that world even though knowledge is socially produced. This is the position taken by critical realism.

I will develop that position in chapter 1. Here I want to suggest some of what it offers to theatre studies. One of the most significant contributions is a rapprochement between history and theory. A theory highlights things to look for in history and ways to understand it, and history may (and often does) present events not immediately explained by the theory, so that the theory must either be refined or rejected (assuming one's theory is falsifiable). The philosophical positions I stake in the first chapter guide the historical research that follows, but only actual historical research can demonstrate whether the theoretical analysis provides good explanations. Conversely, theatre history is not simply a passive object to be worked upon: its twists and turns led to the questions that instigated this book's theoretical investigations, and then impelled further theoretical developments. By the end of the book, questions arising from theatre history result in a revised definition of theatre itself, so that theatre reemerges from "performance" as a distinctive cultural form. Its definition, however, arises not from formalist or stylistic considerations, but instead from the concepts needed to explain aspects of theatre history. In short, critical realist philosophy establishes a true interdependence between theoretical and historical analysis, in which they assist and create problems for each other.

A critical realist approach can provide a highly comprehensive understanding of the body both on stage and in the audience. Critical realism is not limited to semiotic analysis: it apprehends the body not only as a bearer and producer of signs, but also (among other things) as a physiological being and as a social entity. Moreover, critical realism can grasp the interrelationships among these aspects of embodiment, and it can do so in concrete, "operational" terms. It enables discussions about (say) how semiosis, social power relations, and the brain's mirror cells might interact in a stratified analysis of audience response (the stratification being a crucial part of that analysis).

I do not mean to imply that no efforts along these lines have been attempted. Realist historiography has been practiced for some time, and can be found in the work of some (albeit not all) feminists, marxists, members of the *Annales* school, and so forth (see Lovell 22–25; McLennan). Although this is the first book to take an explicitly critical realist approach to theatre studies (or any other realm of culture), other works have upheld some form and level of realism. To pluck out a few titles over the past thirty years, Bruce McConachie's *American Theatre in the Culture of the Cold War* is an explicitly realist history of theatre; Tracy Davis's *Actresses as Working Women*, Jean-Christophe Agnew's *Worlds Apart*, and Eli Rozik's *The Roots of Theatre* are implicitly realist to a significant degree. There have also been several theoretical articles in the realist vein.[2] Scholars such as Rhonda Blair and John Lutterbie are undertaking interdisciplinary research on embodiment within theatre in a manner compatible with critical realism.

The last point I'll raise about critical realism's significance for theatre studies is that it allows a reversal of the usual relationship between a philosophy and the field to which it is applied. Theatre, it turns out, is a surprisingly good model of critical realist theory itself. Just as history can inform theory, the study of theatre can lead to questions and new ideas within critical realist philosophy. In striving to resolve problems for theatre history, I identify gaps and flaws within critical realism and to introduce solutions and alternative conceptualizations. In other words, while in general scholars adopt a theory (such as phenomenology, marxism, or deconstruction) and apply it to theatre, issues of theatre can also lead outward to ideas in philosophy, without turning theatre into a metaphor (as occurs in Goffman, Butler and others). This can happen because within critical realism, it makes sense to ask, "Given that theatrical performance involves X, what must the world be like—what are the *conditions of possibility* for that aspect of theatre?"

4

My study focuses on theatrical performance. In contrast to writers who pursue a highly general and abstract notion of "performance" (or expand "theatre" to cover football games, Catholic masses and political demonstrations), I concentrate on the history and nature of theatre specifically. My analysis of dramatic literature is more guarded because the theory of communication's effect on theatrical performance provides a "big picture": the insight it can offer on the meaning and appeal of particular plays is necessarily limited, because the more individual the object of analysis, the greater the number of forces and counterforces one must account for. My argument is at a middle level and does not aim to explain everything about theatre. Finally, due to space limitations I barely scratch the surface of aesthetics and audience response.

I begin with a brief survey of critical realism, situating it within the conflict between positivist and social constructionist philosophies and their effect on historiography. In a sense, critical realism brings social constructionism and positivism together: on the one hand, knowledge is socially produced and in that respect is relative; on the other, reality is nevertheless independent of our ideas, it is knowable, and consequently there are rational grounds for judging one theory better than another. However, on a fundamental level critical realism opposes both positivism and social constructionism. Against their view that the only things we can call "real" are our (objective or subjective) perceptions, critical realism argues that things are real if they have causal powers, whether or not we can perceive them.

By thinking in terms of causal powers, one can address different levels of explanation and how they are related to each other. Critical realism emphasizes the stratified nature of reality, such as the emergence of life from chemical interactions, and the emergence of living creatures who possess consciousness. Each level involves the rise of new, irreducible powers and characteristics. At the same time, one set of structures and activities may set the conditions for another. For example, geography creates certain economic possibilities, and within certain economic conditions particular types of theatrical production become possible. Thus critical realism provides exceptionally strong ways to explain historical change, which is crucial for an activity as multilayered as theatre.

I then turn to a subject that critical realism has barely touched: semiotics. Charles Peirce's semiotics, which has long shown its value in theatre studies, turns out to be readily adapted to critical realism because it involves connections to the real world, an understanding of the semiotic character of all perception, and a dialogic (rather than hermetic) conception of the unceasing nature of semiosis. My discussion of semiosis leads me to refine critical realism's social ontology, that is, the elements that constitute a society. Most social ontologies identify two basic levels of society—social structures and agents—and many theories attempt to collapse these layers into one, such as by reducing social structures to individual's interactions or by conceiving people as wholly controlled by social structures. Critical realism rejects any conflation of structures and agents. They are distinct, but they interact: structures set the conditions for agents' activities, those activities affect structures, and thus set the stage for the next round of activity. Departing somewhat from "canonical" critical realism, I argue that society has not just two layers, but three: structures, agents, and discourses. This revised social ontology allows one to address multiple types of social causes, with important implications for historiography in general and theatre studies in particular. By the end of the book I will show how these layers are particularly relevant for the concept of theatrical performance. One structure has a particularly powerful impact on discourse and representation: communication.

In chapter 2 I begin to examine communication practices' effects on performance historically. A critical realist approach, including an analysis in terms of communication practices, is applicable to any historical period and place; I can only consider a few examples. I have chosen them strategically, in order to address certain topics, and I do not discuss them in chronological order. I start with the interactions between orality and literacy in manuscript cultures as manifested in two types of early theatre: Greek tragedy and the medieval mystery cycle (specifically York's). Eschewing any notion that theatre's origins lie in religion or ritual, I locate the rise of tragedy in Athens within its social circumstances, of which two are particularly prominent: the shift from an agricultural oligarchy to a mercantile democracy; and the rise of literacy as both an element of the new political and economic structure, and as the foundation of a new mode of cultural practice. Greek tragedy bears numerous traces of a conjunction and collision between oral and literate modes of communication. Medieval theatre similarly arose in a society possessing only speech and handwriting, but the cultural results were quite different partly because one book—the Bible—had become the lodestone toward which all thought ultimately pointed. Thus the strategies involved in oral and written communication entwined in a way that established similitudes (allegory, analogy, and related techniques) as the distinctive feature of medieval thought. Yet the York Cycle used similitudes rather less than other plays, despite being the oldest extant mystery cycle. The discrepancy turns out to derive from York's importance as one of England's administrative and mercantile centers, which gave greater weight to literal meanings and to activity that followed proper legal and contractual procedure, as revealed by several of the play's key episodes.

Chapter 2 argues that orality and literacy affected thought primarily through the practical issues of how each mode of communication stores thought: oral culture, for example, used rhythm and formulaic phrases to help fix knowledge in memory. However, pragmatics alone does not quite explain certain features of discourse, especially during the era of print culture. I close that gap in chapter 3 by considering recent work in cognitive science. Research shows that embodied interactions with the physical and social world generate "image schemas," subconscious models of space, movement, time and other aspects of the world which underlie a variety of metaphors that structure thought. The importance of image schemas' linkage between embodiment and cognition recalls the emphasis that Peircean semiotics places on iconicity. By reconceptualizing the idea that knowledge is rooted in practice, cognitive science provides a new way to think about how certain ideas come to dominate a culture. In particular, communication practices generate many of the dominant culture's crucial image schemas, which play an especially important role in shaping the culture's concepts of selfhood and agency. For instance, modern ideas of individualism and psychological depth derive not so much from the effects of economic competition as the experience of solitary reading.

Because image schemas are elaborated as cognitive patterns which allow a variety of expressive forms, they offer a new way to identify commonalities among performances. The concept of performance strategies specifies the conceptual foundations of disparate elements of performance such as acting style, dramaturgy, and stage design. To provide an example I analyze how the "sentimental" theatre of the early eighteenth century was connected to another change in communication structures. I select this historical moment in order to make chapter 3's other main point: whereas ancient Athens experienced a radical cultural shift due to the introduction of writing, the change in eighteenth-century England involved not a new technology, but a new use of an existing technology. During that period, the first regular, frequent, and sustainable periodicals began appearing. The innovation is significant from a historiographical perspective, since it underscores how a single technology may provide the tools for different communication structures (monographic and periodical print publication) with distinctive cultural effects. Enlightenment empiricism depended on linear and atomistic image schemas, which derived not from print technology as such, but rather from the experience of using print as the main source of knowledge, and the methods adopted to make printed works accessible. These image schemas were also manifested in the new verisimilitude in drama and stagecraft. However, Enlightenment print culture fostered both a public sphere and a private sphere. The two were connected through periodical publication. The most important early periodicals, *The Tatler* and *The Spectator*, were edited and largely written by Richard Steele, whose play *The Conscious Lovers* was also the blockbuster of the period. His method for making his journals successful also shaped a performance strategy he incorporated in his play: sentiment. The underlying image schemas generated an increasingly psychological notion of dramatic character, and the theatre's emphasis upon the actor's gestural expressiveness. The chapter closes with a discussion of modern drama, in which many empiricist assumptions continue, but through various seemingly opposed dramatic genres.

The fourth chapter considers a particular dramaturgical structure: metatheatricality. While there have been several taxonomies of metatheatricality, efforts at explanation have been unsatisfactory. Although it can appear in any era, metatheatricality mostly arises during periods of social change and in particular change in communication structures. Backtracking historically, I turn to late Renaissance England. The introduction of printing had slowly brought massive changes in its wake, strikingly evident in the persistently metatheatrical plays of Ben Jonson. In order to explain why a shift in communication would lead to metatheatricality, first it is necessary to understand the ontology of theatrical performance. In contrast to theorists who define theatre in terms of either mimesis or repetition, I show that ontologically, theatre is a model of society, and specifically of social agency. When communication structures shift, they eventually disrupt concepts of self and agency. The cognitive reflexivity that is inherently part of agency must itself become the object of reflection, in order to transform agency into a configuration that may better suit changed conditions. During these discursive crises, theatrical performance as a model of social agency reflects upon social agency through metatheatricality. For the same reason, the main forms of metatheatricality vary historically. These differences embody forms of agency and knowledge fostered by the emerging communication practices.

I conclude with three brief discussions. The first is the significance of electronic media. One of the most challenging treatments of that issue, Philip Auslander's *Liveness*, raises important questions about how theatre differs from cinematic and televised performance. Its shortcomings lead me to return to social ontology in order to clarify theatre's distinctiveness and its relationships with these and other types of performance, such as puppetry and performance art. The next section addresses some aspects of aesthetics and audience experience, identifying (again on ontological terms) a number of the factors involved. Last, I consider the antitheatrical prejudice, which itself is partly rooted in communication practices. Thus a critical realist analysis illuminates both the history and the nature of theatre. And conversely, the analysis of theatre leads to revisions of critical realism itself.

CHAPTER 1

PHILOSOPHY, HISTORY, THEATRE

> [T]he historian speaks of what happened, the poet [i.e., playwright] of the kind of thing that *can* happen. Hence also poetry is a more philosophical and serious business than history; for poetry speaks more of universals, history of particulars. "Universal" in this case is what kind of person is likely to do or say certain kinds of things, according to probability or necessity.
>
> Aristotle, *Poetics* (32–33)

ONTOLOGY MAY NOT BE THE UPPERMOST TOPIC THAT MAKERS AND historians of theatre consider when they conduct their work, but it's on their minds nevertheless. They—we—always have ideas about what's real, whether there really are causal connections between events, whether we can have cognitive access to an external reality or instead it's all in our minds. Positions on these issues are often most clearly articulated within philosophies of science. Historiography (and theatre practice) generally adopts the presuppositions of a philosophy of science, whether it does so avowedly or unknowingly. For example, positivist theatre historiography defers to or relies on a positivist philosophy of science. Positivism is one of the three major "families" among philosophies of science. The other two are social constructionism and realism. Within the arts and humanities, social constructionist theories of various stripes have sent positivism packing. Yet despite their animosity, social constructionism and positivism actually have much in common. Realism makes better sense than either.

1

Positivism is the modern representative of a philosophical family encompassing empiricism, objectivism, methodological individualism, and most forms of instrumentalism. In the natural sciences, positivism maintains that only physical, observable objects and events can be known scientifically. Reality is independent of the mind; it is knowable, but only through sensory experience, and all knowledge can be reduced to observations. Observations must in no way be colored by personal beliefs or sociocultural contexts: they should be theory-neutral, and hence objective. Analogies and iconic models may initially be useful psychologically for analyzing how an object or process behaves, but past that point, models should be eliminated (and if possible, superseded by mathematical equations), and they should never be viewed as describing actual entities that cause the behavior in question. Positivistic explanation proceeds through logical *deduction*: if cause C, then event E will occur. (Alternatively, one deduces from statistics the probability of E.) Scientific laws are objectively true facts providing a high or even absolute degree of certainty and are wholly independent of the observer's values or conceptions, which after all are not physical realities. Causality is thus linear and mechanistic: a causal claim says only that there is a regular succession from one set of circumstances to another. In fact, causality is really more an expectation, a human construct. Positivists reject the notion of natural necessity (powers and susceptibilities) as depending on evidence that humans cannot observe (see Keat and Urry 9–13, 27–28). Thus they reject ontology, and may even ridicule it as metaphysical mysticism. (Philosophies of science, I should emphasize, may or may not adequately describe the practices and theories of actual scientists.)

Within historiography, positivism requires modification and hedging. History doesn't have invariant regularities, and even statistical probabilities are notoriously difficult to find. Instead, history consists of the objectively identifiable interactions among individuals (sometimes organized groups, population categories and so forth) as well as their material products, and their ideas and expressed intentions. But positivistic historians refrain from asserting underlying causal forces, generally judging them to be subjective and speculative. Historical development results from linear chains of events composed of agents' activities.

Although positivist historiography never stood entirely unopposed, major efforts to debunk it became prominent in the 1960s with the rise of *social constructionism*, which belongs to a philosophical family embracing relativism, subjectivism, conventionalism, and most of postmodernism. The social constructionist who has influenced the humanities most is probably Michel Foucault, but my comments on social constructionism will be more general. One of its key concepts is that ideas about the world are governed by a set of underlying assumptions. Foucault called them *epistemes*, consisting of discursive rules; Thomas Kuhn's similar analysis used the term *paradigm*, which is largely grounded in a set of images or models. Not only are the sciences shaped according to these assumptions, but so are all understandings of the world. Observations are never theory-neutral; technologies hinge on theories as well. Far from progressing in some linear manner, scientific discourses undergo radical shifts, in which one paradigm or episteme supplants another. Ptolemy's paradigm of an earth-centered universe gave way to the Copernican heliocentric paradigm; Newtonian mechanics fell to Einsteinian relativity; the medieval and Renaissance interpretation of the world in terms of resemblances and similitudes was replaced by eighteenth-century ideas of measurement and order that eventually formed empiricism and its successor, positivism. The new system of thought doesn't constitute an advance in knowledge so much as a change in perspective: truth is relative to the conceptual system. Perception itself depends on theories, so that "discursive formations" regulate all areas of mental life. But the episteme or paradigm does not merely describe reality, it actually constitutes "reality" through how it identifies its objects of understanding. Consequently scientists working under different paradigms/epistemes cannot even refer to the "same" object in their studies—they live in different and incommensurable worlds. Discourses have only internally governed rules of validity, evidence, and existence; but because discourses, like language itself, are socially constructed, epistemic shifts are directly connected to social dynamics. For Foucault, the social nature of epistemes ties discourse to power relationships, leading him to coin the phrase "power/knowledge"; indeed, one of the great attractions of social constructionism has been its connection to political critique.[1]

Social constructionist theatre history rightly emphasizes that historical analysis is necessarily theory-based, and that theatre and drama are caught up within larger discourses such as the attitudes of diverse social groups and the exigencies of particular traditions. However, social constructionism suffers from numerous gaps and contradictions. I'll address its politics shortly, but first I want to examine two closely related problems: its weakness in explaining the changes it describes, and the disconnect it suffers between theory and practice. Since the goal of this book is to explain theatre's historical changes by the relationship between theory and practice, these gaps are crucial.

Despite making compelling arguments for the existence of epistemes or paradigms and for radical shifts from one to another, social constructionism barely illuminates why shifts occur at all, why *then*, or why with *that* outcome. The difficulty is rooted in social constructionists' critique of positivist notions of objectivity and theory-neutrality. Social constructionists argue that all perceptions are theory-dependent, and because theories differ, perceptions differ. So far, so good. But from this, the most extreme constructionists conclude that reality itself differs, and even those who do not summarily deny the existence of a world independent of the mind nonetheless give it no role or force. A paradigm's internal *logic* is all that really matters.

For instance, Kuhn says that anomalous scientific findings help trigger paradigm shifts. But if discourses establish self-enclosed, incommensurable worlds—if scientists cannot describe the "same" object differently, only different objects—then there is no window through which nature or argument might present anomalies that could lead to a paradigm's overthrow. Experimentation and theory-testing become inexplicable and irrational. The justifiable argument that all observations are theory-laden does not justify the inference that there can be no effective access to a mind-independent reality. By making that claim, social constructionism implies that theory-based actions achieve their expected results either through luck, or because *all* theory-based actions achieve their results (theory creates reality). There is no clear way for a social constructionist to be *wrong* about anything. In short, social constructionists cannot offer an intelligible relationship between theory and practice, either within theory, or within practice (they do not leave skyscrapers by the window).

Foucault ultimately explains epistemic shifts as an issue of power and its restructuring. The idea that politics affects science is practically a truism by now; but Foucault's idea of power has far too little material or social grounding—power appears to lack any basis or limits. Epistemes can shift as radically as Foucault suggests only if power is essentially total and arbitrary. One might hope that epistemic change arose from political resistance, but he often portrays resistance as venting or even a ruse to fortify the dominant order itself. On this model resistance could never force such an effectively totalitarian rule to crumble or an episteme to be replaced. Again, the self-enclosure of discourse makes practices arbitrary and inexplicable.

Arguably, the goal of these theories is to describe, not to explain, and such theories certainly have a valid role; as I noted in the introduction, there may even be periods when attempts at explaining phenomena may hinder adequate description. In the end, however, a descriptive theory indicates the limit of current knowledge, and ultimately should be supplemented or even supplanted by a more properly explanatory—that is, causal—theory (Keat and Urry 40–41; Bhaskar, *Realist Theory of Science* 211–12). But causality isn't available to social constructionists: because they force all aspects of knowledge into the confines of discourses and their internal workings, they reject causality itself, or (more narrowly) disclaim the existence and hence causal powers of more fundamental social structures.

Social constructionism can only provide arbitrary, irrationalist, interpersonal, hypertotalized, or simply *no* explanations for social and cultural change. Theatre's history cannot consist of anything but stylistic shifts occurring by chance or because Power says so; nor can the world provide any kind of referent for dramatic realism. At best, cultural change depends on interpersonal dynamics; large social forces become incomprehensible and totalitarian powers may exist without underlying structures to support them.

Here social constructionism finds itself in bed with positivism. Clearly, positivism's notion of causality is inadequate for understanding culture and society. As I've noted, positivists conceptualize causality as having a logical structure; this gives causality its objectionable determinist character. But social constructionists conclude that because positivism's concept of causality is inadequate, causality itself should be jettisoned: everything is a social construct, but with its own inner logic. In rejecting causality, they treat positivism's understanding of it as the only account possible, and thus implicitly accept it. Thus both positivists and social constructionists disclaim underlying causal powers, allowing only behaviors and discourses, and so their efforts to explain social change arrive at the same dead end.

Social constructionism adopts other positivist tenets. Its relativism consists of a sort of collective subjectivism that simply inverts the objectivity claimed by positivism, thereby accepting the division between objective and subjective knowledge that positivism supposes. Perhaps the most important doctrine these philosophies share is the perception criterion of reality: only what enters consciousness—whether experiences or discourses—can be accepted as real. Underlying mechanisms are hypothetical or imaginary, not real (a position that can be called *irrealist*). Statements about what exists become translated into statements about our *knowledge* of what exists (a paralogism that has been termed the "epistemic fallacy"). Thus for positivists, perception occurs as an objective reflection of the world; theories can be reduced to experiences. For social constructionists, perception is subjective and constitutive: discourse governs perception and hence the world, and the world can be reduced to discourse.[2] What cannot be perceived cannot be real, according to positivism; perception effectively creates reality itself, according to social constructionism. The arguments of one theorist demonstrates the unity of these philosophies: he maintains that the relation of cause and effect is actually one between signifier and signified; that to be is to be perceived; and indeed that the things of the world "have not any existence without a mind." This postmodernist thinker is Bishop George Berkeley, writing in 1710 as an "empiricist" (Berkeley §§3, 6, 65, 110–16).[3]

In short, although social constructionism is an advance over positivism, its conception of the universe is a half-measure toward the formation of a nonpositivist theatre historiography. Its understanding of knowledge and existence tacitly conserves basic assumptions of positivism. In both cases the root causes of social and cultural change remain largely unexplained, even unexplainable. For a more adequate historiography to emerge, the fundamental assumptions about knowledge and reality need to be reassessed.

2

Another family of philosophies practically specializes in issues of change, whether as alteration, transformation or development: *realism*. The term has an enormously long, complex, and controversial history, made still more confusing for scholars of culture because the word also often refers to certain artistic approaches, themselves not all cut from the same cloth.[4] (I will briefly consider artistic realism in chapter 3.) Nevertheless, it is the correct philosophical term. Contemporary realism began taking shape in the 1960s primarily as a philosophy of science, and hit its stride in the 1970s. Initially it was mainly a British development, but in recent years several variants emerged in the United States, such as "postpositivist realism" and "embodied realism."[5] Due to the rigor of his analyses and his ceaseless pursuit of their implications, Roy Bhaskar became the leading philosopher of what was eventually called "critical realism." But as Bhaskar himself points out, several of critical realism's fundamental ideas derive from the works of earlier writers, including Aristotle, Immanuel Kant, and Karl Marx. Critical realism has advanced mainly in sociology, economics, political science, and law. Explorations of culture are still uncommon, but more are appearing.[6]

From a critical realist perspective, knowledge production may be defined as a socially conditioned activity through which people develop an understanding of reality, and (most of) reality exists independently of their thoughts about it. Thus critical realism conjoins aspects that social constructionists and positivists may find incompatible. How can ideas be socially produced yet inform us of a mind-independent reality? If ideas objectively describe or explain reality, then how can they be socially contingent? The contradiction is only apparent, however, and results from certain faulty assumptions that positivism and social constructionism share.

The first premise of critical realism is that the vast majority of reality exists independently of our present thoughts about it. In the face of some of the most extreme social constructionist theories, this tenet may need more defending than I can provide here, but several arguments can be adduced to support it. Bhaskar develops his through a Kantian strategy: given the existence of knowledge, he investigates the conditions of possibility for knowledge and the intelligibility of science as a social practice (*Realist Theory of Science* 12–17, 21–24 and *passim*). His approach targets positivism. Against social constructionism, which doubts the very existence of knowledge, I think another tack is necessary: the independent existence of reality is the condition for the possibility of *error*. As I pointed out earlier, it's difficult to imagine how a social constructionist theory can ever be proven wrong since it accepts only internal evidence. Yet it is excruciatingly obvious that error exists. Not knowing that fire is hot doesn't stop it from burning one's fingers; believing that we don't need oxygen doesn't liberate the body from breathing; denying the existence of capitalism doesn't protect one from market forces. Such examples demonstrate the independence of both physical and social reality from our thoughts about it. If reality is not simply the creature of our thoughts about it, then it is possible to be wrong about it. And if it is possible to be wrong about something, then it is possible to be right about it too (whether or not anyone ever actually is).

One might object that the social world very clearly depends on thoughts, and wouldn't even exist without them. That is in fact true—but it is true primarily *over time*. At any specific moment, social structures are what they are, regardless of what you or I or even a large group of people think. We cannot eliminate poverty by thinking it away; institutional racism persists despite diminution of racist ideologies. The independence of reality from thought even holds for thoughts: once a thought has passed through the mind, it joins the unchangeable past. Only the thoughts we are having at this instant—not the objects of thought—are truly thought-dependent.

But the assertion of reality's mind-independence does not entail a collapse into positivism. To the contrary, critical realism sharply opposes positivism, and arguably makes a better case against it than social constructionism does. One of positivism's crucial assumptions is its criterion for designating something as real. That criterion is perception: a thing exists only if it can be observed—"*esse* is *percipi*," in Berkeley's phrase. Accordingly the condition for asserting the existence of something is our knowledge of it; we must understand being in terms of our knowledge. We can know our experiences, but not things themselves: ontology is dependent upon, collapsed into, or even disavowed in favor of epistemology (Bhaskar, *Realist Theory of Science* 36–40). Allegiance to perception (or another cognitive phenomenon, such as language) and skepticism toward ontology also characterize social constructionism. When positivism and social constructionism contend that nothing exists without a mind, that mind is undeniably human. In both philosophies humans are central to reality: the world revolves around us. In other words, positivism and social constructionism are radically anthropocentric.

In contrast, critical realism maintains that something is real if it has *causal powers*, that is, the power to create a change, whether in another thing or in the causal entity itself. Causal powers necessarily include not only the ability to create change, but also to be changed: they include susceptibility to the causal powers of other entities. If changes happen—for example, if something moves or acquires a new shape or alters something else—then causal forces are at work. For realism, generative powers constitute reality, and even descriptive terms (like *red*) attribute powers to things (such as the tendency to reflect light of a certain wavelength).

The concept of causality cannot be restricted to the mechanical interaction of discrete objects or to the application of some external force upon an entity. A causal power can act across space (as in gravity), and it can arise from things that aren't physical objects (such as someone's intention to act). Moreover, the causal power does not have to act at all times, nor always act with the same result: the power may be latent or inactive, it may strengthen, wane or alter, and its action may be blocked, diminished or displaced, because action is always *interaction*, either with other entities in its environment or among its own constituent structures. The spotlight has the power to illuminate even if it's off, unless its bulb blows out; two actors may be good individually but acquire a special chemistry when acting together; a fine singer's voice declines with age. Causality concerns potentialities and tendencies—not behavioral regularities, universal laws, logical formulas or linear sequences of events. Exceptions aren't necessarily disproof.

Whatever causes change is a real entity, even if not necessarily a physical entity, and not necessarily one that is understood or even known to exist. It may be possible to demonstrate that a causal entity exists (through perceptions of its effects) despite the impossibility of observing the entity itself. Even the absence of something may be causal. For instance, the relative absence of heat causes entropy, the lack of food causes hunger, Tom Wingfield's ignorance of the gentleman caller's impending marriage in *The Glass Menagerie* causes his sister's heartbreak and his own departure. When positivism conceptualizes cause and effect as separate states marked only by difference, it fails to provide a concept of change. Because critical realism conceptualizes causality in terms of powers, it is able to sustain a concept of change, including ideas of process and work. Realism's aim, then, is to identify causal mechanisms, and determine how they work and how they generate particular outcomes (Bhaskar, *Realist Theory of Science* 79–90, 175–84, 231–40; Harré 185–88, 269–84, 296–314).

If reality consists of causal entities—"generative mechanisms," in Bhaskar's phrase—then it must be stratified. In fact, it is stratified in two senses. One is familiar to most people: the world has "layers" of entities, in which things existing at one layer are composed of entities at a lower layer or compose entities at a higher level. There is a vast array of generative entities ranging from basic materiality (physical and chemical mechanisms), through the biosphere (such as physiological and ecological structures), to the social realm (economic systems, communication, family-gender structures, and so forth).

The world is layered in this manner because of *emergence*. In emergence, new beings (objects, structures, relationships, concepts, et cetera) arise out of preexisting material. They possess distinctive, relatively autonomous causal powers or properties which can neither be reduced to the stratum from which they emerged, nor induced or deduced from it: they really are new powers or properties. Thus life emerged from chemical and physical reality, the species *homo sapiens* emerged within the biological realm, human society emerged from the biological realm, capitalism emerged within the social realm, and specific ways of producing theatre emerged within capitalism. An emergent entity's powers can affect the action of things at the lower stratum, whether through compulsion or constraint. Human intentionality, for example, enables people to act not only upon each other, but also upon biological, chemical, and physical objects (say, by putting apple seeds in the ground, or by drinking coffee), in order to achieve certain goals and purposes. Emergent powers are conditioned by lower strata: the latter determine the power's limits and may explain how it came into existence (for instance, what features of the brain make thought possible, or impossible if the thinker dies), but they explain little about what the emergent power actually is and does (in this example, what thought consists of and what a person thinks) (Bhaskar, *Dialectic* 49–56, 172, 397, 400; Bhaskar, *Possibility of Naturalism* 97–99).

The first type of stratification consists of the layers of objects which compose the world. Understanding these objects is the goal of scientific ontologies, which are substantive theories about the specific nature of an entity and its relationships with other entities. The second type of stratification pertains to philosophical ontology, since it concerns objects' mode of existence. For Bhaskar, reality is stratified into three ontological domains. The fundamental domain is the *real*. All real entities possess various causal powers and susceptibilities which affect and are affected by other entities; and if something has causal power, it is real. Powers create potentialities or tendencies which may or may not be manifested, depending on the circumstances. But at this level, powers exist as a realm of possibilities awaiting their exercise. When (as a result of their tendencies and susceptibilities) entities interact, they produce events, which occupy Bhaskar's second domain, the *actual*. On this view, things may be real but not actual, in the sense that their powers may not be currently exercised: a car has the power to move, even if right now it's parked. The actual may be understood ontologically both as an emergent stratum, and as a small subset of the real, since events and actualized possibilities possess causal powers. For instance, they condition subsequent events. Finally, some fraction of those events are or result in experiences or concepts. These constitute the third domain, which (depending on the account) is the *empirical*, the *subjective*, or the *semiosic*. The reasons for the variance will be taken up later; in all three versions, consciousness and its contents are but the tip of the ontological iceberg, the contingent products of a myriad underlying dynamics and conditions. Critical realism's philosophical stratification of ontology into three domains is at odds with the view that reality must be understood strictly in terms of one domain, an epistemological one of experience, perception, or discourse. By finding that the conscious or discursive realm is but a tiny part of reality, critical realism rejects anthropocentrism, for human consciousness no longer serves as the litmus test of existence. Thus critical realism displaces humankind from the center of the universe (Bhaskar, *Realist Theory of Science* 44–45, 58, 61–62, 243; Bhaskar, *Scientific Realism* 4).

Understanding critical realism's three domains is essential for the analysis of theatrical performance I will be undertaking. I must emphasize, however, that all three domains are real: in particular, thoughts have causal powers since they can affect our actions—they must not be treated as somehow contrasting with reality merely because they are thoughts. (Obviously the *content* of a thought may contrast with reality. Unicorns may not be real, but the concept of a unicorn *is* real and has a real impact.)

Due to its attention to causal factors, critical realism tends not to view entities in isolation: things always interact with other things or change as a result of internal dynamics, and so individual entities always exist and act within a context or whole. Things are constituted by both their components and their relations with others. Changes to one element affect the system of relationships and the dynamics of the elements' interaction. (Consider, for instance, how a play performance can alter simply by a single cast change.) Things belong to or consist of totalities, that is, systems of internal relations; and systems are emergent entities possessing causal powers underivable from their constituents. However, totalities do not have to be hermetic, with all their relations being internal and necessary: they may also have external or contingent relations (including relations with external or internal totalities), forming "partial totalities." In fact, most totalities are partial (or open, if you prefer). Since totalities have two or more elements, the researcher can always switch perspectives from one element to another: if we switch perspectives on totality itself, in its inward form totality is reflexivity (Bhaskar, *Dialectic* 123–27, 272–76, 401, 405; and see Mohanty 139).

Reflexivity is an essential element of human agency. For Bhaskar, agency must be understood as intentional, embodied, and causally efficacious. Reflexivity plays a role in agency because it is fundamental to intentionality, that is, to a person's reasons for acting. Reasons are a form of reflexivity, in which people not only monitor what they are doing, but monitor that monitoring by means of a sign system (such as language) which allows them to assess their mental states and experiences, and thereby develop an understanding of what they are doing, have done, or are considering doing. Such understandings characteristically explain why an agent had taken or would take an action, that is, their reasons for acting. Reasons are themselves causes, when they are acted upon. They provide the purposes and meaningfulness of actions. Thus intentionality and causal efficacy are intimately connected—not, of course, that all of an agent's actions or causal effects are intentional (far from it), but that agents are to significant extent able to envision and *choose* among those possible actions and effects over which they do have control.[7] Reflexivity and its relationship to agency is key to the ontology of theatre, as I will show in chapter 4.

Agents are one part of what constitutes society. Society is more than simply the aggregate of individuals, or the sum of their individual interrelations. It is a complex emergent partial totality, possessing sui generis characteristics because its dynamics and very existence depend on the activities and inactivities of people, most of whom are now long dead. That fact alone (and there are others) make society's ontological structure highly complex, as I will show.

3

I have said nothing yet about critical realism's epistemology, save that like social constructionism, critical realism maintains that knowledge is socially produced. There are three major issues: the mediated, theory-laden character of perception; our access to the world beyond our theories about it; and the certainty of knowledge.

Perception and knowledge are necessarily theory-mediated. We perceive things under one description or another. But one needs to be cautious about what that means. Commonly used examples of the theory-mediated and incommensurable character of perception are the goblet/faces and duck/rabbit drawings, in which one must interpret the picture in either one way or the other, perhaps in rapid succession but not at the same time or with some sort of merge. But such drawings are specially designed to elicit exclusive perception choices, and they scarcely represent normal situations, such as seeing a spotted roundish shape through a microscope versus seeing a paramecium (Keat and Urry 50–54). Here the visual image is the same, and it is the observer's scientific training that differs.

A better example of theory-mediation is color perception. Color pertains to the way we perceive light, which occurs in a continuous spectrum. Different cultures divide the spectrum in different ways, and some may establish far fewer or far more colors than others. The boundaries within the color continuum are socially (and to some extent even individually) determined, giving us culturally relative color theories. However, differences in categorization do not entail that cultures actually see different colors, they simply mean that the continuum is broken up differently; and it turns out that all cultures pick essentially the same wavelength as the best example of red. Although observation is never theory-free and our access to reality is always mediated through signs and representations, nevertheless we have genuine contact with (and may therefore obtain valid knowledge of) the world outside. Definitions of color are established to some extent by the physiology of eyes, and no culture can choose to see ultraviolet.

Finally, most things do not exist as continua: there are real breaks between objects. In any comparison of perceptions, there is at least one element that is independent of the theory under consideration, and so can serve as a reference or identification framework. People can debate whether a sunrise consists of the sun moving upward or the horizon turning downward, but they can agree that the sun looks like an extremely bright yellowish-white disk that moves across the sky: its identification at this basic level has no bearing on the question at hand. Regardless how they understood the sun's movement, the ancient Greeks, Chinese and Maya (among others) all discovered that the solar year is approximately 365¼ days long—which would be impossible if reality were truly a social construct.

Consciously or not, people adopt frames of reference, categorizations, and images of the world's structure. The frames tend to be metaphoric at base, which is where the idea of paradigms comes into the picture. Building knowledge of powers and generative mechanisms involves creating models, which often invoke analogies and images (icons) drawn from familiar sources. The model isn't eliminated later: it remains embodied in theory. For realists, then, models can make existential claims, and theory-construction proceeds through both logic and analogy, both reason and imagination: as Rom Harré puts it, "at the heart of a theory are various modeling relations which are types of analogy.... [T]he prime vehicle for thought is a statement-picture complex."[8]

We may have only indirect, mediated access to entities outside our minds, but since real entities have causal powers, they have direct access to us. That access is part of the force of reality upon consciousness: if we believe we can walk on air, gravitation will quickly show otherwise. But the outer world's access to the mind is far more extensive and graceful than that. From a semiotic perspective, one can say that not only do many signs refer outward to the world, but also that the world points inward to our signs, shaping and molding them. The force of real entities also places significant limits on the sort of perceptions and interpretations we may have of them, and so the range of viable theories cannot be infinite. The powers of the material world usually operate quite independently of the human ability to control, experience, and sometimes even imagine them, and so establish a limit or horizon on the possible ways we may interpret or theorize their activity; but they also reveal the gaps in our knowledge and provide the tantalizing possibility of filling them. In short, facts limit, condition, but also enable and even motivate our interpretations. That said, there remains a range of theories, which can only be narrowed by undertaking practices (experimentation, field research, historical analysis, close reading, and the like) to turn up further evidence. Knowledge depends on both empirical evidence *and* theory-construction. Explanations invoke substantive criteria for validation, not just formal ones (Bhaskar, *Realist Theory of Science* 13–14, 56–59; Lovell 17–18). Through this process we may obtain extremely high levels of certainly about some theory, but absolute certainty is unattainable. Nor is it necessary: knowledge does *not* require absolute certainty.

The issue of certainty is a critical one. The desire for absolute certainty was fundamental to Cartesian thought, and it is no less central to positivism, which excludes all talk of the existence of imperceptible entities and causal forces as speculation: only sensate experience provides the sort of certainty that positivism demands. The impulse toward logicization and mathematization stems from the same root. Social constructionism and critical realism agree that absolute certainty is unavailable to the study of society and culture. However, the two philosophies' next steps are radically different. Social constructionism takes the impossibility of absolute certainty as a warrant for skepticism that things outside the mind can be known at all. By adopting this type of skepticism, social constructionism accepts the positivist notion that absolute certainty is the proper measure of knowledge and that the only permissible concept of certainty defines it as absolute: if it is not absolute, it is not certain, and without absolute certainty there is no knowledge.[9]

Critical realism, in contrast, maintains that there never was nor will be any absolute certainly—not in the human sciences, or even in the physical sciences. Error demonstrates that reality exists independently from our thoughts, and the possibility of error is an ineradicable condition for *all* thoughts about reality. Critical realism is *fallibilistic*: we produce theories which fit the evidence available today, but as we gain more (or other sorts of) evidence, the theories may need to be refined or replaced, and alternative theories will be debated. Our experiences with reality force us to be modest about what we know. As Bhaskar strikingly argues, "To be a fallibilist about knowledge, it is necessary to be a realist about things. Conversely, to be a sceptic about things is to be a dogmatist about knowledge." A corollary of fallibilism is that the merit of a theory lies not in its predictive power (a notion which for the social sciences is ludicrous), but in its explanatory power.[10]

Nevertheless, evidence does accrue, and provides a rational basis for preferring one theory over another. In principle the atomic theory of matter could be completely wrong, but given the ever-increasing data, that's highly improbable; hence it is rational to believe that atoms exist. If the theory is faulty, it is more likely to be incomplete, or correct only within certain boundaries. Or it could be completely wrong yet remain useful for a huge array of circumstances, which is what happened to Newtonian mechanics: Einsteinian relativity proved it incorrect at its very assumptions, yet pragmatically it remains applicable for nearly everything that people ordinarily do. All told, critical realism upholds *epistemic relativism*: all of our knowledge and beliefs are socially produced and historically contingent. At the same time, however, it maintains that there are (or can be) rational grounds for choosing one theory over another: a *judgmental rationality* that opposes the relativist notion that all beliefs are equally valid and none can be preferred over another.[11] It is possible to talk about truth: indeed, it is scholarly and political responsibility. As Christopher Norris puts it, "the postmodern retreat from values of truth and reason" promotes "a placid assurance that change comes about for no better reason ... than mere boredom with the old paradigm"—an idea which he finds symptomatic of "the ethical bankruptcy entailed by [the] slide into an outlook of *laissez-faire* relativism" (*Against Relativism* 3).

The ethical and political implications of social constructionism's relativism about truth are troubling. Relativism rightly opposes ethnocentrism and strives to bestow respect to all cultures. But it also claims that making judgments about a culture's ideas is deeply disrespectful. One must take another culture always and completely on its own terms. Satya Mohanty, however, argues that relativism undermines the very multiculturalism that it (and he) supports. By asserting that there is no responsible way to adjudicate between cultural spaces and that cultural spaces must be seen as equivalent, relativists implicitly deny that there is any particular reason to engage with another culture or take it seriously (Mohanty 116–48). Arguing from a "postpositivist realist" perspective, Mohanty values differences and disagreements among cultures because they can unearth important information, leading to new knowledge. That requires the ability to establish an objective referential framework and the possibility that some of a culture's ideas (including one's own) are right, some partially right, and some wrong. Fallibility is the condition not just for knowledge, but also for moral claims and cultural values. Thus "the realist will favor cultural diversity as *the best social condition* in which objective knowledge about human flourishing might be sought" (243, his emphasis).

One example of social constructionism's failure to engage the Other is its typical hostility toward science. Far from attempting to understand what science is, many (though not all) social constructionists assume a simplistic account of science or rely on faddish popularizations, and don't distinguish science from its positivistic representation, its technological applications, or the political or economic uses of either. Nor is that the only case of social constructionism's self-blindness and arrogance. One of its critiques of science is that it is a pursuit of mastery, as exemplified by Francis Bacon's aphorism "Nature to be commanded must be obeyed." Certainly his approach to science pursues mastery, but it is a mastery within limits imposed by nature's dictates. In contrast, social constructionism's claim that cultures define reality any way they like asserts a mastery without limits at all.

Without the ability to refer to external reality and make truth claims about it, political action becomes effectively (even if unintentionally) meaningless, since exploitation, oppression and abuse cannot be caused by material conditions outside the mind and become in essence the result of a poor attitude or rhetorical manipulation. Ironically, social constructionists' aspirations for social change are undermined by their own ideas. In fact, the refusal to permit a rational basis for choosing between theories has boomeranged into an indefensible defenselessness against ideologies like "intelligent design." The latter's adherents have relied precisely on the idea that all theories are equally valid—and that evolution is "just" a theory—as a key part of their campaign. For that matter, the notion that facts are purely social constructions was almost a point of pride to the George W. Bush administration, for whom the facts were whatever they wanted, who cared only for "truthiness," and whose scorn for science rivaled social constructionism's. Postmodernism indeed—with a vengeance.

Much current theatre scholarship is driven by the author's political and ethical goal of critiquing the status quo, perhaps in some manner subverting it, and even offering some signposts toward progressive or liberatory change. The various forms of identity theory (such as critical race theory, queer theory, and feminist analysis) were all born from such intentions, which I and maybe all critical realists share. But social constructionist arguments tacitly maintain the fundamental philosophical assumptions of the culture its proponents wish to critique. Social constructionism's inability to connect its desired practice (hard as that may be to define: individual liberty, cultural equality, some abstract justice?) with its free-for-all theory undermines its moral legitimacy. It has led to the intellectual and political impasse we now so often see, of scholarship going around in its own tight circle, with little effect or relevance in the wider world. By shying away from the concept of truth, they gut their own ethical and political force. But if one aims to "speak truth to power," one damn well better be able to speak about truth.

Ethical issues come into better focus when one recognizes that material processes, social functions, and meanings are all *real*, are all causal powers in the social world, with real effects. But we live in a multileveled world. In particular, material realities (natural forces, tangible resources, physical actions, bodily states and the like) condition social life in ways that ideas and intentions can control or counteract only to a limited extent, even though it is also true that in certain circumstances ideas are decisively transformative. The statements "He was killed by witches" and "He was killed by an infection" simply do not have the same type of explanatory value, and human lives hang on the ability to say that for medical purposes, one theory is decidedly truer than another. Ultimately, experiences, interpretations, and even society itself are not altogether socially constructed. The human world is irreducibly social, but as an emergent entity it incorporates and manipulates physical and biological realities that are the conditions of its possibility but are scarcely social at all. At the same time, because there are many intersecting social forces, people face real choices from among competing needs and values and their decisions lead to material consequences. Art and philosophy also have material consequences, potentially including political consequences; hence it is quite in order to evaluate theories and theatres politically, even though they may have mixed political implications, and even though that is far from the only or necessarily the most important assessment one can make.

Critical realism provides a more thorough critique of positivism than social constructionism does. Both positivism and social constructionism accept the use of perception as the criterion of reality (in the forms of experience and interpretation respectively). Critical realism instead upholds causality as the criterion of reality, including the reality of things we cannot perceive directly, but only through their effects. That difference alone has several results. Positivism and social constructionism reject the idea of an underlying reality, whereas critical realism maintains that reality is stratified (in more than one way). The former are anthropocentric, while the latter is not. Positivism and social constructionism doubt or deny ontology, and instead are epistemology-heavy, consequently becoming dogmatic about knowledge (or its impossibility); critical realism emphasizes ontology as the condition for all knowledge, and asserts that a condition of knowledge is that theories are inherently fallible even though we may attain a high degree of certainty about them. Because they depend on the perception criterion, positivism and social constructionism conflate being into knowledge of being; for critical realism, perception is just a fragment of stratified reality, and so there can be no such collapse between knowledge and being. Positivism states that there can be a theory-neutral language, whereas social constructionism rightly maintains that there is no such thing as a theory-free observation. Critical realism, however, adds that despite their denials, positivism and social constructionism are not *ontology*-free: the very insistence on the existence only of object-events, perception-events, sign-events and so forth commits them to an ontology, albeit a flat one. As Bhaskar maintains, "Ontology—and realism—are *inexorable.* The crucial questions in philosophy are *not whether, but which*" (*Dialectic* 205, his emphases). Positivism and social constructionism live in contradiction.

However, the philosophical credentials of any particular analysis (whether realist, social constructionist or positivist) do not guarantee its truth or falsity, or for that matter its political leanings. A person can agree with realist philosophy yet reject a specific theory with a realist basis. Realism does not stand or fall according to particular theories, but as a continuing program. And as a program, realism's strength is especially manifest in studies of history and society. The fact that action and communication are meaningful, purposeful, materially efficacious social activities makes critical realism particularly intelligible as a philosophical basis for theatre historiography. The tension and interplay between world and stage, idea and embodiment, conventions and technology, demand a multileveled and multifaceted understanding of existence. Further, even more surely than theory, theatre is a "statement-picture complex." Every performance embodies models, analogies, or icons of the world, presenting concrete theorizations of reality. Even the lightest comedy relies on certain understandings of existence. In a sense, then, theatre is a model of realist philosophy itself. Theatre is philosophical, as Aristotle might say. To turn toward its history, we must consider the conditions of theatre's own possibility: semiosis, society, and the structures of communication.

4

Underpinning the thesis that perception is necessarily mediated, there is a theory of signs. It goes almost without saying that signs and representations are fundamental to social life. In theatre studies, it is widely understood that theatre produces signs of signs. On stage you can represent a car by bringing on a car, but you can also use two chairs next to each other; an audience normally understands an actor's laughter not as a sign of her own amusement, but her character's. In this section I will sketch the basics of a critical realist semiotics, which has implications for the philosophical ontology I've just described and for the ontology of society. The latter not only affects sociological and historical research, it also plays a crucial role in my analysis of metatheatricality and theatricality itself.

The currently dominant understanding of the sign was developed in the early twentieth century by the Swiss linguist Ferdinand de Saussure, who defined the sign as having two parts: a meaningful component called a "signified," and the mental image of its spoken or written form, the "signifier." (Versions of this analysis go back at least to John Locke.) The relationship between the two is a social convention. Signs are distinguished only by their differences; the structure of differences forms a linguistic system (*langue*).

The linguistic system as such can only be understood by examining it during a single historical moment (synchronically) rather than across time (diachronically). Saussure named the study of sign systems "semiology," and argued that all sorts of social practices could be analyzed semiologically. That understanding laid the basis for structuralism and a hefty part of poststructuralism, supplying much of the impetus behind the "linguistic turn" and linguistic analogies.

However, the Saussurean sign involves nothing akin to a referent or object, and if it doesn't exclude the extra-mental world altogether, certainly gives it no role within the signification process. For that reason alone (and there are others), it cannot be incorporated into critical realism. Bhaskar breaks with this conception of signs, and argues that "the centrepiece of any adequate theory of meaning must be the semiotic triangle." He illustrates his idea with a diagram, the essence of which I present in figure 1.1 (Bhaskar, *Dialectic* 222–23). Bhaskar observes that nominalism customarily elides the signified, whereas post-structuralism (with Saussure) elides the referent; and he proposes that all three components of the semiotic triangle may have many other semiotic triangles attached to them.

Bhaskar's semiotic triangle bears a striking resemblance to Charles S. Peirce's concept of the sign. The value of Peircean semiotics for theatre studies has long been recognized (Elam; Carlson). His semiotics has sometimes been treated as a sort of footnote to Saussure that classifies signs as icons, indexes, or symbols, but in truth Peirce and Saussure have deeply dissimilar theories of signs. To keep them distinct, I will use "semiology" to refer to Saussurean theories, and "semiotics" for Peircean approaches. Even though Peirce can sometimes be eccentric and occasionally he makes odd swerves into both empiricism and idealism, large portions of his thought reveal a realist bent and with certain modifications many of his key ideas can be appropriated into critical realism.

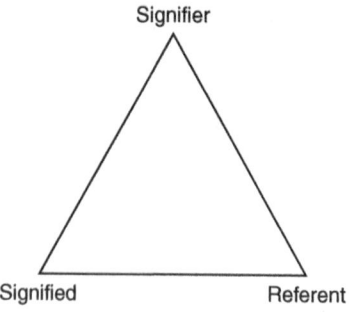

Figure 1.1   Bhaskar's Semiotic Triangle.

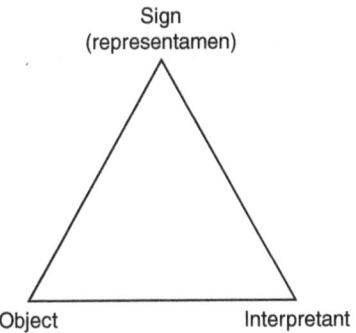

Figure 1.2   The Peircean Sign (basic version).

In its most basic form, the sign for Peirce has not two parts, but three.[12] These are the sign, object, and interpretant (see figure 1.2).[13] Unfortunately Peirce used the word "sign" both for the entire semiotic unit *and* for one of its parts, so he can be confusing; occasionally he adopted "representamen" for the part, and I will use that term for clarity's sake. Roughly speaking (but only roughly), the representamen is equivalent to the signifier, the interpretant to the signified, and the object to the referent. Thus it is comparable to Bhaskar's semiotic triangle. By recognizing the referent as a force within signification, Peirce's theory of semiosis satisfies realism; as I will show, it possesses other realist features, and at the same time upholds some of the most valuable contributions of post-structuralism.

Peirce's briefest definition of a sign is "something which stands to somebody for something in some respect or capacity" (*Collected Papers* 2.228).[14] This definition describes an operation or process aiming toward some effect or goal. A sign in Peirce's definition is always active, never static; it consists of an interaction between the sign-interpreter and another entity (human or not) (*Collected Papers* 5.484). Semiosis is an *act*, a practical action in the real world. The sign is also fundamentally mediative, as it enters between and so connects two things (the object and its interpretant).

The sign is mediative in another sense as well. For Peirce, the sign actually has *two* objects: the "dynamical object" and the "immediate object" (see figure 1.3). The dynamical object is the real object of reference in the world. Peirce defines the real as "that whose characters are independent of what anybody may think them to be"—an independence he accords even to dreams, once they have been dreamt (*Collected Papers* 5.405). Thus, as in critical realism, past experiences, concepts and fictions are all real, whether or not their referents are. For Peirce, the dynamical object in some way influences or corresponds to the sign. In contrast, the immediate object is the object as the sign presents it, that is, as a perception or mental image.

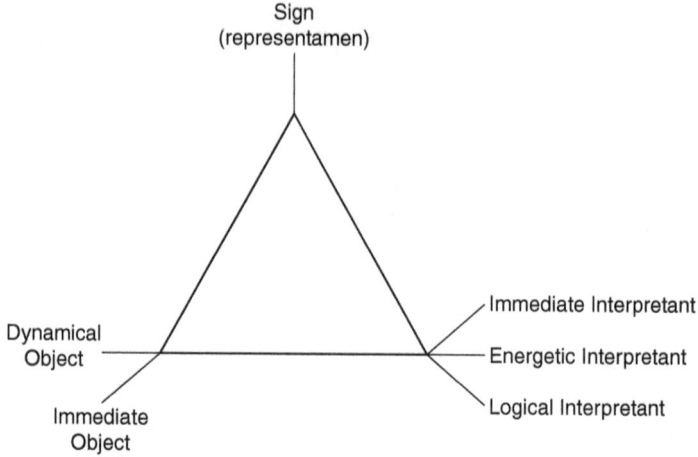

Figure 1.3   The Peircean Sign (elaborated version).

From the latter perspective, the object of a sign can only be another sign, and we can only obtain experience through signs. Knowledge consists solely of signs. Here Peirce anticipates social constructionist arguments concerning the semiological, theory-laden character of all perception. Nevertheless the dynamical object remains an extra-mental influence upon semiosis. Consequently the immediate object tends to give at least a hint or indication of the dynamical object, and knowledge of the dynamical object is possible, even if mediated and perhaps approximate. Signs, then, mediate our interpretive relation to the world (4.536, 4.539, 5.311, 5.473–74).

The sign (representamen) itself can have three main forms.[15] These are the icon, the index, and the symbol. The distinction derives from the relationships the representamen can have with the object. A relationship of similarity, analogy, or another comparably shared quality produces an icon (a category that includes not only pictures, but also metaphors, conceptual models, mathematical formulas, and so forth). An index is related to a specific object through a real relation, either by being its effect (the smoke produced by a fire, the rise of mercury in a thermometer), or by referring to it (an arrow toward something, a pronoun, a synecdoche). A symbol bears a conventional relationship to the object, and applies to the object as a general category (the word "dog" has only a conventional connection to actual dogs, and applies to all dogs). Saussure's semiology consists only of symbols in Peirce's sense. Often sign-types (relationships between signs and objects) are combined and "impure." For example, the "happy face" ☺ is a conventionalized icon (an iconic symbol); "experience," in one of its meanings, conjoins indexicality with conventionality. But the basic distinction is generally sufficient (*Collected Papers* 2.247–49, 2.276–306).

The interpretant is by far the most complex notion. There are three major points. First, any interpretant can become the object for a subsequent semiosis—and subsequent semiosis is the norm, at least among humans. Put phenomenologically, we live in a world that is, for us, one of unceasing semiosis; we are constantly developing our dim perceptions into fullblown concepts, rethinking our past, and so forth ad infinitum. Conversely, if one tries to trace a semiosis backward, one simply comes upon somewhat less-developed signs, never to an object free of an interpretant. So infinite semiosis, at least in principle, occurs in both directions (*Collected Papers* 1.339, 2.274). Bhaskar appears to have arrived at a similar conception when he speaks of the semiotic triangle possibly being attached to many other semiotic triangles.

Second, an interpretant need not be a concept. Hence the Peircean interpretant is not equivalent to the Saussurean signified. Peirce preferred to describe the interpretant as a "significate effect," of which there are several kinds. His analysis changed somewhat over the years, but the best account posits three types of possible interpretant—"possible," because after the initial one, it is contingent whether further interpretants arise. The start is the "emotional" interpretant. The term is a bit misleading since Peirce has in mind not the grand emotions such as joy, fear, sorrow or rage, but low-level feelings such as recognition, acceptance, interest, or uncertainty. Next, the "energetic" interpretant is a sort of action, possibly of the body (a response to a command or to a traffic light), but more likely a mental effort, a basic idea (Peirce is not terribly clear about this). Finally, there is the "logical" interpretant. It may be a concept, but a concept may always be followed by another logical interpretant. The *ultimate* logical interpretant, he argues, is a strengthening, weakening, or alteration in a *habit*: a habit-change. Such habit-changes need not arise gradually: Peirce notes that even a single effort of thought can produce it. At a social scale, such interpretants inculcate what Bourdieu terms *habitus*.[16]

Unlike the signifier, the interpretant is not anthropocentric. All that Peirce's theory requires for semiosis to occur is the presence of a mind or even what he called a "quasi-mind," which forms an interpretant—a significate effect—from the sign. "Thought is not necessarily connected with a brain," he wrote, noting that his semiotic analysis attempts to encompass non-human thought (*Collected Papers* 4.551; see also 4.536, 4.550). The dance of the honeybee may signify nothing to us, but be highly meaningful to another honeybee; antibodies "recognize" chemical markers on cells. Semiosis does not require human consciousness.

When I began describing the Peircean sign, I emphasized its mediative character. For humans, that makes the sign inherently dialogic and social. Peirce frequently argued that thought itself is dialogic. Likewise, V. N. Voloshinov, whose effort to develop a marxist (and, it has been argued, critical realist) theory of language remains vital to any understanding of the social nature of discourse, called thought "inner speech."[17]

Unlike Saussure, Peirce does not privilege language as the model through which all sign-production must be understood. Instead, Peirce is concerned with the variety of possible signs from the very start. And a Peircean sign is not coterminous with a single word, a simple signal like a traffic light, and so forth: a sign may be of any size and complexity. Propositions, arguments, experiences, triptychs, jazz riffs, plays, rituals, thoughts are all signs. More, according to Peirce the self is a sign, both constituted and manifested in and through signs. Here too Peirce contrasts with Saussure: where Saussure defined semiology as a branch of general psychology, Peirce argues the opposite—since the self is a sign, psychology is a form of semiosis (*Collected Papers* 5.313–15, 6.270; Saussure 15–16). Voloshinov similarly emphasized that "[t]he reality of the inner psyche is the same as the reality of the sign" (11–13, 25–39, quoting 26, emphasis removed). The view that the self is a sign corresponds with theatrical performance, in which the character is a semiotically constructed "self." In this sense one might call a dramatic character a "virtual person," or as I will explain later, a virtual agent.

Much more can be said to flesh out the critical realist theory of signs. However, my focus here is on the implications of semiotics for social ontology and ultimately for theatre. What I have presented so far is sufficient for that purpose.

5

Earlier I discussed reality's stratification into three ontological domains. The *real* consists of entities possessing causal powers and susceptibilities. Entities interact in various ways and so produce events, which constitute the second domain, the *actual*. Finally, some events are or result in conscious activities. These belong to the third domain, which Bhaskar originally called the *empirical*, consisting of experiences; later he expanded the domain to include concepts as well, under the term *subjective* (*Realist Theory of Science* 56–59; *Dialectic* 11, 393; *Plato, Etc.* 23, 42, 204). As I've argued elsewhere (Nellhaus, "Signs"), Bhaskar's account of the domains has two shortcomings. First, defining the third ontological domain as the "empirical" or even as the "subjective" raises several concerns, including a risk of cultural bias, epistemological individualism, and anthropocentrism. But as Peirce shows, psychology, experience and subjectivity are categories of *signs*.

Thus the third ontological domain consists of meanings embodied in signs and semioses. Because sign-production is incessant, I will call it the *semiosic* domain.

The second weakness in Bhaskar's account of the three domains is the vagueness of the criteria used to differentiate domains. At some points he argues that the subjective is a subset of the actual, and the actual a subset of the real; at other points he indicates that in some sense, the subjective is "above" the actual, and the actual over the real. These descriptions are hazy. What distinguishes the domains, I believe, is *emergence*. The domain of the real consists of powers and susceptibilities; hence we can define it as the domain of possibilities or conditions of possibility. From these arise events and new entities; but these occupy a new and emergent domain, the actual. Actualities not only are governed by underlying structures and generative mechanisms, but also may act upon them. Actuality is a new property, which cannot be reduced to mere possibility. Likewise for semiosis: among the many actual events, some involve interactions in which with a mind (or quasi-mind) forms an interpretant of an object. Signs emerge, possessing a new property or power: meaning. When people act on signs (that is, their reasons for acting), the signs act upon actualities and even possibilities.

These revisions of the ontological domains bear implications for the ontology of social entities. As I've noted, society is an emergent totality that arose from the natural and biological world. It remains tied to that world through geography, weather, environmental changes, resource usage, and so forth. But society has characteristics that cannot be reduced to biology, and so it needs to be analyzed on its own terms. Bhaskar provides the basic foundation stones: social structures are only relatively enduring; social structures are in some measure dependent both on agents' activities and their concepts; and neither structures nor agents can be reduced to the other. Agents act on the basis of given structural conditions, and their actions (or inactions) ultimately reproduce and/or transform those structures (*Reclaiming Reality* 33–38; *Dialectic* 154–60). These are absolutely essential concepts; nevertheless, they do not provide a fully workable ontology of society.

Peirce himself, having few interests in social analysis, has little to say on the question. But a way to connect philosophical to social ontology can be inferred from an undertheorized aspect of Margaret Archer's critical realist social theory. When Archer addresses ontology, she (like Bhaskar) focuses on the need to distinguish between structures and agents, a distinction that allows us to investigate their different powers and the ways in which they interact; she calls this position "analytical dualism." In particular she emphasizes that structures pre-date agents' actions, and that social reproduction or transformation post-dates those actions (*Realist Social Theory* 12–16).

The critical realist concept of social ontology, even in this bare-bones sketch, bears comparison with a somewhat similar analysis. Anthony Giddens's structuration theory treats structure and agency as inextricably interlinked and at every moment mutually constitutive. On this view, structures are "virtual" until instantiated by agents—a theory that is modeled on Saussure's concepts of *langue* (language) and *parole* (utterances). In contrast, critical realism views society's strata as interrelated and interactive, but still ontologically distinct, analytically separable, and real (not virtual). Rather than being simultaneously mutually constitutive, they are mutually transformative *over time*, in a rhythmic or cyclic sense. People are born into a social structure not of their personal making, but given to them from the past, the result of the activities of the long dead. Having been thrown into this social structure, they receive various enablements and constraints from their position within it, and as they work their way through the possibilities, choices and necessities presented to them, they reproduce and transform that social structure, until they die and leave it for the succeeding generation. Even though billions of these cycles proceed concurrently across the globe, what any particular agent finds is not a mutual constitution of structure and agency, but rather a set of given conditions which the agent subsequently acts within and upon (Archer, *Culture and Agency* 149–61; Bhaskar, *Possibility of Naturalism* 31–44; Bhaskar, *Dialectic* 154–64).

However, when Archer actually applies her theory to social developments, she clearly presumes a more complex ontology, since her theory explicates social change in *three* realms: structure, agency, and culture. She refuses to treat culture as being simply "inside people's heads," because much of it isn't. Instead, large portions reside in the world's cultural archives and repertoires. Thus knowledge can exist embodied in a document or artifact, without anyone currently possessing that knowledge. In each of the three areas (structures, agents, culture) Archer finds a similar cycle of initial conditions, social interaction, and eventual elaboration that sets the stage for a new round of activity. Each area possesses its own unique set of emergent properties, leading her to speak of structural emergent properties, people's emergent properties, and cultural emergent properties (*Realist Social Theory* 172–94).

Archer's implicit social ontology corresponds strikingly to the three ontological domains as I redefined them via Peirce: the real (possibilities given by underlying structures), the actual (events), and the semiosic (meanings and sign-processes). On first sight the equation of agents with events may appear unwarranted. However, social agency concerns a person's location within a set of socially positioned practices and her ability to act within that location (an ability, however, that depends on being embodied and having intentions). Agents *act*, and what keeps agents in their locations within the system of positioned practices is the system's continuous functioning so that the positions are constantly being (re)produced: they are events.

Instead of a two-tiered social ontology consisting of structures and agents, we have (for the moment) a three-tiered social ontology of structures, agents, and culture. That arrangement accords semiosis a clearer place in the theory of social dynamics. The homology with philosophical ontology is more than an analogy or a coincidence. It arises because agents act materially, they depend on social structures for their positions and resources, and they are thinking beings who produce signs when they experience, conceptualize and communicate.

However, things are not quite this simple. Two alterations are necessary. First, although the three tiers establish social ontology, they will not suffice when one examines the ontology of specific *practices* such as material production, interpersonal activity, and theatre. In certain ways the tiers seem to intersect. For instance, economic production cannot occur without semiotic activity such as imagining a product and ways to produce it. The product not only has economic value, it also becomes part of the cultural sphere (say) by being a status marker, since choices of food, clothing, and entertainment are as much indexes of social position as wealth is (see Bourdieu). Similarly, discursive practices cannot occur without the use of some sort of physical material, such as speech sounds or marks on paper. The effectiveness of a discourse, its authority for its audience, is conditioned by the speaker's social position. For these reasons Voloshinov describes the sign as simultaneously material, sociological, and meaningful (33). Finally, intentionality plays a role at every level. Intentionality is the emergent property distinguishing human agency from its biological substratum (Bhaskar, *Possibility of Naturalism* 335; Bhaskar, *Dialectic* 51). However, while only people (not structures or signs) can have intentions, intentionality marks and orients people's products, including structures and signs, so that these too exert some form of goal orientation or motivating pressure, such as a sociological function, a set of interests, or a discursive (illocutionary) force.

Thus social structures involve *both* material resources *and* embedded concepts, even if the former weigh more heavily than the latter in the analytical balance (Archer, *Realist Social Theory* 145–47, 175). Cultural activity primarily depends on systems of meanings, but also requires material resources, especially human ones. Agents consist of people, who interact with each other but also depend on and produce structures and discourses. The simultaneously material, sociological and meaningful character of each tier leads to my second adjustment. As we see, cultural elements form part of all levels of social ontology, even if they do so in different ways and to different extents in each. Consequently it is misleading to call the tier that consists principally of meaning systems "cultural": more accurately, it is discursive, understanding that term as encompassing not just verbal expressions but also visual and aural imagery. Social ontology thus consists of structures, agents, and discourses.

6

Social ontology is constituted by a sort of "double emergence." On the one hand are structures, agents and discourses, which parallel the real, actual, and semiosic ontological domains. On the other hand, social practices necessarily have material, sociological, and meaningful aspects, which we may call the phenomenological dimensions of social activity.[18] The phenomenological dimensions of practice correlate with the three main modes of explaining people's activities, delineating in what manner, to what end, and with what understanding people act.

I'll illustrate with the York Corpus Christi Cycle. The York Cycle dramatized events from the Bible, from Genesis to the Last Judgment. It is the longest and oldest of the extant mystery cycles (the best known is the Wakefield Cycle). Each biblical story was presented as a short play or "pageant" staged on one or occasionally two wagons and the grounds immediately around it. The pageant wagons were towed through York, stopping for performance at a dozen or so stations, to be replaced by the next pageant in the sequence. Thus it created a procession of plays through the city that began at dawn and probably concluded past midnight. The York Cycle's processional staging has been well analyzed in terms of the three modes of explanation, and I discuss the cycle in more depth in chapter 2 as a case study of the interactions between oral and literate culture.

Technical explanations focus on material realities to show how social structures, practices and forces operate, divulging their dispositions to act in certain ways and generate certain effects, because the practical manner in which people accomplish an activity affects their behavior and attitudes. A technical explanation of the York Cycle's processional staging might focus on how York's narrow streets couldn't accommodate the festival's audiences. Processional staging resolved this problem, and recent re-creations have shown that it was a brisk and efficient staging method.

People generally do and say things for a purpose. We identify such purposes through *motivational* or *functional* explanations, which concern the intentions, roles, and interests behind agents' actions: reasons are causes. However, people may not recognize or understand their reasons; they may achieve, miss, undercut or exceed their intended goals; practices and people can lose their functions, gain new ones, or change their approach; and the goals, practices, and effects may not be acceptable to others. To return to my example, York's processional staging developed largely around the strength of the craft and merchant guilds, each of which took responsibility for a single play and its pageant wagon. The guilds' participation may indicate their eagerness to join in the festival; or it may reveal a civic regime that the powerful merchant guild enforced but the poorer trades resented; or it may even show both.

Sorting through agents' motivations, some theorists have distinguished between immediate interests, which focus on what is possible within given social relations, and fundamental interests, which concern the reproduction or transformation of social relations (Wright 88–91). This useful contrast may be further refined by aligning it with social ontology. Thus immediate interests pertain to how one may influence the behavior of other agents; fundamental interests, to the reproduction and transformations of social structures; and discursive interests, to attitudes, beliefs and values insofar as they direct and justify agents' behaviors. (The stratification of interests implies that there are also multiple levels of possible social conflict.) The distinction between immediate, fundamental, and discursive interests applies to theatre: a play's immediate objective is to show characters' actions in a dramatic situation; its fundamental objective is to establish the theatrical relation between stage and audience; and its discursive objective is to materialize scriptive imagery, language and ideas.

Agents have an understanding and rationale for their actions, and the meanings of action influence the intention to act. Thus, *hermeneutic* explanations disclose the meanings behind people's activities. Practices not only have methods and goals, but also significance: along with the pragmatic and purposeful aspects of their activities, people act for symbolic ends or in symbolic ways, and produce meanings in the course of their activity. York's processional staging may be analyzed hermeneutically as a deliberate echo of Jesus's entry into Jerusalem, and of royal "triumphal" entries into medieval cities. In addition, by beginning at Holy Trinity Priory at the town's outskirts and ending at the Pavements in the city's center (where public punishments took place), the procession's path echoed the movement from the Creation to the Last Judgment. These symbolic elements helped to consolidate the pageant's political and religious functions.[19]

Taken together, society's ontological levels and their phenomenological dimensions can be represented as a grid, as shown by table 1.1. I have attempted to indicate what sorts of social elements occupy each grid cell (more could easily be added). Due to the mixed character of all social practices, it is sometimes difficult to decide where to place certain features of society. Nevertheless the majority are, I think, clear.

Working counterclockwise, in the lower left cell I've placed the material structures of society (forces of production and human bodies)—the practical, even technical aspects of the activities that meet human and social needs

Table 1.1 The Ontological and Phenomenological Dimensions of Social Activity

		Phenomenological Dimensions of Practice *(Explanatory modes in italics)*		
		Material *(Technical)*	**Sociological** *(Motivational/Functional)*	**Meaningful** *(Hermeneutic)*
Ontological Levels of Society *(General ontological domains in italics)*	**Discourses** *(Semiosic)*	Texts, sounds, visual images, locutionary acts (material signs/ representamens)	Illocutionary forces, intended meanings Psychological processes (inner speech) Discursive interests, ideologies, and ideological motives Power as ability to choose, interpret, and express	Discursive articulations or formations; reasons/reasoning Theories, novels, plays, music, dance, films, other cultural products Symbols
	Agents *(Actual)*	Habits/habitus Institutions, organizations Communities	Intentions Immediate interests Social interactions, memberships, alliances, oppositions Power as ability to act	Discursive and performance strategies Identities as self-images, other-images; identifications Social imaginaries Indexes
	Structures *(Real/Possible)*	Forces of production (e.g., economic, communicational, familial) Bodies	Social positions Social relations of production Fundamental interests Power as domination, exploitation	Image schemas, basic-level categories; meaning structures; structures of feelings Icons

of whatever sort (food, shelter, companionship, children, knowledge, and so forth). Out of these material processes emerge social relations and forms of power such as domination, subordination, and exploitation (at the cell right). People occupy places within the system of positioned practices from which they strive to sustain themselves and improve their lot, but under continually changing conditions. Thus, intentionally or unintentionally, they both reproduce and transform that system.

From both the material and sociological dynamics emerge meanings in the form of basic concepts and images, which are usually or principally iconic. Capitalism, for example, generates images of the individual as the source or origin of all action. Basic categories and image schemas (to be addressed in chapter 3) conjoin to form meaning-structures that act as generative principles for higher-level forms of meaning. Image schemas provide the basis for two related sets of agentially oriented ideas (first cell up). The first set comprises discursive and performance strategies, which are essentially methods of acting upon or implementing given image schemas. As I will explain later, they are an inherent part of dramaturgy, staging, acting and many other aspects of theatre. Discursive strategies are also embedded in philosophical matters. Examples include anthropocentrism, the objective/subjective divide, methodological individualism, and the perception criterion of reality. Thus discursive and performance strategies are indexes to concepts of the human/world relationship. The other set of agentially oriented meanings consists of the images of Self and Other that constitute ideas of social identity and establish various other types of identifications and social analogies, such as between the civil rights movement and the feminist movement (cf. Laclau and Mouffe 135–36, 153–56). For example, American melodrama employed varying strategies of identification (common ground, antithesis, and the assumed or hegemonic "we") to suit changing goals and pressures (McConachie, "Cultural Hegemony" 45–55). Essentially these are social imaginaries. Since identity-images are distinguished according to agents' social positions, they are indexes of agents' locations in social space (see Bourdieu).

Continuing counterclockwise from the upper right cell, the specific articulations and transformations of meaning-strategies and identity-imagery occurs in theories, plays, and other cultural products. Discursive products depend on Peircean symbols, and they are grounded in discursive and performance strategies which are constituted at the agential level. Currently many theorists call discursive products of all sorts "texts" (such as "spectacle texts") which are "read" by "readers." However, the metaphor prejudices the analysis of theatre, dance, music and other non-written discursive products. Writing is not a good paradigm of all semiosis.

Discursive articulations supply explanations, justifications and/or rationalizations (whether real or pretended) for agents' actions, which take the form of intended meanings (next cell left). Psychological dynamics are a significant part of intentionality, but these too are socially conditioned and social in form, as indicated by thought's character as inner speech. Like agents and structures, discourses are connected to a specific form of power: the power to choose, including the choice of how to interpret and express things. Expressions, of course, must take material form (upper left cell), such as speech, texts, paint or sound. The material forms constitute a society's cultural archives and repertoires. But the materials of expression are not the sarcophagi of meaning. Because everything in the discursive stratum points toward semiosis, the materials used for expression can be thoroughly "alive," rich with semiosic possibility. Technical explanations in this instance must be analyzed as technique. Art in particular urgently grasps materiality as a major or even the sole source of expressive effect—sometimes sensual, sometimes fervid, sometimes suasive, and sometimes (for want of a better word) spiritual, as though precisely by embracing the material world we transcend the material world.

The semiotic process may ultimately generate habits, habit-changes, and habitus within agents. This is part of the organization and institutionalization of agents (next cell down). Thus the individual body as a mode of agency has structural and semiotic effects incorporated within it. So too do collectivities, such as organizations, informal social groups, governments, and communities. Transformations in such modes of embodied agency can, of course, transform the material structures, which are the condition of their existence.

At the center is embodied intentional agency (both individual and group), which provides the motive force behind social processes. To be sure, agents are not "pure origins" of action: they necessarily act under conditions and imperatives not of their choosing, and their choosing may have unintended consequences. Nonetheless society exists and changes only because agents act. The ordinary human power to act in the world and especially to interact with each other enables people to try to fulfill their intentions and satisfy their immediate interests. Interests and the values that accompany them often compete: for example, succeeding at work, meeting family obligations, acting according to religious precepts, supporting friends, and so forth. Moreover, they are directly tied to one's overlapping memberships, necessarily drawing upon larger social resources and conflicts. Thus on the one hand, discourses are critical for establishing identities and alliances, differences and oppositions, and consequently there can be struggles over meaning. Yet on the other hand, there would be no point to those struggles, no stakes involved, were it not that the processes of forming and maintaining alliances, oppositions, and organizational arrangements often consume limited resources, dedicate the future use of others, can seldom readily be undone—and ultimately reproduce or transform the fundamental structures of society, including the structures of power.

7

Critical realism's resolution of society into structures, agents, and discourses can be used for several modes of research. One is in historical analysis. Most historiography traces the ways in which certain individual or group ("corporate") agents act. Within a critical realist approach, one would attend to the social structures and discourses that preconditioned and motivated the agents' actions, as well as how the agents transformed them and thereby prepared the ground for the next cycle of social and cultural action. Alternatively, the historian may focus on the history of a social structure, but would recognize the importance of discursive conditions and (still more) the ways that agents' actions and interactions reshape the structure. A history of ideas and cultural activities would explain their development not just according to their logical and analogical elaborations, but also in terms of their emergence from, motivation by and intervention within social affairs and even structural conditions.

For critical realism, then, historiography concerns the irreversible choices people make (individually or collectively), and how structural and discursive forces limit, condition, enable and motivate those choices. This formulation offers theatre historians considerable leeway to work within. One may focus on anything from the daily life of a performer or the travails of a specific play production, to the underlying, stubbornly enduring social structures governing theatrical "paradigms." Economics, politics, gender, technology, reception, aesthetics, and many other areas can be the subjects of realist theatre histories. However, critical realism charges theatre historians to recognize the causal links tying particular events and practices to underlying social structures and dynamics in order to explain the emergence, form, timing, and mode of existence of some aspect of theatre. It is not enough to discuss the development of set technology, the meanings of a play, or the declared goals of a certain performance tradition, without considering how such things emerge out of social dynamics or what they mean in terms of social agendas and discourses; nor to identify a pattern, trend, or issue in culture without showing how underlying social forces brought it about.

It is now well understood that one cannot attribute all major social processes to the workings of one structure alone. Sociocultural development is considerably more complex than that. Of course, realist historians (like all others) usually *focus* on only one social structure—it is impossible to write exhaustive history. Case in point: this book concentrates on communication structures, although it considers their relationship to economics to some extent, and somewhat less to gender.[20] Moreover, critical realists may disagree vehemently over what structures exist, what their powers and susceptibilities are, how they operate, and so on. There will always be "many histories." Nevertheless, from a critical realist perspective history involves the interaction of all three strata of social ontology, and it may include yet further strata such as the natural/geographical environment, the capacities and physiology of the human body, or the mind's complex and multilayered cognitive structures.

In addition to historiography, the structure/agents/discourses framework can be applied to sociological analysis, which places agents at the center of a synchronic analysis of society. For theatre that might mean looking at economic conditions, funding sources, audience composition, aesthetic norms, and so forth. However, much depends on how one defines "social." On the one hand, positivism typically defines society as the interactions among various agents, be they individuals, cultural groups, corporations, governments and the like, whereas social constructionism takes society as principally discursive, although it may frame discursive transactions in terms of intersubjectivity. On the other hand, a social constructionist argument can readily address agents' activity insofar as they are the beings that utter some discourse toward one goal or another (or in some extreme accounts, agents are "spoken by" discourse), and positivist research does often consider the sorts of ideas that agents express. To some degree positivists tend to take, dare I say, the positive view, bringing notions of progress and triumph in its wake. In contrast, social constructionists strongly lean toward finding bad intent, leading to a characteristic hermeneutic of suspicion, or as Auslander forthrightly (proudly?) proclaims, paranoia (*Liveness* 121–24).

Critical realism distinctively includes social structures in its definition of "social." But it is important to recognize that structures are not the same as institutions, companies, and similar organizational forms. ExxonMobil is a capitalist corporation, but it is not capitalism. Structures are social relationships, especially relationships with material resources, including human ones. Even though structures are everywhere oriented by intentions, they are not in themselves intentions or even intentional. They are *pre-* and *post-*intentional. Pre, because they are preconditions for agents' actions. Post, because they are the outcome of agents' actions, now embedded in the conditions that set the stage for the next round of activity. This is hardly to say that in critical realism intentions don't matter—quite the contrary, they do matter, because reasons are causal. However, they don't matter in the way they do in positivism and social constructionism. It's important what a person, a corporation, a government chooses to do. And sometimes suspicion and paranoia are amply justified. However, from an analytical perspective the first order of business is to understand the *conditions of possibility* for whatever intentions might be acted on, conditions which affect everyone in a given society no matter what their aims might be, and which may lead the best intentions to a terrible end or for that matter, evil to unexpected good.

A third realm for thinking in terms of structure, agents and discourses is ontological analysis, through which one attempts to determine the manner and conditions in which some particular practice or social entity exists. Its focus is on the nature of a practice or institution as such, for instance the features of any sort of economy that make it an economy, not a religion (although the two may be conjoined in some society). Efforts to define theatre are ontological. Historical, sociological, and ontological forms of analysis may and sometimes must be combined. My discussion of metatheatricality in chapter 4 involves exactly that: I will undertake a principally ontological analysis of theatrical performance, but in order to do so I will draw on theatre history and certain elements of its sociology.

8

Before conducting that analysis, I need to resume my discussion of semiosis, particularly especially as a social practice. Signs are not merely mental activity: they are also material, since they require sounds, writing, visual symbols, or at least synaptic activity; and they are social, particularly because they are the fundamental means by which people interact and form groups. All told, signs are but one part of a much larger system: communication. Communication it is not equivalent to the discursive stratum, because it has its own structures and agent-positions along with its discursive content. Raymond Williams pointed out that means of communication are themselves means of production (*Problems* 50). We can go farther: because communication practices produce signs and involve both material resources and social relations, they should be considered *modes* of production. The system of communication practices constitutes a fundamental social structure comparable to the economic system and sex/gender system.

Means of communication are not inert conduits of information: in a manner that I will elaborate later, the formation of ideas is affected by material practices. My hypothesis is that communication practices have a general effect on discourse, especially formally and methodologically. The activities one learns in order to communicate through speech, writing, and so forth, affect the structure and methods of thought. Historiographically, then, the social use and development of speech, handwriting, printing and electronics may form the primary basis for discursive and performance strategies, and changes in communication practices are the major cause of epistemic shifts.

This position differs from technological determinism, which claims that the means of communication directly determine the form and content of thought; and from social constructionism's view that a mode of communication's effects, or at least its most important ones, are entirely socially determined, and result strictly from (say) schooling, cultural imperialism, or class ideology. I'm arguing instead that communication connects technology, social relations and semiosis, and that it should be conceptualized as possessing various powers, dispositions and susceptibilities. For example, because sound is ephemeral, oral cultures use stock phrases, rhythm, or other types of verbal patterning to preserve ideas across the generations. Since texts are generally quite durable, those techniques are unnecessary in a print culture; but the latter displays its own difficulties as soon as one tries to locate a particular statement *somewhere* in a book, *somewhere* in a library. Thus the materiality of communication conditions the production and retrieval of discourse. However, to a crucial extent, the social conditions and methods of a technology's use shape the powers that it actually exerts, to what extent, and in what manner. Conversely, the technology itself is usually shaped by social interests. Changes in how a mode of communication is used, or even in attitudes toward that mode, can have a substantial impact on discourse and performance strategies.

Modes of communication are comparable to modes of production, and they can be analyzed through similar concepts. For example, communication has a "cycle" akin to the economic cycle, which progresses from production, through distribution and exchange, to consumption (Marx, *Grundrisse* 83–100). Consumption in this case involves practical issues of reception, such as public gatherings for oratory and the development of silent reading. One must also bear in mind that reception isn't a passive activity: the emergence of an interpretant is necessarily dialogic. Audiences aren't tied to a speaker's intentions and they are quite capable of (say) responding with derision or turning a speaker's utterances to unanticipated uses. So in a sense, communication's moment of consumption is also a moment of production. The communication cycle involves an additional moment as well, which I locate just "after" production: preservation. Unrecorded speech is evanescent, whereas writing can endure. Both pose problems of storage and retrieval—orality promoting various types of repetition or patterning, the amassing of texts leading to catalogs, indexes, and related organizing systems. Preservation and retrieval methods have further implications for the production of speech and texts, and ultimately for the production of meaning itself.

Modes of communication also have forces and social relations. The forces of communication comprise the materials, procedures, skills, and institutions which people use to produce discourse; the relations of communication pertain to social roles, divisions, and power. However, typically people engage in several modes of communication: they converse, they handwrite notes, they peruse magazines, they watch television, and so forth. The uses of and access to different modes of communication vary according to social class, gender, region, institution, and even individual; the relationships *among* modes of communication alter the powers of each mode. Consequently, it is impossible to develop an adequate social analysis of an isolated mode of communication. Instead, the primary object of study must be the combination of communication modes and the relationships between them: all together, the *communication framework* as a partial totality. The communication framework, not an individual mode, shapes discursive and performance strategies. The communication framework cannot be adequately analyzed in isolation either: other social forces, such as economic and gender relations, shape communication frameworks in crucial ways, and are themselves affected by communication structures.

Communication frameworks vary not only with each society, but also with each social group. Because social groups have differing access to and uses of speech, writing, and so forth, there are usually several communication frameworks in a society, including subordinated ones. In general, however, a single framework (and with it, one mode of communication) is socially dominant. The dominant mode of communication is the chief repository and productive force for a culture's ideas, values, and beliefs. Its dominance does not derive from simple numerical preponderance; were that the crucial measure, speech would still be the dominant mode in Euroamerican culture. Instead, dominance is a cultural, social, and political matter. Whenever a mode of communication becomes dominant, the other modes continue to be used (and may even gain new applications), but they become subordinated to, conditioned by, and generally less authoritative than the dominant mode. (An example of such subordination is the metaphor of theatrical performance as a "performance text.") As a result, the character and development of each mode of communication depend on its position within the communication framework as a totality. Handwriting, for instance, changed from an aid to oral performance in antiquity, to the indispensable servant of religion and education during the Middle Ages, to its current marginal use for notes, letters, and document drafts, but also its crucial legal function for signatures. However, one cannot assume that a new mode of communication *will* become dominant: for example, some cultures or subcultures have possessed writing but remained basically oral. Nor can one assume that subordinated modes are marginal for everyone: sometimes they are tied to subordinated social groups, as suggested by as African-American traditions of storytelling and oratory, so called women's talk, and songs in the union and the Civil Rights movements. Such practices can present forms of accommodation to the status quo, but also strategies for subverting it.

One can characterize the social relationships within a communication framework along several lines. *Deployment:* the communication modes are organized into institutions that address certain collectivities (schools and students, churches and congregations, broadcast stations and audiences, and so forth). *Access:* people may have open access to a certain mode, be excluded from it, choose not to use it, be forced to express themselves, make decisions based on cost, and so on. *Permeation:* a society's level of dependence on a mode, and the social status accorded its use (for instance, television is vitally important for most people, yet still often considered "lower" than newspapers and live theatre). *Utilizations:* the roles of a communication mode in providing valid evidence or identification (such as documents versus oral testimony as legal evidence), the use of speech or writing to preserve thoughts and experiences of the past and to direct thoughts and actions in the future, audience responses such as talking back, and other functions.

The concept of a communication framework points to some further aspects of social ontology. Although a mode of communication is analogous to a mode of production, the fact that it produces signs means that economic analysis as such generally plays a secondary role in the study of communication's effects (even after commodification), whereas communication's material character implies that traditional ideological critique is inadequate. Without question, ideology (or more broadly, discourse) is influenced by economic relations; for that matter, it is also affected by gender relations and all other social dynamics, and it influences them in turn. But the classical notion of an economic base and ideological superstructure, which has long been subject to criticism, has to be supplanted by a more multidimensional theory. Discourse has its *own* primary "base": the communication framework. The notion of discourse's relative autonomy from economics becomes much more concrete and gains a specific materialist and critical realist explanation: discourse has relative autonomy because it is primarily governed by a different underlying social structure. Similarly, gender is most directly shaped by dynamics such as sexual embodiment and family structures, which interact with economic and communication structures. No single base is primary for everything. But this position does not lead to a pluralism in which everything always counts more-or-less equally. One cannot make that assumption for a society as a whole, still less for an understanding of a particular social process.

Communication frameworks generate power relations of their own, among them divisions of official competencies, such as the distinction between the literate and the nonliterate, and degrees of educational training; the formation of discursive communities based on shared language, founding texts, and so forth; and most important, the division between mental and manual labor (which Marx called the first true division of labor: Marx and Engels 159). Interestingly, Bourdieu argues that social space is organized along two major principles, economic capital and cultural capital (Bourdieu 176, 260 and passim). These correspond to the mode of production and the communication framework. (Social space is also organized by gender, a point that figures in chapter 3.)

But even though cultural capital is usually subordinated to economic capital, mental labor wields crucial power. It produces the main discourses defining society, social positions, identities, ethical conduct, the possibilities and methods of social change, and so forth, often setting the terms under which political opposition attempts counter-definition. The issue bears on both social ontology and social relations. When Percy Bysshe Shelley wrote, "Poets are the unacknowledged legislators of the world," he overshot and his reasons were Romantic ones (513). But from the vantage point of analyzing communication frameworks, he was essentially on the mark. Since society is concept-dependent, the people and communication structures which most immediately control the formation of concepts possess a form of power. Journalists, novelists, artists, talk show hosts, playwrights, scholars, intellectuals of every stripe do reshape the world, even if that power is usually felt only in the long term. That may be a good thing, it may be a bad thing, but in either case it's a reality—a reality that underscores the importance of adopting a theory that gets the nature of reality right.

A Peircean understanding of signs and semiosis recognizes connections between mind and world that are unavailable in Saussurean semiology, and permit a redefinition of the three ontological domains as the real, the actual, and the semiosic. It also underlies a social ontology consisting of structures, agents and discourses, each of which bears material, sociological, and meaningful aspects. This ontology provides the backbone for realist historiography. In the following chapters, I use that ontology to show how one social structure, the communication framework, affects the history of theatrical performance, and ultimately helps define theatrical performance itself.

CHAPTER 2

ORALITY, LITERACY, AND EARLY THEATRE

THEATRE HAS MORE DIRECT TIES TO SOCIAL DYNAMICS THAN MOST OTHER arts, a marked emphasis on embodiment and agency, and a unique conjunction of modes of communication. Paradigmatically, theatre nearly always combines speech and writing. The fact of their combination has always been front and center. Unlike film and television scripts (which are read almost solely by scholars and fans), drama has been literature essentially since theatre began; unlike music scores, which are always understood as different from and only one contributor to music itself, play texts are sometimes seen as equivalent or even superior to their performance. The combination of speech and writing makes theatre especially sensitive to changes in the relationship between the two, and their relationship to other social dynamics.

In order to show how a communication framework generates the core features of performance strategies, I will look at two examples of theatre in cultures that possessed *only* speech and handwriting: classical Greek tragedy, and an early play from medieval England. The comparison between them shows the inadequacy of technological determinism, because their profound differences cannot have derived from the mechanics of orality and literacy alone. By examining Greek tragedy I will of course face the question of theatre's "origins," for which there is scanty evidence; it would be helpful to compare classical tragedy with the comedy, but we know even less about that. There is however considerable evidence on medieval theatre (albeit not its "origins").

1

The invention of Greek tragedy was once explained as a natural evolution from dithyrambs, Dionysian rituals, or cults of the dead. Although those ideas refuse to die, they have received extensive criticism from classicists, who have shown that theories of theatre's origins in ritual or religion don't stand up to historical, anthropological, or logical analysis.[1] Gerald Else has proposed an alternative, that tragedy was invented by two theatrical geniuses, Thespis and Aeschylus. But neither evolution nor genius explains why this innovation was needed, how it was possible, and why it was accepted. These riddles concern tragedy's social circumstances. Two upheavals mark the sixth century BCE, the period when tragedy arose. On the one hand, the country's political and economic structure drastically changed. On the other, literacy became increasingly central to economic, political, and cultural activities. Together, these shifts created both the need and resources for a cultural innovation, tragedy.[2]

Greece's economic and political structure was distinctive. By the eight century BCE, Greek land was owned by individuals or extended families ("tribes"). In some areas, however, the villages eventually banded together to form a *polis*, combining agricultural lands with an urban center. Compared to most other areas of the Mediterranean, the decentralization of land ownership gave the Greeks greater political and economic independence, and weaker local monarchies (Austin and Vidal-Naquet 50, 57–58; Finley 123; Hammond 72–86, 97–98).

During the seventh and sixth centuries BCE, most of the *poleis* were struggling through social conflicts, which usually involved demands for land redistribution, but the rise of increasingly wealthy merchants and manufacturers also unsettled the traditional, agrarian basis of power. Across Greece, "tyrants" (autocrats) overthrew many of the old aristocratic oligarchies to carry out the demands of the lower and especially middle classes, or at least to provide political stability. In an effort to avert tyranny, the Athenians installed Solon as archon during the years 594–91 to mediate changes in the system by legal means. Eschewing land redistribution, he chose instead to institute debt relief and eliminate the possibility of citizens becoming slaves. He also promoted a diversification of the Athenian economy by encouraging commerce and artisan manufacture. He may have obligated citizens to teach their sons a trade and offered citizenship to foreign artisans; his constitution included landless laborers as citizens. Hence it became possible to be a citizen through labor and trade as well as through land ownership. Further, Solon trimmed the aristocracy's hold on power, expanded the role of the Assembly and included within it a judicial body in which citizens conducted their own prosecution or defense. These were the first steps through which Athens slowly placed the state's claims above those of the tribes.[3]

Tyranny eventually arose in Athens anyway: some forty-five years after Solon, Pisistratus attained power. Pisistratus respected the Solonic constitution in form, but held power behind the scenes, achieving a period of relative political stability. Though he did not make major changes in the political institutions, Pisistratus (like Solon) aided the interests of the rising artisans and merchants both economically and politically, and attracted talented refugees—among them, artists and poets from Ionia, where Persia had overrun the Greeks. He paid special attention to public works, religion, and festivals. In particular, he anchored his power by building the importance of the state (which he controlled) over the aristocratic families, and by obtaining popular support (even if Athenians chafed under imposed rule). Such actions were typical of sixth-century tyrants.[4]

Until fairly recently, the scholarly consensus was that in 534 Pisistratus introduced a new contest, at a civic event which he also invented or reorganized: tragedy, at the annual City Dionysia. On this view, his innovation provided him with a unique showpiece which flaunted Athens's talents. It invoked Dionysus, the god of the people, and in so doing moved the populace away from aristocratic rituals. The City Dionysia was placed under a secular authority that Pisistratus could control. And unlike most other festivals, the City Dionysia was open to foreigners and occurred at the opening of the shipping season when many visitors were likely to attend, so that Athens might build a new regional reputation. But the scholarly consensus has been challenged by W. R. Connor, who argues that it depends on faulty evidence. His position is that although Thespis may have won a prize for his *tragoidia* (proto-tragedies) in 534 BCE, it was in a rural setting; the City Dionysia however began quite a bit later, perhaps as late as 501—after the establishment of democracy in Athens. In that case the City Dionysia was created to celebrate the growth and power of Athens under its new regime.

In either event, performance competition in general caught the public imagination: the emerging democratic government rapidly developed the City Dionysia (or the festival that would become the City Dionysia) starting around 509, first with dithyrambic contests, then satyr plays, perhaps next tragedy (if Connor is correct), and finally comedy in 486. The festival's value to its community can be seen in its economic underpinnings. Financial support for the tragic contests derived from taxes. More significantly, paying for tragic choruses became one of the chief public services which Athens's wealthy residents, whether citizen or foreigner, were both required and honored to perform: required, because it was the best way to get things done; honored, because the religious and competitive elements involved allowed the rich to show off their public spirit. Citizens boasted about how much they had spent, which was comparable to equipping a battleship. Since paying for a chorus was a public service, Athenians most likely felt that tragedy greatly contributed to the vitality of their democratic order. Theatre tickets were not free, but probably between 450 and 425 a fund was created to subsidize tickets for the poor. The fund again suggests the importance of theatre to the democracy. By then Athens had developed an empire and much of its revenue came from tributes paid by other *poleis*. It is worth noting that the tribute payments were displayed at the theatre at the beginning of the City Dionysia: the festival had become a symbol of Athens's wealth, power, and vitality, and so was the most suitable venue for further displays of the city's ascendancy. Tragedy's public functions explain why it was an open, civic, state-supported spectacle, unlike the private Senecan drama, or today's commercial theatre.[5] A core part of the public, and a major source of financial support, were the merchants and artisans who were slowly becoming an ever-greater part of Athenian life.

2

I have described the political rationale behind the state-sponsored Dionysia. But tragedy itself arose for other reasons. The culture was changing in fundamental ways primarily because literacy was becoming increasingly important. Prior to Pisistratus, Greek culture had essentially been oral. Speech was the Greeks' medium for transmitting knowledge, beliefs, and traditions. The spoken arts were central to *paideia*, the total process of enculturation, maintaining the values and heritage of Greece. The epics, crowned by the Homeric poems and sung by minstrels who traveled from city to city, were at the heart of *paideia* (Havelock, *Preface to Plato* 47). However, until the early sixth century, Athens apparently was a cultural backwater: bards seldom visited, nor are any known to have been born there (Else 46–47). Then, sometime during the sixth century, competitions in the rhapsodic performance of Homer's epics were added to the Panathenaia.[6] However, competitively or not, Homer's poems had been sung for centuries; why was this newcomer, tragedy, moving in?

It seems that by this time the rhapsodic tradition was decaying or at a crisis in its development; after all, life in Greece had changed considerably since the twelfth century, the time of the Trojan War (Else 67–68). In addition, the Greek alphabet was devised sometime around the middle of the eighth century BCE. In the late sixth century BCE, reading and writing began to displace oral culture, and clearly became ensconced by the fifth century. In Athens, unlike elsewhere, literacy extended beyond a scribal or elite caste, and a significant part of the public (including merchants and artisans) were able to read and write.[7] So with the rise of literacy and the decline of Homeric performance on the one hand, and the changing political and economic environment on the other, Athenians probably felt an increasing need for a *paideia* with a new mode of transmission, one that could pose a kind of alternative to the traditional *paideia*. The new cultural form, tragedy, was intimately involved with the rise of writing in Greece.

Today, we think in a manner that is indelibly marked by literacy. But the Athenians of pre-classical times did not. Tragedy arose in the classical period during the transition period between orality and literacy as the socially dominant mode of communication. This transition affected the way the playwrights composed drama, and they could not have composed the tragedies as we know them unless they had first become literate. Tragedy was the main art form in which these two modes converged, combined, collided, remaining deeply oral yet increasingly shaped by literate consciousness.

The theory that in some manner theatre emerged from literacy is not itself new. Some scholars have seen the causation as direct. Derrick de Kerckhove speculates that "Greek theatre was one of the developments of the phonetic alphabet" (23). Ong concurs: Greek drama was "the first western verbal art form to be *fully controlled* by writing" (*Orality and Literacy* 148, my emphasis). Their proposals are ill-supported and deterministic. Havelock, who believes that drama arose simply as an Attic supplement to Homer, nevertheless sees in tragedy a "tension between the modes of oral and written communication," which eventually gives way to the literate orientation (Havelock, *Literate Revolution* 261–313). Although this argument is better, it too is thinly made. Jennifer Wise's more satisfactory account of tragedy's debt to literacy is particularly attentive to theatre's interlinking of written and oral modes of communication. She also takes somewhat greater note of the social context and preconditions for literacy in Athens.

All of these writers emphasize the importance of the alphabet (or more accurately, phonetic script) as opposed to syllabic and logographic forms of writing, which they contend promoted abstract thinking processes. I consider that claim dubious, and so I do not attribute any cognitive role to the alphabet as such until two millennia later, when it gained an added application. Nevertheless phonetic script was central to the rise of literacy in classical Athens in one respect: alphabets use only twenty to thirty characters, and so they are far easier to learn than all other scripts, which greatly facilitates the spread of literacy. In saying that, I do not mean that alphabetic writing was necessary to the creation of theatre—the development of theatre in China puts the lie to that notion. The Greek alphabet did, however, bear on the particular way theatre arose in Athens.

Syllabic and logographic scripts utilize numerous symbols, making learning difficult and restricted to scribes, clerics, or aristocrats (Ong, *Orality and Literacy* 85–93). Such scripts were satisfactory for the theocratic, despotic states such as in Egypt, Persia, and Mycenaean Greece, where aristocracies had an interest in constraining the spread of knowledge and keeping laws under personal control.[8] The Phoenicians developed the more-or-less phonetic writing that served as a prototype for the alphabet. Phoenician script, like Hebrew, did not have separate signs for vowels. The Greek alphabet introduced vowel signs, largely because its words often began with vowels or contained combinations of sounds that the Phoenician script could not represent. Consequently Greek script possessed several advantages: it represented phonemes in an explicit and generally unambiguous manner, it had the flexibility to transcribe words in other languages, and most importantly it was relatively easy to learn.[9]

The Phoenicians were traders, and their commerce took them throughout the Mediterranean world. During that era Greece and particularly Athens had an economic and political structure that made alphabetic writing worth adopting. Its decentralized economy was becoming ever more involved with commerce and manufacture—trades that utilize writing for orders, inventory, accounting, loans, insurance, and contracts. The merchants and artisans involved in such pursuits would naturally prefer a simple form of writing, and evidently they were indeed the first to use alphabetic writing, along with the scribes; the upper and lower classes became literate rather later. Writing was also important for legislation and litigation, both of which would become more vital as Athens's democracy and population grew, even if oral methods still predominated (Havelock, *Literate Revolution* 187–89, 201; J. Fine 415–29; W. Harris 50–51, 72–73).

The argument that writing had a deep connection to the establishment of tragedy depends first of all on evidence that writing was prevalent and important enough to have had such effects by the end of the sixth century. Because direct evidence is scarce, inferential arguments must do. Ultimately the crucial issue is the effect of writing on those who used it most. But the extent of literacy within Attica is relevant, because it is on that basis that the audience would understand, accept, and even desire certain differences between epic and dramatic performance.

Without question, only a tiny number of Greeks could read or write before 600 BCE. For the sixth century, the clues are sparse. We know that Solon wrote poetry, and probably his constitution. It appears that Thespis wrote his *tragoidia*. The rhapsodic competitions instituted at the Panathenaia were based on a written version of the Homeric epics. And apparently, laws began to be written in the sixth century at the insistence of the middle (and possibly lower) classes, in order to wrest the laws from the whim of the aristocracy. This codification implies that by then there was wide knowledge of writing, or at least knowledge of its significance. Writing had clearly begun to play an important role in public and semi-public life. Schools were established even in some small towns. The advance of literacy may have been expedited by Solon's reforms at the beginning of the sixth century: if he did require every citizen to teach his son a trade, and if the trades were the first to utilize alphabetic writing extensively, there should have been pressure on citizens to learn writing. Still, one should not exaggerate the extent of literacy during this period; in the late sixth century the level of literacy in Greece as a whole was perhaps just a few percent, albeit probably higher in Athens.[10]

Evidence for the fifth century is firmer, though, scarcely clear cut. William Harris amasses evidence on the increasing uses and functions of writing, and the greater presence of schoolteachers. He suggests that wealthy males were almost always literate, and that literacy in Athens had spread beyond the elite and was necessary for various activities in public life. But universal literacy was nowhere on the docket and the majority of citizens couldn't read or write. He conjectures that in Attica as a whole the literacy rate was still below ten percent (a figure which factors in the exclusions of women and slaves), but Athens itself probably had a much higher literacy rate (65–115). It seems likely, then, that literacy became reasonably common in Athens during the early or mid fifth century. Theatre audiences were perhaps somewhat more lettered than the rest of the city (86–87, 108–111). In any case the evidence overall suggests that some sort of threshold was passed during the fifth century, and writing had come to play a central role in Athens's cultural affairs.

The process of submitting plays for the dramatic composition depended on the development of not merely literate but literary writers and readers. The distinction involves the differences between orality and literacy arising from the fact that speech is aural, whereas writing maps words onto a visual form. That affects two related issues: the uses of sight and hearing, and preservation, here memory. In orality, information is stored principally in oral forms, but visuality nevertheless could serve memorization. A speaker typically uses language to create "visual" imagery in the listener's imagination. Often such mental images (and their drawn or painted depictions) are iconographic and require verbal exegesis in order to unpack the meaning condensed within it (a feature crystallized in the Art of Memory, to be discussed later). In contrast, literacy stores knowledge primarily through visible material: consequently it promotes seeing and display over imagination (Ong, *Orality and Literacy* 117–23; Havelock, *Preface to Plato* 189). Thus one can expect that a change from an oral culture to a literate one would bring ultimately bring a change in the character of visuality in its wake.

But that doesn't mean such a shift happens quickly. It is questionable whether literacy had become extensive in Greek culture by the fifth century BCE, or for that matter anywhere in Europe until about two millennia later—it was only with printing that literacy became truly hegemonic. However, we can see how literacy affected the tragedies at several other levels, involving the implications that oral vs visual means of storing knowledge had upon memory (rather than the senses).

As many researchers have found, in oral composition thought is fixed and made memorable mainly through formulaic structures: verse, proverbs, epithets and other regular patterns of speech and thought.[11] The Greek rhapsodes utilized a fund of well-worn phrases, epithets, and speech patterns, to which they could make alterations and add unique material as needed: their compositional method is one of "theme and variations." A natural part of the formulaic method is the use of meter. Greek tragedy uses meter as well; however, they use iambic trimeters instead of the epic dactylic hexameter (and only occasionally the "danceable" trochaic tetrameter), since as Aristotle observed, "iambic is the most speech-like of verses."[12]

The dramatists' diction is also distinguishable from the formulaic patterns of oral culture. Oral composition also tends to preserve archaisms in formula (Ong, *Orality and Literacy* 47). But Aristotle comments that in tragedy, "Just as iambics were adopted, instead of tetrameters, because they are the most prose-like of all meters, so tragedy has given up all those words, not used in ordinary talk, which decorated the early drama and are still used by the writers of hexameter poems" (*Rhetoric* 166). Aeschylus's *Oresteia* is riddled with strange, often grotesque twists of phrase and image, rupturing the norms of speech and weird enough for even Aristophanes to travesty (77–80; see also Hadas 180). Conversely, Aristophanes ribs Euripides about his fluid, "natural" speech (80–83); it would seem that by Euripides's time, archaisms were more thoroughly shed. A turn from formalized to everyday speech, prosy and vernacular, is characteristic of verbal art in increasingly literate societies; so too, somewhat paradoxically, is the expansion of vocabulary (Ong, *Orality and Literacy* 103–08). The reason may be that writing allows one to choose words more sensitively.

These changes in rhythm and diction, particularly as they appear in Euripides, are related to growing literacy. This is not to say that formulaic material vanished, but the shifts in diction and rhythm of the playwrights' work appear to reveal significant movements away from orality and toward literacy. Such transformations are never smooth. It seems likely that the verbal and dramatic grotesque that we see in Aeschylus are symptomatic of transitions in the relationship between orality and literacy: witness its appearance in Gothic art, Rabelais, and so forth (Havelock, *Literate Revolution* 283–92, 299–308; McLuhan 266–67). Aeschylus may have been especially wrenched by the shift from orality to literacy, which the later writers had more clearly passed, although their works too have features bequeathed by oral composition (Havelock, "Oral Composition").

Literacy also affects narrative structure. Oral forms seldom demand strict chronological sequence or causal necessity. On the one hand, rhapsodes recall epic episodes according to their associations or their sense of the audience. The epics interweave several stories, launch into digressions, jump backward and forward, and so on. On the other hand, storytellers tend to use formulaic patterns of action. Storytelling uses a single narrative, but generally it has a narrow repertory of plot structures with a particular rhythm and a "non-logical" organization, such as the ritual use of three incidents (Ong, *Orality and Literacy* 141–47; Hawkes 67–79, 90–95). In contrast, the Greek tragedies tell a single story, in a step-by-step fashion. Their plots focus on a single crisis; one action sets up the next, through a linear sequence of causes and effects. That linear structure probably derives from the need to sequence ideas when writing.

Narrative structure bears a concept of time and causation. Time in oral culture is multiple, patterned, or simultaneous: for example, the ancestors coexist with the living in the present. Epic (or mythic) time is set in an indeterminate past and wanders freely back and forth according to its own inner rhythm, like memory: it is non-linear and discontinuous. The implicit concept of time in tragic narrative is linear and continuous. However, Greek tragedies actually fuse the two kinds of time: the tragic, linear plot joins with the epic, nonlinear choruses (Romilly 5–31). As we saw with diction, orality and literacy were amalgamated to form tragedy.[13]

The characters in epic and storytelling tend to be externalized or "flat," having little or no internal development (Ong, *Orality and Literacy* 151–55). But as Ong puts it,

> The first approximations we have of the round character are in the Greek tragedies.... Sophocles' Oedipus and, even more, Pentheus and Agave and Iphegenia and Orestes in Euripides' tragedies are incomparably more complex and interiorly anguished than any of Homer's characters. In orality-literacy perspectives, what we are dealing with here is the increasing interiorization of the world opened up by writing. (Ong, *Orality and Literacy* 152)

Else concurs, writing that tragedy involved "a new, inward apprehension of what it means to be a hero and die a hero" (68). The conjunction of actor and chorus reveals other evidence of an oral/literate collision. As Else observes, "Greek tragedy, by the peculiarity of its form, is committed to a special kind of double vision: the hero's view of himself and the chorus's view of him.... Thus the original form of tragedy—single actor and chorus—established a tension which is of its essence" (44). If literacy creates a sense of personal depth and complexity that was largely unknown in oral society, then very likely literate individuals were seen and saw themselves as both valuable and disturbing to the traditional community. The combination of chorus and actor was a product and a symbol of the concurrence of (and transition between) the group oriented oral culture and the individualizing manuscript culture.

But "culture" is perhaps too small a word here, because the two embodied different ways of being—and being effective—in the world. The oral culture concerned itself with the relationship between humans and gods, enacted not just in rituals (occasionally represented on stage) but also in choral hymns constantly addressed to the gods, and in lamentations, which bear the marks of older ritual forms; notably, the chorus nearly always consisted of people below the protagonist's rank (Else 58, 71, 75). The concept of agency posited by literacy was at this time more or less heroic, but comparatively individualized and less wholly dependent on the gods: the tragic hero is "irreducibly separate" (Else 69). As literate culture developed, the number of actors increased from one, to two, to three; the emphasis shifted from plot to character; and contests for actors were added to the City Dionysia in the mid-fifth century. Simultaneously, the chorus took a smaller and smaller practical function in the plays (Pickard-Cambridge, *Dithyramb* 232–34).[14] A new orientation toward individuality was taking shape. Even under Aeschylus the chorus was showing signs of strain: in *Agamemnon* he has a long passage (the longest among the extant tragedies) in which the chorus is broken up and each member assigned a separate speech.

Writing and theatre have similar semiotic structures. In alphabetic writing systems, the written word is a sign for a spoken word, which is a sign for a concept: writing is a system of signs of signs.[15] Acting too is a structure of signs of signs, for actors produce words and actions, and these signs in turn become signs of the characters. In fact, all things and actions in theatre tend to become signs (if not signs of signs, then signs of themselves), to the point that audiences may mistake actual injuries for part of the performance (Veltrusky 565–67). In theatre, there is a fundamental and inescapable doubling movement that creates signs of signs and replaces every real thing with an image.[16] Their semiotic homology certainly doesn't demonstrate that writing caused theatre, but it does suggest that writing opened up a conceptual space which theatre then occupied. It seems doubtful that fictional re-enactments of religious rituals in tragedy could be tolerated without that semiotic framework. There are only a few modes in which one can imitate a religious ritual without actually performing it: childhood play, rehearsal, and parody are the main alternatives other than theatre. Otherwise the dangers of blasphemy could be quite real, as Aeschylus could tell us, having been brought to trial on the charge of revealing the Mysteries in a play (Hadas 177–78). It seems plausible that the rise of literacy fostered the ability to see things other than writing as signs of signs—theatre specifically, but also beyond: the *theatrum mundi*, a notion that emerged during Hellenistic times and possibly earlier.

If tragedy were instituted as both a political showpiece honoring Athenian power and democracy, and a means of protecting Athens's Hellenic heritage (the two aspects support each other), that would explain several things. In order to fulfill the particular political roles it was assigned, tragedy would have to be a major public event, rather than an amusement for the aristocracy or an informal entertainment at the marketplace. In addition, despite being performed at an event honoring Dionysus, tragedy had to be serious, not humorous or bawdy, since like the epic source material that dominated the plays themselves, tragedy's motive was the inculcation of the Athenian *paideia*.[17] At the same time, having tragedy at the Festival of Dionysus made political sense, since Dionysus was a god of the people, among whom most notably were the merchants and artisans whose democratic rule and self-celebration provided the City Dionysia's raison d'être. (In this regard it is worth mentioning that comedy may have arisen, some forty or so years before tragedy, from farce in Megara, which prided itself on its democracy. Literacy was probably less developed than in Athens, but one gets the impression that these performances were long on jokes and slapstick but short on plot and character: literacy would be less necessary for this genre. See Aristotle, *Poetics* 19; Rozik, *Roots* 156–60.)

But we cannot underestimate the need to replace rhapsodic *paideia*, which was straining under the ancientness of the songs and the change in consciousness inaugurated by rising literacy. Merely composing new songs would not do the job: another genre had to be developed which would meet the new mentality being nourished (whether or not welcomed) by the merchants and artisan manufacturers upon whom both Pisistratus and the democracy depended. The playwrights worked with particular political and cultural demands and specific resources to create a transitional amalgam of the old and new techniques of *paideia*.

Within the ancient world of the Mediterranean, Athens was exceptionally capable of supporting tragedy. It was populous and wealthy. Its comparatively mixed and decentralized political and economic organization, particularly its vibrant merchant and artisan activity, encouraged literacy and individual creativity (a kind of "decentralized knowledge"). Athens wasn't as weighted by the culture of the past as other places in Greece, and so was more open to cultural innovation. However, the notion that literacy *per se* has certain specific and inevitable effects (say, the "spread of rationality") cannot be sustained: its effects depend on other conditions, especially political, economic and gender relations. (This accords with the critical realist argument that a generative mechanism's actual effects are through its interactions with other structures and entities.)

In developing *tragoidia*, Thespis probably took techniques from earlier kinds of performance (such as dithyrambic choruses and iambic poetry) more or less as "raw materials." However "dramatic" the preexisting materials, the concept underlying his creation was radically different, fundamentally new. The inclusion of tragedy in the City Dionysia, an increasingly literate and civic environment, and a strengthening grasp of the nature of the new medium, set the stage for Aeschylus's addition of a second actor; the number of actors eventually increased, the dramatic role of the chorus shrank, and plot, character, and the other elements approached the qualities that now typify theatre. However, it was not yet theatre as we know it. As Else maintains, *tragoidia* lacked conflict, and instead was the enacted self-presentation of a hero and his situation or fate, placed in a relationship with a chorus representing the hero's followers and dependents, or citizens of his state (65–66). In those respects it was still deeply rooted in an aristocratic and epic culture, and it was mainly a rural art at this time. But the same political, economic, and cultural pressures that led to the invention of tragedy also led to its dissolution. During the fourth century, with the transition from orality to literacy solidified, the old tragedy became more and more a thing of the past. Theatre and drama remained; but the future belonged to a more fully literate performance.

Although my argument specifically concerns Greek tragedy, the intertwining of orality and literacy through which tragedy arose appears to have had similar effects elsewhere: as many have observed, noh and ancient Sanskrit theatre, both of which arose out of early manuscript cultures, have striking similarities to Greek tragedy. (And as the development of noh suggests, an alphabet *per se* is not necessary to the creation of theatre.) The conceptual basis of theatre is unlike that of rituals, dream re-enactments, and other kinds of performance founded entirely in orality; in ways that I will more fully elaborate in the next chapter, the new communication framework that incorporated writing was a generative mechanism (a causal power) which produced a conceptual space for theatrical performance; and this conceptual space has remained, even in theatre's filmed and televised permutations, throughout the career of generalized literacy. Tragedy was emergent in the critical realist sense: a new causal entity drawing from the dynamics at play within a complex totality. The complexities of a communication framework are yet more visible in another theatrical fusion of oral and literate cultures, the theatre of medieval England.

3

Medieval culture had a strong propensity for similitudes: the perception of likenesses and resemblances also embodied in symbolism, analogy, allegory, and related techniques. Similitudes were incorporated within the literature, art, sermons, political thought, music theory, and public punishments of the Middle Ages; they lurk in the background of logic and theology, and in the discursive strategies of even those writers who criticized analogical thought (Allen 180). The theory of the fourfold interpretation of the Bible (literal, allegorical, moral, and anagogical) was practically doctrine. Nature itself appeared composed of signs. Natural phenomena took the guise of a text, the Book of Nature. Writing and nature mirrored each other's being. I will call this habitual use of similitudes "figural thinking." It held sway from the patristic writings to the Reformation, and continued to be commonplace long after.[18]

In theatre, the importance of similitudes is obvious in the morality play. For example, *The Castle of Perseverance* (written around 1440) depicts allegorical characters such as Avarice and Humility, and they engage in allegorical actions for Mankind's allegiance. The key similitude in the mystery play is more subtle to modern eyes: allegorical characters are few, and instead the plays tend to use "typology," the idea that people or events in the Old Testament (the "types") prefigure and are fulfilled by people or events in the New Testament (the "antitypes"). An example appears in the York Corpus Christi Cycle, which was first produced in the late fourteenth century and is preserved in a script largely written around the same time as *The Castle of Perseverance*. In its *Abraham and Isaac* play, Abraham's near-sacrifice of Isaac corresponds to God's sacrifice of Jesus. The play suggests this through both stage imagery and language: Isaac is somewhat over thirty years old, he willingly submits to his father's command and carries the wood for the sacrifice on his back, he uses phrases that recall Jesus, and so forth.

At the same time, the York play has no allegorical personifications. Its action is not directly a model of human life or the fate of the soul. And it has one unusual quality: several plays present remarkably lifelike details. Pilate, for instance, receives hot water when he washes his hands at the end of Jesus's trial, and Herod worries about his delicate skin. These plays have been attributed to a "York Realist."

I turn to medieval theatre now because from the perspective of communication frameworks, fifteenth-century England is both similar to and radically different from classical Greece. The similarity is that both societies possessed writing only in handwritten form. But the differences are profound. In the Middle Ages official literacy was almost entirely in a learned language, Latin, rather than a vernacular; reading was dominated by one particular text, the Bible, which was supported by a vast devotional and exegetical literature sometimes produced on a nearly industrial scale; and intellectually, medieval life was structured by figural thinking of a sort we seldom find in Greek culture. The contrast exemplifies the inadequacy of technological determinism.

Among medieval English plays, the York Cycle is particularly interesting for the present study above all because it is one of the earliest. The extant manuscript dates from the period it was performed, and there is far more information on how the cycle was performed than for most other plays of that era. (The manuscript of the better-known Towneley or "Wakefield"

Cycle, in contrast, is from at least a century later, and it is unclear how it was performed.) But given its cultural context, the York Cycle's intertwining of similitudes and naturalism needs to be explained. We must understand why and how medieval discursive strategies let realistic qualities flower within figural thinking and concealed similitudes within naturalistic representations; the particular factors that led to the York Cycle's atypical "realism"; and what its realism consists of.

The first issue, however, is to identify the dynamics that generated figural thinking. Too often, the similitudes' ever-presence is taken as an unexamined fact—an attitude that displays complacency toward the causes of cultural change, leaving us with the "series of styles" theory I criticized earlier. But figural thinking did not spring from nothing: its roots lie deep in the fundamental structures of medieval society, and particularly the communication framework.

English society and culture endured massive changes during the fourteenth century. The Black Death killed a third or more of the population, and plague remained endemic in Yorkshire for many years. The resulting labor shortages brought higher wages to the peasant and a greater demand for services to the urban artisan. By the 1380s craft guilds and merchants were leveraging themselves into greater power both nationally and in the major towns: York, then England's second city, reached the height of its prosperity and population during the following decades, and in the 1390s secured many rights and charters from Richard II. The peasant revolt and heretic movements of the period had little impact in Yorkshire (Tillott 54–113; Hey 89–96; Coldewey 79–80; Moran, *Education* 3).

York was the northern seat of governmental administration, served as England's capital from 1298 to 1304, and was often involved in the country's political, parliamentary, and military affairs. As the site of one of England's two archbishoprics, York was a center for ecclesiastic administration as well. These political and religious institutions required the use of texts and placed a premium on literacy skills. They also helped to make York an educational center, although not a university town (Hey 69; Coleman 46–49; Courtenay, *Schools* 151–67, 185–90, 196–98).

Language itself was changing. At the beginning of the century, French was the vernacular of choice among the literate, but with the growth of the merchant and artisan classes, English started to displace it. The late fourteenth century brought the works of Chaucer, Langland and Gower, achieving the first literary triumphs in English. The vernacular ferment included the earliest English interludes, morality plays, and Corpus Christi dramas.

Among the transformations of the fourteenth and fifteenth centuries were changes in manuscript culture. Formal education spread, manuscript production expanded, the manner and content of reading altered. We can analyze the development of manuscript culture in York in terms of four intertwined aspects of the social relations of communication. *Access* concerns the extent to which social groups can use a mode of communication. A mode's *deployment* is the scope of its use within institutional contexts (such as schools and scholars, churches and parishioners, or theatres and audiences). A mode's *permeation* of social life consists of the degree and manner of a society's dependence upon it. *Utilization* pertains to the employment of a mode for different purposes. The character of these four aspects varies regionally as well as chronologically; the discussion that follows concerns only England.[19]

Access: In the Middle Ages, the literate population was anything but separate from the oral culture. Well into the sixteenth century, aristocrats and clergymen regularly participated in popular oral culture by attending the same sermons, hearing the same minstrels, and joining the same festivals (Burke 24–29, 277–78). But few people could read and fewer still could write—although recent research indicates that the extent of reading skills was greater than once thought (see for example Garrison). The literacy rate is difficult to assess, partly because of the limited evidence, but also because of problems in defining medieval literacy, which at the time was understood as Latin learning. Memorizing a Latin phrase by ear could allow someone to claim the legal benefit of clergy, and so count as a *litteratus*; in contrast, those who could read English but not Latin would not be considered *litterati*. Also we tend to assume literacy includes writing, but in the Middle Ages reading and writing were separate.[20] Nonetheless some appraisal of the literacy rate is helpful, and according to one calculation, in the early sixteenth century twenty to twenty-five percent of the men in York Diocese (a very large part of England) could read at a minimal level. One can reasonably guess that in the late fourteenth and early fifteenth centuries, when the York Cycle was developing, around ten to fifteen percent of the men in York itself could read.[21] Most readers were male and at least moderately wealthy, although sometimes education was provided to the poor. It is unclear what percentage of guild members could read; a few trades must have required literacy, and it is worth noting that tradesmen in London were described as *litterati* by the mid-1400s. Since the guilds were responsible for producing and (usually) for acting the York plays, one may reasonably surmise that there was generally at least one person in each guild who could read, and the use of actors' "sides" suggests that a fair number of guildsmen could; but it's possible that many performers learned their parts orally.[22]

Deployment: Schooling was not the only route to literacy in the Middle Ages: since the primary goal of reading was for prayer, it may well have been taught at home (Clanchy, *From Memory* 13). But schools were scarcely unimportant. Recent studies of England as a whole and of Yorkshire in particular have shown that schooling in the Middle Ages, though far from universal, was considerably more available than previously believed; the education revolution once assigned to the Renaissance actually started much earlier (Orme; Moran, *Growth* 278–79 and passim; Moran, *Education* 8–9 and passim). The point bears on our understanding of the print revolution: the printing press was created to respond to the demands of an already growing readership, and so some features of print culture had begun before Gutenberg, even if they could only coalesce and accelerate afterward. Outside of basic education, other important and expanding centers of manuscript culture included bureaucracy, trades, and universities. It has been argued that lay literacy grew out of bureaucracy, which York certainly possessed (see Clanchy, *From Memory* 19). Nevertheless the dominant institution of manuscript culture in the Middle Ages was the Church—or more accurately, the Bible itself. The Church was strong, but the rise of lay literacy broke the ecclesiastic monopoly over literate practice and the Church became subject to vigorous criticism. However, whatever battles were engaged over the status and quality of the Church, whatever words of wrath might issue from the lips of Langland or the Lollards, the Bible was unassailable.

Books were essentially luxury items, but between 1325 and 1475 the production of books in English leapt by perhaps twenty-fold; more Latin books were also produced. To meet the demand, the book trade expanded and became more organized. Even so, most books were copied by the actual user or else produced by non-professional clerics for specific buyers (Meale 201–38; Edwards and Pearsall 257–78; Pearsall 1–10).

Utilization: The Norman conquerors began a new era in the use of documents for law and administration, and established conditions in which bureaucracy became increasingly necessary. Until the middle of the thirteenth century most evidence for legal proceedings was taken orally, but by the early fourteenth century written documents were usually preferred. Other changes took a similar turn, such as the increased reliance on texts for reference or the use of seals and letters to authorize transactions (Clanchy, *From Memory* 25–78, 253–327; Musson 105–6).

However, oral procedures continued even within literate culture. Oral methods were customary for teaching reading, and oral performance remained crucial at the university, where lectures and public disputations were central to academic life; at court, where argument before the bench continued; and at the pulpit, where the art of preaching had revived. In fact the verb "to write" often meant "to dictate to a scribe." Oral activity, then, was prominent in teaching readers, writing texts, and conducting business.

The books that the laity read included romances, histories, legal texts, vernacular poetry, and ballads; but the most popular works were various kinds of religious writings—saint's lives, service books, psalters, books of hours, missals, and many other devotional texts.[23] The devotional character of these books was often part of their design, especially among the fanciest manuscripts, for pictures and illuminations helped stimulate meditation. The Bible too was sometimes read, but read or not, it clearly played a dominant role in medieval literacy, circumscribing the limits and purposes of reading, and drawing all writing to itself as the central reference book (Coleman 58–156). However, reading for pragmatic, business purposes was on the rise, due to the growth in commerce, administration, and law. By the fifteenth century, in fact, law had displaced theology as the subject most frequently studied at the universities (Parkes 557–61; Courtenay, *Schools* 365–68).

Another, quieter revolution had also occurred in the manner of reading. Reading aloud had been the norm for centuries; in the Middle Ages reading was basically a speech act which recovered an author's thoughts (Clanchy, "Introduction" 6). But as Paul Saenger has demonstrated, reading silently became common practice among monastics by the twelfth century and increasingly among the laity during the fourteenth and fifteenth centuries. Texts prompted speech progressively less; their utilization turned toward stirring inner thoughts. As more and more private citizens learned to read, reading itself became more private.

Permeation: Texts had permeated social life to a significant but by no means unequivocal extent. Religion, education, administration, and some trades depended on them; most people did not. Possessing books conferred status, but they could also symbolize beliefs, as suggested by the books owned by an unlettered peasant convicted of Lollardy in 1415 (see Hudson). However, many people viewed penning a text as a lowly manual labor. Oral performance remained an important and valued skill, including (perhaps especially) among the literate.

The area in which books pervaded most deeply was of course religion. "The really significant point," M. T. Clanchy writes, "is not the proportion of the population which could read (in whatever sense), but the fact that the dynamic of literacy was religious" (*From Memory* 13). The privilege Europe gave to a single text, the Bible, sharply distinguished medieval manuscript culture from its predecessors. When theologians like Saint Anselm in the eleventh century wished to prove the existence of God *without* recourse to Scripture, their very efforts attested to the Bible's importance. The Bible was the "Alpha et O" of knowledge and truth. It was the principal and in a sense the only evidence.

However, for those who worked with texts daily, changes were brewing. Scholars, lawyers, merchants, and administrators had a growing role in society and worked with other sorts of texts. Their demand greatly stimulated the book trade. They could, and to some extent did, pursue text-based forms of reasoning independent of Holy Writ. Still, not until several centuries later did the Bible cease to dominate culture and so cease to address every person as a soul that must hear its message. In sum, manuscript was the dominant mode of communication, in the sense that it was indispensable for most institutional operations and many cultural activities, but it was embedded in an oral milieu and this circumstance often left its traces in cultural artifacts.

4

The earliest performances of the York Corpus Christi cycle may have been around 1350. From early on, the pageants (individual plays) were performed on wagons that were taken on a procession along York's major streets. Performances apparently began at dawn, and the procession stopped to present plays at a number of stations. If the play was done in its entirety, performances may have been both exhaustive and exhausting, running nonstop from the Creation at dawn to the Last Judgment at one in the morning. Indeed, that may be the most religiously effective way to do it.[24]

The Corpus Christi cycle was organized by the city, while responsibility for the individual pageants lay with the craft guilds. For the most part one guild was assigned to one play, and stayed with that play throughout the cycle's history. Although tremendously expensive to produce, the York Cycle was (from at least one perspective) "the city's proud and solemn celebration of itself" (Stevens 17), a value distinct from its economic or political benefits. Despite the drastic decline in York's economic state after the early fifteenth century, its cycle play continued to be performed until 1569.

The text appears to be the oldest extant Corpus Christi play, and it is the only manuscript that is contemporary with its period of performance. Despite the religious content, guild control and other circumstances make it likely that some or all of the playwrights were laymen. (In fact the Trial plays, in which Jesus is brought before Pilate, harshly criticize the Church by aligning it with Jesus's persecutors.) The pageants are written in a variety of stanzas, nearly always incorporating alliteration. The original scripts may date as far back as the 1390s, but the plays by the "York Realist" were probably written in the 1440s; the only extant copy was compiled in the 1460s or 1470s. Annotations in city documents and the manuscript indicate that this copy was not used as an acting script, but instead as an archive and a way to monitor the performances.[25] Nevertheless it is clearly tied to actual performance.

To address the way the medieval communication framework shaped the York Cycle, is it useful to analyze the communication cycle in terms of production, preservation, distribution, exchange and consumption. I'll take the oral dynamic first. The Cycle's performance strategies reveal many traits of spoken discourse. Syntactically, in oral discourse parataxis (additive or modular construction) and simple coordination usually predominate over hypotaxis (subordination, relative clauses), and the York Cycle follows suit.[26] Likewise, verbal formulas appear frequently in the text. Clearly, under conditions of predominantly amateur production the playwrights would have strong motives for scripting language with fairly simple constructions that the performers could readily memorize and speak, and that the audience would quickly understand as well.[27]

As Erich Auerbach has shown, parataxis on the syntactic level is frequently matched by parataxis on the structural level (96–122). A modular or mosaic approach appears throughout medieval arts and literature; the strategy is closely akin to the episodic structure found in epics and tales. Theatrically, the modules can be spatial, as in the ring of settings (simultaneous scenery) of *The Castle of Perseverance*, or temporal, as exemplified by the York Cycle's beaded string of pageants (see Coleman 199–201). Scriptural material was typically seen as a chain of scenes, even if the exact division varied: works like the *Biblia pauperum* divide and select the biblical stories in much the same way as the York Cycle. The use of typology also implies a modular perception of Scriptures. Non-scriptural texts like the *Canterbury Tales* were apparently viewed in a similarly segmentary fashion.

In oral distribution and exchange, the stage/audience dynamic is the principal arena. The York Cycle frequently takes advantage of the possibilities for direct address to the audience. Characters deliver sermons and harangues, occasionally they speak aside, once in a while they even enter from the street. Many of the direct addresses to the audience are spoken by villains such as Satan and the Devil. This strategy creates intimacy between villains and the audience in order both to drive home the message that it is easy to slip into evil ways, and to confront the audience with that evil. But the playwrights also use it to instruct the audience directly, to include the audience in the sacred events, or simply to wrap up the pageant; some two-thirds of the plays end with this kind of address to the audience (Collier 195–96).

Direct address also helps create the spatial circles that appear in various forms in medieval stagecraft. When someone talks to a group, it tends to form a circle with the speaker at the center. Thus circular or semicircular positioning naturally arises in oral performance. It is representative of communal participation, and also connects to the modularity discussed earlier. A simplified circular (or semicircular) form in medieval theatre was the *locus* and *platea*, a modest scenic stage within a neutral acting area. In the performance of the York Corpus Christi Cycle, the individual pageants consisted essentially of a small *locus* and *platea*, sometimes perhaps modified by the use of a second wagon; and communal sensibility took symbolic form through a circle formed by the religious and dramatic processions, which started from the outskirts of town, led across the River Ouse, and then traced a loop through major streets of the city and into the market area (Twycross, "Places"; Weimann 73–74).

The York Cycle clearly was shaped by orality's moments of production, distribution, and exchange; what of writing's? One might assume that as a visual medium, writing encouraged pictorial elements in the play. But evidently this was not the prime area where manuscript culture affected the York Cycle. There are scenes drawn from devotional images inspired be the Bible, proofs through visual evidence, images of light and darkness, and so forth, but such things do not markedly differ from most of oral culture's visual elements. Instead, writing's effects were strongest where it interacted with orality, particularly at the point in the communication cycle where oral culture required the greatest effort: preservation. This is a crucial juncture in the communication cycle because preserving ideas, ensuring their continuance into the future, involves preparation and constant work.

Oral compositions often use verbal patterning and repetition to retain the spoken word in memory. In the York Cycle, the use of rhyme, alliteration, and rhythm all aid the actors' memory, and probably the audience's as well. Since the stories and to some degree the language would already be familiar to the actors, the script aided memory rather than replaced it. The text was subordinate to oral performance, serving its production: the York Cycle is perhaps more word-oriented than any other Corpus Christi play, and its prosody had the very practical function of helping assure that its textual web remained reasonably solid in performance.[28]

But composing a written text does somewhat more to oral performance than secure the delivery of its language. Formulas and other patterns help an oral culture preserve speech, but they seldom become as fixed and elaborate as words organized through writing. Writing in the service of speech can amplify its features: the *literary* use of formulas, meters, alliteration, and rhyme probably took features of oral composition to new heights of consistency and rigor (see Goody 99; Gellrich, *Discourse* 195–99). The York Cycle is thoroughly a literary work, as demonstrated on the verbal level by its careful alliteration, intricate stanzaic forms, and delicate word chains that occasionally link stanza to stanza.

Finally, we come to the moment of consumption, that is, the reception and interpretation of a discourse. There is scanty evidence of how medieval audiences responded to performances, but at least some authorities of the time hoped that the play would serve the same function as a devotional text: as a spur to reminiscence and retrospection. In psalters, books of hours, and related manuscripts, text and image were linked by the silent reader to instigate meditation and devotion. This effect was, in a sense, one of the medieval book's powers; and similar conjunctions were probably used in staging the cycle plays.[29] The flowering of lay devotional literature thus came about in the midst of (and probably resulted from) the great increase in silent readership among the laity within a milieu that maintained strong ties with the oral mentality. Sanctity and piety were closely associated with reading.

The communication cycle played a crucial role in structuring the medieval discursive formation, and so conditioned many performance strategies in the York Cycle. However, its effects only begin to identify the ways medieval communication practices influenced discourse. A communication framework conjoins the communication cycle with the social relations of communication, and in so doing generally it arrays preexisting discursive "tactics" (principally analogical, logical, and inferential techniques) into a generative structure—it establishes a dominant discursive strategy. In the Middle Ages, analogy gained special preeminence, leading to figural thinking; in other words, the creation of similitudes became the discursive norm.

5

The York pageant of *The Building of the Ark* is crowded with symbols. The wood of the ark comes from "high trees" (*York* 8.73), and "tree" alluded to the cross.[30] The dimensions of the ark had a numerological explanation, in which for instance the ark's thirty cubits in height symbolized Jesus's thirty years of human life. Noah's work took "a hundereth wyntres" (8.114) because that equaled the period of grace. Even God's instructions to hew the wood square (8.74) held a higher meaning, as a glance toward the coming of the New, and four-square, Jerusalem (Beadle, "Shipwrights' Craft" 60). Symbols are embedded throughout the cycle.

In the dominant medieval view, the material world everywhere contained signs, inscriptions marking the likenesses of things and ideas. "This sensible world is a certain book having divinity intrinsically written in it," wrote the twelfth-century scholar Bernardus Silvestris, "The single creatures are letters and notes of something which is in divinity" (qtd. in Allen 194). Saint Augustine had expressed a similar view (*Confessions* 322–23). Medieval thinkers borrowed from platonism or neoplatonism; but why would people so many centuries later accept such ancient theories as relevant and defensible? The manner of production and preservation in the communication cycle, and of deployment and utilization in the social relations of communication, came together to establish figural thinking.

The semiotic chain. Writing frequently served as a mnemonic device, helping the reader recall words or ideas that were originally spoken or heard, and as a restorative mechanism to recover an author's thoughts. This is especially clear in the use of writing for professional purposes to assist oral delivery, such as a sermon, lecture, or legal argument; but elementary readers usually read texts aloud too, whether because they lacked silent reading skills or because their intent was to recite certain prayers and services. In this role writing functioned as a supplement to speech; writing which transcribed speech then helped to restored it to life. Semiotically speaking, under these conditions the spoken word was a sign for a referent, and alphabetic writing was a sign of a sign. Writing was in fact understood as imitating speech (Gellrich, *Discourse* 13, 20). But if the medieval use of writing prompted speech, and speech referred to a thing or mental image, what did the referent refer to? The vibrant and universal oral culture attached symbolic meanings to physical objects (as explained shortly), so it was reasonable to expect another referential link. By following this semiotic chain, we find that (in a non-Derridean sense) speech, like writing, could also be a system of signs of signs—the referent could be a sign as well. The written word "tree" recalled the spoken word "tree," which recalled an image of a tree, which recalled the cross.

Thus, the text of *The Building of the Ark* presents written speeches about the ark, which became performed speeches about the ark, which were accompanied by a staging of the ark being built, and the ark itself traditionally symbolized the Church. Judson Allen finds a similar pattern in Chaucer's *Legend of Good Women*, a poem about Alceste which Chaucer dedicated to Queen Anne. According to Allen, what one finds in the book (itself a container of remembrance) is a daisy as a symbol of remembrance; what one finds in the daisy is Alceste, the thing to be remembered; and what one finds in Alceste is Queen Anne. The sequence makes the poem "a literal emblem of the medieval act of reading, of understanding" (270). In the twelfth century, Hugh of St. Victor described the process in theoretical terms:

> The idea in the mind is the internal word, which is shown forth by the sound of the voice, that is, by the external word. And the divine Wisdom, which the Father has uttered out of his heart, invisible in Itself, is recognized through creatures and in them. From this is most surely to be gathered how profound is the understanding to be sought in the Sacred Writings, in which we come through the word to a concept, through a concept to a thing, through the thing to its idea, and through its idea arrive at Truth. (Qtd. in Gellrich, *Idea* 100–1)

Everything in the medieval world thus becomes a sign of a sign, in a chain of meanings that ultimately culminated in God and the divine purpose.[31] But of course this was only known through a text, the Bible, the embodiment of God's Word.

Although silent reading was becoming increasingly common in the later Middle Ages, the movement from text to speech did not end. True, texts no longer always led to outward speech, but the two were still often associated. Oratory, preaching, disputation and the like still had high status (not to mention entertainment value); education in reading continued to begin with pronunciation and reading aloud. Silent reading may have loosened the link with the practical materiality of speaking, but it still retained the idea of speech: oral delivery may have become idealized, "purified," when it was less performed. Thought and meditation were cast as the interior speech prompted by the writing within the heart, and silent reading encouraged meditative associations. Perhaps the expansion and textualization of interior speech also helped foster the notion of an inner truth hidden within material phenomena (cf. Briscoe; Saenger 401–2; Gellrich, *Idea* 117).

Validation. The perception that the world was inhabited by signs developed through another dynamic as well, concerning the truth value of images and physical symbols, and utilizing texts for validation. In oral culture, physical objects were invested with symbolic meaning, often through gesture and ritual. (For that matter, texts and letters of the alphabet could have symbolic and magical qualities.) Ceremony was a vital or even central element in many legal and religious transactions, partly because of its memorializing function. Many rituals used physical objects, which became imbued with social or religious symbolism and power.[32] For this reason the feudal contract was quite different from a modern, wholly textual contract. For example, in the course of transferring a parcel of land, a knife might become a token and symbol of the exchange; few people would need to prove a symbol's validity or interpret its meaning, because both arose from the performance of actions. If a question arose later, the participants (or their descendants) could provide oral testimony. But when writing became privileged, the *litterati* felt it necessary to validate the symbols of agreements, miracles, and other signs by attaching textual evidence, just as they did with oral witness. Human memory was no longer adequate; the truth of the past seemed better assured by documents. From a literate perspective, images were deeply ambiguous, polysemous, requiring textual authorization and limitation. They were figures endowed with inner meanings which one sought by following their connections with written material. So now physical objects and visual images were incorporated into a textual realm. Only through texts could meaning be secured or even established.[33]

Using texts to secure truth affected medieval views of language itself. Increasingly, textuality became the model for language. Augustine evidently based his conception of language and reality on rhetoric, which has an oratorical focus; but in the Middle Ages, Anselm grounded his ideas in grammar and Aquinas cast his analyses in terms of Aristotelian logic, both of which depend on written texts as method and model. The nominalists seem to have been even more committed to a textual orientation: they accepted a contractual interpretation of the sacraments,[34] pursued sophisticated explorations in logic and linguistics, relied on optics and visual evidence in their epistemology, and applied mathematical and geometrical analogues to logic and theology.[35] Thus both in the mainstream and in the margins of manuscript culture, validity was secured by textualizing discourse.

The world now was not simply one of signs, but one of writing. However, the symbols and rituals produced in oral culture could still keep their vitality, provided they found textual validation. Validation through writing and the semiotic chain fostered the medieval interpretive impulse in which everything was a sign, every sign was secured by a second sign, and that sign was upheld by yet a third, trading back and forth between textual proof and ritualistic symbolism. And yet the shuttling between signs did not devolve into an infinite regression of signification: the Bible's status as evidence without equal stopped the semiotic chain on one end as the ultimate sign of God and on the other end as the sacred tomb of that venerable but dead language, Latin, which was learned only from texts.

Thus to validate events the York Cycle often quotes prophecy, a motif similar to typology. After Mary gives birth, she recalls Balaam's prophecy that a star would rise and a maiden would bear a son (*York* 14.100–3), thus confirming her child's identity. The Magi quote Scriptures when they meet with Herod, in order to demonstrate that they have good reasons for seeking the baby (*York* 16.210–34). In *The Entry into Jerusalem*, Jesus consciously stages his arrival according to the prophecy of Zechariah, becoming its fulfillment and gaining its sanction; and when the citizens of Jerusalem speak of his coming, they marvel only briefly at the miracles he performed, for they are far more interested in his prophetic warrant.

The relationships between speech and writing within medieval manuscript culture provided dynamics that led to the view that the world was full of signs of divine creation, "signatures" of a higher being. The view bifurcated meaning, since each linguistic term pointed both to its immediate referent or literal sense, and also to what the referent itself signified, its figural sense. Further dynamics of manuscript culture made the relationship between the two senses a similitude.

Textual memory. The problem of preserving discourse and memory had several facets. Just as texts could remind the reader of images, images could recall texts. Memory had to serve official and practical speech, when logic and persuasiveness took priority. In classical times there was an Art of Memory geared toward the needs of political debate and public speaking. The Art was revived during the twelfth century, when writing was again pivotal in governmental and ecclesiastic institutions, and it remained popular and important among the laity until the seventeenth century, when figural thinking faded to the background. It was often part of standard rhetorical training. Treatises about it taught their readers to construct mental images that condensed the basic issues of an argument, or sometimes the very words. Human (or at least anthropomorphic) figures were traditionally considered the strongest images. But the best spurs to memory are similar or connected to what needs to be recalled. Such imagery included visual parallels, metonymies, and sometimes puns. Texts could thereby be kept in memory through images full of similitudes; by interpreting the image, one recovered the text. From personifications in the mind it was a short step to actual pictures that served as reminders, and from there another short step to allegorical pictures (Yates 1–26, 50–105, 261–62; Coleman 171). Allen likewise notes the memorization of texts and the textualization of memory. He observes that truth for medieval people was usually based on written authority. Everything to be remembered was "transformed into something bookish, or literary—a placed image preserved by the artificial memory" (269). The Art of Memory clearly helps elucidate the importance of similitudes for medieval thinking.

Oral memory. Although the symbols and rituals of oral culture now had to be validated by texts, the *way* in which they were validated was essentially oral: in the Middle Ages people tended to use texts as if they were repositories of oral culture. The Bible, for example, was treated less as a coherent volume than as a collection of independent stories which drew their value from their ethical meaning; hence the *Biblia pauperum* and the York Cycle could represent the Bible by gathering its key stories. Such stories contained the culture's memory and could supply exempla precisely because they were memorable. Thus there was a reciprocal relation between truth and memory, for whatever was selected to be memorized had to appear important, exemplary, and true, while at the same time the true had to take a form that could be memorized. In oral culture, verbal patterns and formulas fixed memory; stories were often retold because their similarity to an occasion or concern could influence present understanding. Imitation and similitude thus underlie the structure of oral thinking. The texts that validated oral material thereby took up many of the reiterative, analogical, and symbolic methods of oral culture.[36] Even though discourse was retained in texts as well as in memory, memory effectively dominated, and so orality guided the investment and retrieval of meaning in texts. In medieval culture, references to truth were references to oral constructions, even when embodied in texts.

These points illustrate the complex interaction of speech and writing in medieval England. Medieval manuscript culture involved not only altering oral culture to suit literate needs, but also appropriating literate resources to accommodate an oral mentality. On the one hand the need to perform orally made writing a mnemonic aid and brought about the Art of Memory; on the other hand writing dominated speech institutionally and encompassed everything within a textual framework, yet operated in a heavily oral milieu and so reestablished oral methods in the written word and complied with oral methods of handling texts.

6

The relationships between speech and writing in the Middle Ages established a semiotic chain and an order of validation that bifurcated meaning into literal and figural senses. We can see how figural thinking shaped the York Cycle and its performance in numerous ways.

The best-known physical symbols in the play are craft images, which appear throughout the York Cycle. About two dozen pageants have clear-cut connections to the guilds that presented them, and several others have associations that seem likely. These plays either incorporated the guild's tools or handiwork in the performance, or else presented a biblical event or a patron saint to which the guild was dedicated. Some ties are obvious: the Shipwrights produced *The Building of the Ark*, and the Bakers performed *The Last Supper*. Some connections have to be inferred and may hint at how the plays were staged, as in *The Expulsion*, performed by the Armorers: in medieval art the Angel usually wielded a sword when driving Adam and Eve from Eden. Such connections placed the trades of the medieval city into salvation history, and reinforced the audience's perception that even the most everyday object had a symbolic meaning joining it to Scriptures. The whole world could serve as a memento of biblical events and the imminence of the Last Judgment (Justice 47–58; Stevens 32–34).

Costuming supplied other physical symbols. While ordinary characters generally wore more-or-less ordinary clothes and little or no makeup, those on the extreme ends of the moral continuum usually wore masks or bold, abstract make-up. God and the Angels probably put on faces of gold or red; devils wore some kind of hideous mask or else blackened faces; a few supremely evil humans, such as Herod (but not Pilate), may have had a mask or more likely a helmet. Much of the clothing also had emblematic characteristics.[37] Such costuming emphasized the characters' religious significance, while mingling it with the more prosaic world of ordinary humanity.

Some characters in the York Cycle are explicitly moral analogues of others. Diabolical figures like Pharaoh and Herod (and to a lesser extent Judas, Pilate, Annas and Caiaphas) are portrayed as Satan-types. Isaac and Moses are like Jesus in part because each speaks with calm confidence and shows obedience to God (see Beadle and King 33, 88, 125; Collier 209). There are several stock "everyman" characters (another moral type), including the Janitors (porters) in *The Entry into Jerusalem* and *The Conspiracy*, and the Beadle in *Christ before Pilate 1*. Joseph too is clearly a stock character—the old man wedded to a young woman.

Analogies between Jesus and other characters are generally typological. The most developed typology in the cycle occurs in *Abraham and Isaac*. Another type for Jesus is Noah, whose father said of him that he "shalle be comforte to mankynne" (*York* 9.32) and indeed Noah proves to be humanity's deliverer by performing God's will. The Flood itself anticipates the Last Judgment, as Noah recognizes (*York* 9.301–2). Moses prefigures Jesus, in a scene that parallels the Harrowing of Hell. Actions could also be the subject of typology: the raising of Lazarus, for example, prefigures the Resurrection (see also Collier 208, 213; Beadle and King: 21, 33; Woolf 223.)

Allegory is of course another major form of similitude in the Middle Ages. The York Cycle actually has little allegorical language, and unlike other mystery cycles (such as *Ludus Coventriae*) it has no allegorical characters. Instead, the York Cycle develops allegory through performance. For example, its procession traveled from the Holy Trinity Priory at the edge of town, to the Pavement, where goods were weighed and sold and where public punishments were exacted. As Martin Stevens emphasizes, the path signified the movement from God and Creation to the Last Judgment. At the center of the cycle is *The Entry into Jerusalem*, widely considered the pivotal pageant. When Jesus is greeted by the Citizens, Jerusalem becomes an allegory for York; at the same time, the actual city becomes the stage for salvation history in the making (Stevens 50–77). The performance of the York Cycle was encyclopedic in scope: all occupations, all of the city, all of history was incorporated in its presentation. If ever there was a theatre of the world, this was it.

Sound often had a figural meaning as well. Probably music was played at various points in the performance, often for practical functions such as covering movement across the playing area or indicating the passage of time. It could also have a symbolic purpose, representing the divine order and the music of the spheres, the harmony of the soul, or the carnality of the flesh (Rastall, "'Alle Hefne'" and "Music").

Finally, most the York Cycle's verse is alliterative. Rhythm, rhyme, and alliteration—likenesses in sound—were not only mnemonic tools, but also similitudes on the phonemic level. Like music, poetic technique can foster a sense of concord and internal symmetry, and posit a common nature underlying the "syllables inscribed in time," in Augustine's phrase (Augustine 322; see also Vance 275–78).

7

Figural thinking is not the only artistic strategy in the York Cycle. Some pageants—most of the Passion sequence and a few others—have been attributed to a single writer/reviser, called the "York Realist." The nature of this aesthetic realism (which is not equivalent to philosophical realism) has been much debated. J. W. Robinson argues that the realism arises from the many physical details presented in plays, creating a sense of naturalism. Examples include Herod's pause to have his gown straightened (*York* 31.73–74) and the Beadle's offer of hot water for Pilate's hand-washing (*York* 33.443). Robinson suggests that the York Realist arrived at these details through logical extension of the narrative (not the Scriptural) material. He acknowledges that some plays outside the Realist group also have realistic details, but he feels they are less developed and formally different from the Realist's work.

Clifford Davidson has pursued these ideas further ("Realism"). He maintains that the concrete details were meant to increase the emotional power of the performance and give the audience the sense of direct, personal acquaintance with the events—especially with the sufferings of Jesus. The York Cycle thus becomes a meditational aid conjoining traditional (and rather abstract) iconography with naturalistic particularism and psychological motivation. Davidson links the naturalistic details in the York Cycle to a more widespread increase of interest in particulars and verisimilitude stemming from the rise of nominalism. Nominalistic ideas had circulated Europe from at least the twelfth century, but is associated in England with William of Ockham, who flourished in the early fourteenth century. Nominalism opposed medieval philosophical (and broadly platonic) realism, which asserted that universals—shared "common natures" or characteristics like blueness—existed in reality outside of the mind. Ockham argued instead that universals had no real existence except as a name for similarities that humans perceived: universals were concepts, and only individual objects existed outside of the mind. Davidson holds that such a philosophy led to an artistic emphasis on particularity, resulting in the realism of the York Realist.

Davidson's argument is very suggestive. Nonetheless it seems unlikely that nominalism had much influence on the York playwrights. Recent research indicates that nominalism soon passed out of fashion; that there was little connection elsewhere with theatre and nominalism; and that York was very traditional both culturally and religiously (it was little affected by humanism, and although Lollard ideas made their way to York as part of the play's religious context, the Lollard movement did not). Moreover, even if nominalism had influenced the composition of the plays, we would still need to explain the rise of nominalism itself.[38] It seems far more likely that the York playwrights remained in the tradition of medieval philosophical realism. One might also speculate that artistic attention to realistic details was a local tradition, but York used similitudes resplendently in the York Minster windows and in a royal entry for Henry VII (Davidson, *From Creation*; Anglo 21–28). The entry in fact used most if not all of the York Cycle's pageant wagons.

Arguably, the York Cycle's realism is an illusion created by the modern reader's view that representing physical particulars constitutes realism. (One should really call it "aesthetic empiricism.") However, I think the York Cycle displays another sort of realism—one that concerns social relations, not physical details. The Trial plays especially reveal a close familiarity with the language and procedures used in the law courts—a familiarity that is appropriate to York as the legal and administrative center of northern England for both religion and government. The York plays underscore how Herod, Pilate, Annas, and Caiaphas protect their political power and condemn Jesus without the proper authority or legal foundation. The "bishops" Annas and Caiaphas worry that Jesus threatens the power of their "church," and repeatedly charge that Jesus claims to be a king and so superior to Pilate. Robert Brawer observes that Pilate is portrayed as an adroit but self-serving administrator, who ridicules the priests and underlings within his jurisdiction, and focuses on preserving his position. As Lawrence Clopper notes, the York Cycle exhibits an "acute awareness of political maneuverings," and he notes for example that Herod sees Jesus as a little more than a political pawn, albeit an entertaining one. Through these depictions the York playwrights critique unjust pursuits of power, including by the Church. Ironically, the city's official text of the York plays may have itself have been an instrument of power: Sarah Beckwith suggests that its use to monitor performance was aimed at quelling improvisation. But in scripting the Trial plays, the York dramatists depicted not only how such power is conducted and the all-too-familiar arrogance, violence and pettiness of the men in authority, but also what it means when proceedings are or are not conducted "by the book."[39]

The sense of aesthetic realism derives from another source as well. Although the play has various instances of typology, another form of prefiguration plays a still greater role. The York playwrights concentrated on the process of events rather than their cyclicity, and organized scenes to take advantage of their sequentiality rather than their typological value. Time and history are thereby ordained by God through *prophecy* and fulfillment, not through figure and fulfillment (Collier 208). The New Testament plays almost always accompany events with references to prophecy, and some of the Old Testament plays do as well. Jesus is constantly praised as a prophet without peer.[40] These references create expectation in the audience; and as the expectation is consistently fulfilled by the dramatic action, the plays encourage the belief that the final prophecy, of the impending Judgment, will also be fulfilled (see Collier 220–40). They are the source of the York Cycle's overall theological force.

Prophecy and typology are grounded on different uses of texts. Typology requires the Old Testament writings to be taken as literal and historical materials which prefigure and are fulfilled by people and events in the New Testament. This leads to a common medieval sense of the Bible as complete and self-contained (Gellrich, *Idea* 19–20, 31–32, 38–42). Typology is thus attuned to the symbolic power of action and its interconnection with other actions (and the repetition of symbolic action is a brief definition of ritual).

Prophecy, like typology, portrays the text as evidence; but unlike typology, it also utilizes the text as a directive—prophecy constantly points outside the text to future action. Prophecies fulfilled within the Bible showed that God kept his promises, and so amassed evidence that further promises would be kept. The emphasis on prophecy, then, treated texts not only as the means of validation, but also as verbal promises—as contracts or covenants. It arose within the York Cycle because, unlike other mystery cycles (which were produced in more rural towns), York was then England's second largest city, and the cycle was firmly controlled by the craft and merchant guilds. The guilds' business activities and the city's administrative functions made contracts important. Prophecies *are* contracts, promises made by God through the voice of the prophet. The play's focus on prophecy affects its interpretation of Jesus himself. At the end of *The Entry Into Jerusalem*, eight of the town's leading citizens hail Jesus's arrival. The seventh declares him "the texte of trewthe the trew to taste" ("the text of truth, the true to test," *York* 25.534): Jesus is the text of truth both because he fulfills prophecy, providing the evidence that tests their verity; and because as the First Citizen proclaims, he is a "prophette preued withouten pere" ("prophet proved without peer," *York* 25.489) whose words, now embodied in the Bible, shall test true.

Thus the York Cycle's orientation toward prophecy derived from an approach to the use of writing. The attitude toward texts was pragmatic and businesslike, not mystical or hermeneutic. Scripture was holy in itself, but its interpretation took the same skills that York's merchants already possessed. Just as the York Cycle is urban and bourgeois as a civic ceremony, so too is its preoccupation with politics, law, and contractual relations. Prophecy still belonged to a discourse of patterning or figuration, but its contractual nature brought an emphasis on sequentiality and the literal truth of words unequaled by typology. The pragmatic orientation brought its own sense of realism. In a sense, in prophecy the words themselves—their meaning, coherence, precision, and truth—are at stake.

Many facets of the York Cycle reveal the growth of lay literacy, concentrated in business and administration, and elsewhere crowned at the universities by the displacement of theology by law. The end of the ecclesiastic monopoly on literacy helped the urban middle strata to take their devotional activity into their own hands in cultural forms like the York Cycle.[41] Many of these people's interests and concerns were consequently incorporated in these plays, leading to the realistic representations of social relations and the depiction of concrete details. The growth of a reading public, then, was behind the literalism and artistic realism of the York Cycle.

This change in the communication framework has two main aspects. The first is an alteration in the deployment and utilization of writing, assigning it increasing importance for pragmatic purposes and in secular institutions. Administration, law, and business focused on a text's literal meaning, its reference to immediate, concrete, and possibly legal activity, rather than its allegorical, moral, or spiritual echoes. In the later Middle Ages this interpretive approach was evidently also applied to the Bible, so that much art took its imagery from a literal reading of Scriptures (Pickering 165–66, 273–85; and see Allen 198–205).

The second aspect of the growth in lay literacy is its expansion of access to texts and deeper permeation of writing into social life. But this raises a question of how texts were understood by the part of the audience who had access to few books, worked with a small set of manuscripts, or read only occasionally, and most importantly, who received only indirect or infrequent instruction in how to interpret what they read—in short, who lived primarily in an oral culture more or less separate from the developments in manuscript culture. The signs here point to a tendency toward literal interpretation that converges with the literalism of the pragmatic readers. Brian Stock describes how texts could make a deep impression on peasants even when they couldn't read, through the internalization of Scriptures interpreted literally as instructions for physical conduct; he calls this a "re-ritualization of religious behavior." Stock's brief example is from the eleventh century, when few peasants could read. Carlo Ginzburg's more extensive consideration of the issue, which looks at a later period when the lower social strata read more frequently, points in the same direction. He finds that Menocchio, a sixteenth-century miller being examined for heresy, read in a manner that combined oral and literate culture. The result was that in Menocchio's "mental and linguistic world, marked as it was by the most absolute literalism, even metaphors must be taken in a rigorously literal sense." This reading was closely tied to a practical logic and materialism sometimes described as "peasant rationalism."[42] It thus seems likely that the problematic of the literal and the figural, the conjunction of idealist universals and naturalistic particulars, addressed the needs of both the oral and the literate cultures.

8

Between the eleventh and twelfth centuries, writes Stock, medieval thinkers began to use standard dichotomies such as visible/invisible, material/spiritual, image/reality, and word/text, to formulate something like a semiotics of culture. Phenomena had a kind of grammar, logic, and rhetoric, which (once understood) would reveal meanings (327). Marcia Colish likewise points toward these dichotomies and their unification when she argues that the Incarnational point of view and the typological approach to symbolism led Dante to express spiritual realities "in tangible, material, earthly terms, in the terms of daily life" (215–16).

The impulse to unite the universal with the particular goes as far back as Augustine. The York playwrights followed the same path. They saw Jesus both as God with supreme powers, and as a man who suffered torments and crucifixion; Joseph, Mary, and the infant may have been a holy family, but they remained a family. Word had to be made flesh for them to know it as a word, and the Feast of Corpus Christi, as a celebration of the Incarnation, would certainly have emphasized that viewpoint.

The unity of the universal with the particular is essentially the core problem of reading and interpretation in the Middle Ages, that of seeing the divine in the mundane. The contrast is equivalent to the distinction between literal and anagogical meaning, but it can also be expressed through the distance between appearance and reality that creates dramatic irony, in which the audience interprets better than the character. The York playwrights incorporated dramatic irony often. Elza Tiner has shown that the York Trial plays use multiple levels of meaning so that Annas and Caiaphas convict Jesus on the outward, intentional level, but on an unintended level they convict themselves and reveal the truth of Christ; or they attempt to vilify Jesus but implicitly praise him. The plays' uses of verbal irony and related tropes and figures similarly produce double meanings along the lines of a legal argument versus its theological implications.[43] And of course the York Cycle stages the large theological ironies. Jesus enters Jerusalem as both a pauper and a king, and as a king he comes in order to be slaughtered. He is judged on earth, but in heaven he is to be the ultimate judge. In these ways, dramatic irony and paradox in the York Cycle pass beyond ornamental usage to become thoroughly structural and constitutive.

The York Cycle fuses the particular with the universal through other means as well. One of the simplest and most direct methods was anachronism. By peopling the plays with "dukes," "bishops," and "citizens," the dramatists quickly made the characters' basic social positions and moral types clear to the audience, who could then concentrate on the action and its moral significance.[44] This technique implies a figural conception of character. In anachronism, the guild imagery makes a similarly figural leap through time (Homan). In the same manner that types and antitypes are linked "vertically" in divine eternity, so too is the anachronism joined with its biblical analogue. Perhaps another combination of the universal and the particular is the coexistence of masked and unmasked characters on stage, a contrast between those who live in the world of abstract being and those in the realm of natural appearances. Such a contrast is likely to have been staged with the supernatural characters on one side and the humans on the other, as many medieval paintings and illustrations suggest.

In medieval philosophical realism, universals were understood as common natures, essences shared by similar individual entities—similitudes, in fact. The Latin term for this common nature was *species*, and the separate entity was the *individual*; thus there are different individual dogs, but they are of the same species, that is, they have the same essence or common nature, recognizable by the similitude between them. Species, then, were likenesses or similitudes, understood as existing independently of the observer (an idealist realism).[45] Species as likenesses were generated across space to meet the viewer's eyes, and from there multiplied into the mind (Tachau 6–11). Species that were similar to each other were of the same *genus*: a dog is an animal. However, the individual object was also distinguished by its *accidents*: particular but nonessential characteristics or circumstances, such as a dog's color, age, friendliness, and so forth. Thus each individual had accidents differentiating it from others of its species and genus.

As we've seen, this medieval platonic realism emerged out of the relations between speech and writing, which made similitudes the dominant strategy in medieval discourse. Thus unlike today, medieval philosophy and language theory emphasized similarity over difference. Whatever the strategy of artistic similitude—the likeness of promise to enactment found in prophecy, of earlier story to later story described in typology, of things and actions to moral beliefs and attitudes established in allegory, or of human action to cosmic or social event embodied in ritual—the particular and literal object was constantly imbued with the universalities and figural meanings.

Medieval theatrical space was organized on the same principle. Whether the staging used one location, several emblematic locations, or a procession of pageants, it regularly divided the playing areas into a *locus* and *platea*. The *locus* was a particular place in which individuals found themselves. The *platea*, in contrast, was a generic space where all species were united under one universal. The difference between the two was further underscored by a contrast between the *platea* as the realm of play, presentation, and audience engagement, and the *locus* as the domain of fiction, a mimetic representation existing independently of the audience (Munson 197; Weimann 73–85; Agan). The contrast is analogous to the one between the interactive character of speech and the self-enclosed appearance of text; the contrast may in fact have been one of the conceptual resources that writers and performers drew upon when constructing the cycle plays.

In performance the division between these spaces was always crossable and often crossed.[46] But in its underlying concept, the *locus* and *platea* consist of a realm of the particular at the center, a general realm surrounding it that quickly merged into the spectators' universe. In order to see the particular place and people in the *locus*, the audience has to look through the *platea*, the general acting area. Or one can say that everything that is particular must pass through the general on its way to the audience. As Cami Agan points out, the two spaces force the audience to be aware of both the historical situation represented on the *locus* and the cosmic situation presented by the *platea* (160–61, 164). The poles of the *locus* and *platea* set up a tension in which everything has to be read through a generalizing filter, revealing its species or essence, as emblems or moral types. People on the stage represented, even through their individuality, typical relationships to God. Consequently, there was little pursuit of the modern sense of "character" (bearing internally governed consistency or psychology) either because the emphasis was not on personal motivation but on fundamental moral meaning, or else because fragmentation, incongruities, and enigmas were themselves significant, being representative of a God who works in mysterious ways (Mills; Clopper; Auerbach 192).

The similitudes, then, were the conceptual foundation of medieval acting, both because rhetoric and oratory trained speakers to present likenesses or human behavior, and because similitudes were the metaphysical basis for the species that actors presented. The question of whether the acting was "naturalistic" or "stylized" in modern terms, probably unanswerable in any case, is historiographically less important than gauging what medieval actors and audiences most likely thought acting did, which guided both performance and viewing. If good acting was seen as "natural" (as John Elliott claims), then it must be realized that "nature" consisted of species: abstractions that most people understood as real and a part of everything in the world. The presentational and symbolic use of masks and costumes reveals this emphasis. So too does one of the York Cycle's other important performance strategies, that of having different actors play the same characters in different pageants. This performance strategy probably would have interfered with audience attempts to see these characters in a way that would preserve their psychological and corporeal identity, but it would not have blocked reading the representations as pointers toward a higher nature. Indeed, the strategy would have promoted such readings because it drew the audience's attention to the underlying *species* or type.[47] The very variety of particulars became the doorway to the universal, just as masks did not hide the actor so much as reveal the moral type.

The amalgamation of the universal and the particular, of the figural and the literal, is particularly intense in the Corpus Christi plays, which were bound to the most important text of all in medieval culture, the Bible. In the morality plays, where the script had more independence from the Scriptures, the allegorical impulse was pursued more fully, and other textual sources could more easily be introduced, as happened when humanism finally took root in England. Yet the Corpus Christi plays as a genre also had stronger ties to oral culture than moralities had, for they necessarily addressed themselves to the common people, whereas the morality play's very openness to other textual influences ultimately drew it toward the masque, a genre that principally addressed the educated elite. The social balance between speech and writing thus influenced the strategies of performance. It is not surprising that mystery plays such as the York Cycle, as the "highest" cultural event in which oral culture and literate culture could still meet, were highly popular theatrical forms. It was at this nexus within manuscript culture that the mysteries of the guilds confronted the mysteries of existence.

That the guildsmen who produced and most likely performed the York Cycle were expected to confront this mystery and see the divine hidden in the mundane is clear from pageants like *The Supper at Emmaus*. The play incorporates many of the themes and techniques I've discussed. It tells the story of how, after the crucifixion, two pilgrims meet a third, who turns out to be Jesus. The play's several devotional themes include the sufferings of Jesus, the importance of faith, and the hidden divinity in everyone. It has two references to prophecy. The first concerns the promise of Jesus's resurrection, about which the two pilgrims are troubled and confused. The second prophecy is cited by Jesus when he chides the pilgrims for their weak faith: he reminds them of the prediction of a savior who had to die. This textual reference encourages the two pilgrims, who ask the unrecognized Jesus to stay with them so they can learn more. Both references are dramatically ironic, since the audience knows what the pilgrims do not, that the risen Christ stands before them.

The play's versification helps to point out other themes. It is written in an eight-line alliterative stanza up until the characters enter the "castle" at Emmaus, when the verse shifts to a four-line form. The entrance into the castle signifies the mutual acceptance of the pilgrims and Jesus; anagogically, it underscores the theme that the soul must believe in order to gain entry into heaven, making the play as a whole an anagoge for individual salvation. In addition, the stanzas throughout *The Supper at Emmaus* are linked together through repeated words. The technique highlights the notion of process latent in the play's allegory of the individual soul as a pilgrim seeking holy truths, moving from fear to faith. The emphasis on process is typical of the York Corpus Christi play, and typical of other products of medieval culture, such as the pilgrimage of the *Canterbury Tales* (Allen 85–88; and see Reiss, *Discourse of Modernism* 77).

The Supper at Emmaus closes by emphasizing process in one other way: as one pilgrim says, "Here may we notte melle more at this tyde, / For prossesse of plaies that precis in plight" (*York Play* 40.191–92). They must make way for the next pageant. This theatrical self-reference is another instance in which the York Cycle crosses the line between stage and world, fiction and reality, as when characters address the audience or enter through the crowd. Likewise, the cycle often assimilates the world (or a part of it) within the play, such as in its use of guild products. Nevertheless it is a striking moment. It doesn't sound like a wink to the audience. Most likely this is metatheatricality with a spiritual purpose, creating a similitude between the procession of plays and a procession of pilgrims, with no less holy a goal. But that is what's so striking. Generally literature of this type refers outside of itself to the world and the divinity that explains and fulfills it. Here, instead, it refers to its own earthly actions as a sign of its holy purpose. The significance of the play is in the outside world, but in this one moment the York Cycle asks the audience to think of meaning as contained within the performance itself (see also Allen 33–34, 150–51).

It was completely sensible for people in the Middle Ages to perceive Nature as a book: it was a consequence of the nature of the Book. Where everything is symbolic, the world becomes text and text becomes world. Nature and writing were together united in the image of Jesus on the cross, whose bodily wounds (as the medieval poet John Lydgate has it) are written through remembrance into the heart, to be read each day. The idea of the body as text was central to the tradition of *imitatio christi* (Kimmelman 39–44). This Incarnational conception was celebrated at the Feast of Corpus Christi—the occasion for the performance of mystery plays. Theatre, which embodies texts, was the text closest to the living body: a standard medieval defense of the stage proposed that if (as many theologians claimed) paintings were books for the unlettered, then theatre was a superior devotional aid, for "the one is a dead book, the other a quick."[48]

In a sense, then, theatre was less like a text than a text was like theatre. Texts were understood to move outside themselves to engage an audience in a simultaneously ethical and symbolic context. The likely result was that the audience's experience and enjoyment of the performances were significantly different from the typical ones today, even though they are not wholly inaccessible to us. In medieval performance, all events and entities become incorporated into the universe of the play. When medieval plays are performed today, the interpenetration of world and text continues to be exerted on audiences.[49] Unexpected and uncontrollable incidents, rather than being distractions as they usually are during indoor performances, become part of the performance, open to interpretation as somehow commenting on the performance: rain falling, geese honking overhead, dogs barking, a child wandering through the playing area. The actors performing their text in the open air become natural inscriptions, and then nothing will untwine what is natural from what is inscribed. The play truly is a "quick book."

9

Among the various differences between the classical Greek and the medieval European communication frameworks, the most outstanding is the contrast between Athens's decentralized system of knowledge production versus the Church's centralized institution and the supreme position of one book, the Bible, to which everything in life had to be connected. Even outside the Church, the importance of the Bible was substantiated by the universities, where theology was for centuries preeminent. The decentralization of knowledge in Athens promoted a competitive, practical, eristic literacy, exemplified by Euripides's iconoclasm, and the diverse pursuits and arguments of the Sophists. In contrast, the Bible's role encouraged the production of similitudes, emphasizing the presence of God's signature in all things.

Analysis of these early forms of theatre reveals various structures consisting of material, social, and semiosic relationships. These structures are often highly imbricated in their resulting products, not in the sense of being inextricable even to the point of indistinguishability, but rather as a complex, dynamic, open totality comprised of distinctive systems which affect each other through numerous causal, logical, and analogical interactions. Communication plays a pivotal role in these interactions, and does so in ways that cannot be reduced to textuality, intersubjectivity, or neutral conduits of information. Communication itself has structures, agents, and discourses—the latter both as content and as style, which I call discursive and performance strategies.

By attending to the material aspects of communication, including the role of the physical means used (speech, handwritten manuscript, and so forth), I've indicated that semiosis does not consist solely of meaning; or more exactly, semiosis is not all propositional or discursive content. The argument counters the current trend in cultural theory, which not only defines cultural activity primarily as discourse, but still worse, detotalizes even that by conceptualizing cultural objects as *texts*. The metaphor conflates all forms of semiosis into the model of a single form of communication, writing. Even setting aside the ethnocentrism of that approach, the conflation conceals various aspects of other modes of communication and distorts many others. Indeed, it even distorts the nature of writing, either abstracting it from the human dynamics that create and shape it, or collapsing all of society into it.

Within theatre studies the metaphor converts audience experience into an intellectual exercise of decoding signs and observing how they relate to each other. That is certainly part of what happens when we see a show, but just as certainly it is not all.

Rather than narrow the analytic frame as postmodernism has done, critical realism broadens it, embracing the fuller range and systematic complexities of the structures underlying cultural production. The concept of communication accomplishes that task: it encompasses the meaningfulness of semiotic activity (iconic, indexical and symbolic), its social aspects (interpersonal, collective and structural), and its material means (speech, intonation, gesture, drawing, music, handwriting, printing, electronics, et cetera). That last aspect of communication also emphasizes that semiosis is, first and foremost, an *embodied* activity. The point bears on our understanding of how audiences experience and enjoy performance, in which (as we will see) embodiment plays a crucial role.

A communication framework, then, is a system of practical, social, and semiotic systems that generate certain strategies of discourse and performance. They are generated not simply as intellectual fashions: instead, they emerge from the practical procedures and social exigencies of everyday communication.[50] What we see by comparing the two theatrical cultures considered here is not simply differences among institutions and styles, but rather underlying structural dynamics—specifically, social structures, agents and discourses—that cause the emergence of new and characteristic ways of thinking and acting.

I have discussed those dynamics from the "external" perspective of how structural and discursive preconditions establish agents' possibilities of action; but they also affect the constitution of agency itself, helping to shape its inner structure. In addition, although I have emphasized the importance of practices, I've only scratched the surface of what that entails. To address these aspects of communication and performance, the next chapter again picks up the thread of critical realist theory.

CHAPTER 3

EMBODIMENT, AGENCY, AND PERFORMANCE STRATEGIES

CRITICAL REALISM IS COMMITTED TO THE POSITION THAT KNOWLEDGE IS fundamentally social. Knowledge develops through individual and collective research, institutional resources, social approbation, cultural values and traditions, and other societal features. In addition, however, ideas arise through embodied activities. Since the 1970s scientific evidence has mounted to support the role of the body in the mind, in a detailed and operational way, bringing a whole new meaning to the philosophical theory of the "primacy of practice." Meshing evidence from various fields, including neuroscience, psychology, linguistics and ethnography, the "second wave" of cognitive science has forcefully and provocatively demonstrated that thought is fundamentally embodied and metaphoric—that myriads of images emerging from everyday physical activities not only make ordinary experiences intelligible, but also structure abstract thinking, including science, political analysis and philosophy. The imagery operates largely subconsciously and affects the very structures enabling discursive knowledge, extending beyond propositional thought to certain forms of unconscious and nonpropositional thought. Communication practices have a particularly important role in shaping knowledge. Consequently cognitive science has particular ramifications for our understanding of theatre, where embodiment, communication and agency all come together.

To explore these interconnections, I am going to skip over several centuries and consider the bookends of what I'll call the "Age of Empiricism": the late seventeenth and early eighteenth centuries at one end, and the late nineteenth through mid twentieth centuries at the other. I will turn to the Renaissance in the next chapter, because the introduction of the printing press initiated massive cultural changes and their impact bears upon the nature of theatre itself. The issues in that discussion are best addressed if I take up other matters first.

Theatrically the era I will treat here is characterized by a new definition of artistic realism, bearing a distinctive and growing emphasis on aesthetic, psychological, and even scientific verisimilitude. Philosophically this brand of artistic realism was allied with the positivist family of theories (initially, empiricism). I will pay considerable attention to the period's beginning phase, particularly the early eighteenth century when civil society was established, and when the play *The Conscious Lovers* broke box office records. The link between these, which makes the moment especially attractive, is the rise of the periodical press. Newspapers played a crucial part in the formation of civil society; the development provides another example of how a change in the *use* of a communication technology can have as important an impact as the introduction of a new technology; and one of the people most involved in periodical publication was Richard Steele, editor and contributor to *The Spectator* (one of the most renowned periodicals of the eighteenth century) and author of the play *The Conscious Lovers*. It is only poetic justice that this age of sometimes severe Cartesian separation between mind and body should be approached by first examining their deep connection.

1

Cognitive science has developed in many directions, but I will be drawing on only one of its theories, which has been synthesized in the individual and collaborative work of linguist George Lakoff and philosopher Mark Johnson. Its key finding that thought is deeply shaped by human embodiment. Embodiment influences cognition through experiences with the world's contents and structures. For example, our concepts of source, path and goal emerge through our sensorimotor experiences of travel, which we apprehend as infants when we crawl about and when we see things move (Johnson 19–21; Lakoff 271–75). Kinesthetic interactions of this sort provide general forms for organizing perception and cognition in terms of numerous iconic models, including "container," "force," "link," "cycle," "part/whole," "up/down," "center/periphery," "hot/cold," "front/back," "balance," and so forth. Lakoff and Johnson call these models *image schemas*. Unlike full-fledged images or mental pictures, they lack particularity and detail: they are abstract patterns—tropes, if you will, of space, time, connection, and action.

As we build upon our experiences of the world we turn image schemas into metaphors that help us conceptualize other sorts of things, particularly abstractions. We might apply the path schema to materialities like temporal progress (we look "toward" the future), goals (someone takes her "first step toward" a new career), reasoning (one can wonder where an argument is "headed"), and social relations (two people may be "going together"). Image schemas regularly structure thought through this sort of metaphoric projection, such as by using concrete examples of the image schema. For instance, a road is a type of path, and so we generate metaphors such as "Their relationship reached a crossroads" or "He's in a dead end job." Rather than simply reporting an experience, metaphors form part of the experience itself. Through these means people generate image schemas that fit many different situations. Thus image schemas are highly dynamic (Johnson 27–30, 48–51, 98, 113–17).

Lakoff and Johnson focus mainly on image schemas emerging from individual kinesthetic experience, but they also discuss schemas arising from social life. From the examples they offer, they conceptualize "social" in two senses: the aggregate of many individuals' experiences with common socially produced objects or activities, such as "She felt like a fifth wheel" or "They're cooking up something"; or experiences that depend on social relationships or institutions, as in "sister organizations" and "Here's my two cents."

Virtually all of our thoughts, perceptions and knowledge—basic concepts such as interiority and part-whole, logical operations such as syllogisms, even scientific theories—build upon image schemas. They are not conveniences: they are wholly interwoven into the cognitive unconscious, and structure thought and meaning themselves (Lakoff and Johnson, *Philosophy* 16–59, 161–66, 247, 380–82; Lakoff 281–92). However, that fact does *not* imply that metaphors have free play or are indeterminate, that knowledge is wholly cultural, or that all we can know are metaphors. Image schemas emerge from human interactions with the real world, so their applicability is also constrained by reality. Consequently metaphors often establish genuine knowledge of both the world outside the mind, and the world within it.

Cognitive science's case for the fundamental role of imagery in thought correlates with Peircean semiotics, which holds that icons are integral to symbolic (conventional) signs such as words. "Symbols grow. They come into being by development out of other signs, particularly from likenesses or from mixed signs partaking of the nature of likenesses and symbols.... Now every symbol must have organically attached to it, its Indices of Reactions and its Icons of Qualities" (Peirce, *Essential Peirce* 2.10, 2.193–94; and see 2.278, 4.531). It turns out, then, that Peircean semiotics is not only a fruitful theory for cultural analysis and for understanding theatre's semiotics, but also has scientific support.

For Lakoff and Johnson, cognitive science jettisons empiricism in favor of "embodied realism," a philosophy which is consistent with the major elements of critical realism (see Nellhaus, "From Embodiment" 117–18).

However, although Lakoff and Johnson recognize that image schemas have social determinants and a shared, public character, they never delve into the nature of social determination, and they derive the shared and public character of image schemas primarily from the human body (Johnson 175, 190). Ultimately cognitive science must be incorporated into a more socially oriented theory. Integrating it within a theory of communication practices provides one step in that direction.

2

Cognitive science enriches our understanding of culture by showing how image schemas play a role not just within particular thoughts and expressions, but also in the ongoing exercise of cognition (understanding "cognition" as the brain/mind system which generates unconscious as well as conscious mental contents; see Hart 319). First, image schemas are central to categorization. Categorization is a neural necessity that evolved for survival: it winnows down millions of inputs and groups them in various ways in order to produce distinctions and identifications. But even though categorization is cognitive, our embodiment conditions its possibilities. As a result, the vast majority of categories arise unconsciously through our embodied experiences. And categories are nearly always structured by image schemas.

Categories are the basis of concepts, which "allow us to mentally characterize our categories and reason about them.... What makes concepts is their inferential capacity, their ability to be bound together in ways that yield inferences" (Lakoff and Johnson, *Philosophy* 19, 20). By generating inferences, concepts (or concept-relations) exercise causal powers (Lakoff and Johnson, *Philosophy* 116–17). Often we infer through metaphorical entailments—elaborations and metaphorical applications of an image schema. For instance, the "containment" schema can entail notions of protection from external forces, restraint of forces within the container, relative fixity of location, presentation for or blockage from view, and transitivity (if A is inside B, and B is inside C, then A is inside C). Likewise, the metaphor "love is a journey" entails the ideas that a romantic relationship can make progress, lose direction, get stalled, move too fast, run its course, hit a bump in the road, and so forth: all things that can happen on a journey, which is an advanced metaphor describing personal experiences over time (Johnson 22; Lakoff and Johnson, *Philosophy* 64–69).

Different metaphors for something evince different aspects of their target. For instance, the schema "love/desire is food" ("Hi, honey"; "He's starved for affection"; "What's your taste in men?") expresses the combination of need, want and pleasure in sexual or romantic feelings. Other common metaphors for sex and desire include heat ("What a hottie!"), force ("They're attracted to each other"), games ("He's a player"), and insanity ("She's crazy for you") (Lakoff 409–15). Complex realities, experiences, and abstractions often require multiple metaphors, and few thoughts about subjective experiences (reflexivity) occur without them. Such variety results in rich arrays of entailments (Lakoff and Johnson, *Philosophy* 59–72).

Entailments allow people to produce new conceptual links. Typically this happens by applying an image schema to perceptions or experiences as a metaphor for understanding them. But one can also obtain a new understanding by switching perspectives on a given image schema—many have "flip sides." For example, containment: a box can protect wineglasses, but Pandora's Box prevented evils from escaping. Path: Oedipus both leaves Thebes, and heads for Athens. Force: Clov pushes Nagg into his bin, and Nagg feels himself being pushed. Multiplicity/mass: you can see the trees, or the forest. Reversals of this sort are also possible with more complex images and metaphors. We have seen an example in the shared but inverted assumptions of positivism and social constructionism, and toward the end of this chapter I will discuss some "flip side" dramatic genres.

Literal meanings do play an essential role in subjective experience. Terms for bodily activities and everyday objects are literal, the perception "these two shapes are similar" is literal, and so forth. It is nearly impossible to be wholly literal in abstract reasoning, and generally we adopt image schemas to map the abstraction as a whole. So, for example, we often think about similarity through the schema of physical proximity: "these two shapes are close." Literalness (of some type) establishes constraints on meaning that allow a metaphor to be apt. "Similarity is proximity" probably derives from the experience of finding similar things at the same or nearly the same location: this is a background literal element. Through its mappings, a metaphor must adequately describe at least some of its target's properties; if it failed to correctly identify any aspect whatsoever, then it would fail to be useful. However, knowledge can seldom be completely translated into literal terms, because what makes understanding different from simply possessing information is what organizes the information, puts it into a context, describes what it represents, and connects it to our experience. The mind may rely on perceptions to generate knowledge, but as evidence of things that in some cases aren't themselves directly perceptible: inference and pattern-seeking step in, and image schemas provide those patterns. In the absence of such relationships, bits of data are—to use a telling metaphor—lifeless (Lakoff and Johnson, *Philosophy* 58–59, 72–73).

Primary image schemas, their metaphoric applications, their combinations with other image schemas and their entailments form vast and intricate networks of iconic cognitive structures that permeate and stimulate reasoning: thought proceeds not simply or even principally through propositional logic, but also through analogical consistency. The pursuit of consistency promotes the systematization of concepts around a basic model or image. More than one image may be valid: light can be understood as consisting of particles *or* waves, each model successfully explaining part of light's behavior. Likewise, Bhaskar argues that models are indispensable for scientific theories in order to provide explanations and describe newly identified levels of reality (Bhaskar, *Plato, Etc.* 20, 21; Bhaskar, *Realist Theory of Science* 159–63, 166–68, 194). As Lakoff and Johnson show, models and metaphors underpin philosophies on a range of topics (they consider time, causality, mind, self and morality). In fact, Lakoff and Johnson demonstrate that syllogistic logic is itself founded on the metaphors "categories are containers" and "predication is containment" (Lakoff and Johnson, *Philosophy* 380–82). For example, the major premise "All elephants are mammals" says that the set "elephants" is contained in the set "mammals"; the minor premise "This is an elephant" states that a particular entity is within the set "elephants"; and the conclusion "This is a mammal" uses transitivity to place that specific elephant within the set "mammals." Theatrical performance involves models as well. In short, images are fundamental to all scientific theorization and cultural elaboration.

Thus knowledge arises through the interplay between agential intentionality and embodiment acting within the world. At the heart of the process is metaphoric imagery. Image schemas enable us to conceptualize things that we cannot perceive directly, including the relationships among things that we *can* experience directly. The pervasiveness of image schemas supports the position that there is no theory-free perception. However, it also demonstrates that we are not locked inside a prison house of language: we do have cognitive access to independent reality, and we can test metaphors for adequacy and suitability to their object.[1]

If people can only perceive the world through concepts that emerge from their embodied interactions with the world—if a condition of possibility for knowledge is the body's powers and susceptibilities—then our knowledge is inherently shaped by our human corporeality (which provides a basis for common understanding). But by the same token, if perception is conditioned by our bodies, then other bodies may perceive differently, and perhaps develop other knowledge within certain fields—but not in all. Our *way* of knowing is anthropomorphic, but knowledge as such need not be. The limits on perception are not the limits on knowledge. The proverbial Martians might have different bodies and senses than we do, and consequently different perceptions of the world, but they would conclude that the water is *in* the jug (if it is)—and by one method or another, they would also find that water is H_2O. What human embodiment and the consequent anthropomorphism of knowledge do underscore, however, is the fallibility of our insights into the world, and the boundaries of humanity's place among the multitudinous species of the planet.

3

Theatre involves characters. Even if the figures on stage are mere shapes moving about, audiences tend to anthropomorphize them. Characters are depictions of human agency, and so the concept of agency is important to theatre. Bhaskar regularly refers to "embodied intentional agency"; cognitive science not only supports this concept, but also demonstrates that agency is not an aggregation of discrete qualities or powers (embodied + intentional + agential) but instead is a complex dynamic totality. Cognitive science vigorously underscores the "embodied" part and elucidates the role that embodiment plays in intentionality as well as the sheer ability to act (in both the everyday and theatrical meanings of the term). For just as surely as the mind is in the body, the body is in the mind.

But agency is not merely embodied in a general sense: it is structured by particular image schemas which may vary from culture to culture, establishing socially specific concepts of agency, and different experiences of selfhood. It is important to make a distinction here. Although the *concept* of self differs among cultures, all cultures must possess a *sense* of self (initiated by the distinction between self and not-self). One learns a concept of self only after establishing a sense of self. The case for the chronological and structural priority of the sense of self is in fact based on the experience of embodied encounters with the environment, and the necessity for continuous practical activity in the world (Archer, *Being Human* 121–24). The sense of self is embedded in the human capacity for reflexivity, which is connected most immediately to the experience of *error*: when things don't do what one expects (for instance, the pretty bug bites), one must distinguish between oneself (and one's ideas) and the rest of the world. As Peirce puts it, "*error* appears, and it can be explained only by supposing a *self* which is fallible" (*Essential Peirce* 2.20; his emphasis). Earlier I pointed out that error produces the recognition of a mind-independent reality. Now we see the converse: error discovers the existence of selfhood, the mind as separate, and this new awareness is a rudimentary form of the reflexive self-monitoring that Bhaskar considers critical to intentionality (*Possibility of Naturalism* 35, 81–82).

Expressions of the *sense* of self utilize certain image schemas, which—precisely because they derive from embodied experience—provide metaphors for the *qualitative* experience of being engaged with an outer and an inner world. But because selfhood has many qualities, people's metaphors of selfhood engage a range of image schemas. The most common are the self as an object, a location, an inner essence, or a person. Evidence suggests that the various schemas for selfhood may be universal, not just Western. Self-as-object metaphors appear in sentences such as "She held herself back from laughing," "He forced himself to eat the soggy sandwich," and "They got carried away." Self-as-location metaphors include "He's out to lunch," "I was beside myself," and "She's very down-to-earth." Essential-self metaphors contrast outward appearance with inward being. In one variant, the "inner" self reflects the true person, which is masked by a public persona: "She acts tough, but she's really a marshmallow." Alternatively, the outer or customary self may be genuine, the inner one unpleasant and false: "He wasn't himself yesterday." Or the true self may need to be found: "He went on a journey of self-discovery." Finally, the self is imagined as a person in expressions like "She's punishing herself because of what happened," "Take care of yourself," and "He persuaded himself that they were right" (Lakoff and Johnson, *Philosophy* 267–87). For theatre studies, as I will explain later, two particularly important self-as-person metaphors involve projection onto another person, either by putting oneself in another's shoes in an advisory manner ("If I were you, I'd do X"), or by empathically adopting the other's viewpoint or experience ("I see why you feel that way"). These projections of self bear on audience experience.

Metaphors about selfhood attach to certain ontological elements of the self. According to Archer's critical realist sociology, humans are simultaneously *persons*, who develop a personal identity and qualities of self as they interact with the natural, practical, and social realms; *agents*, who occupy positions or roles within society; and *actors*, who play each of their agential roles in their own manner and to their own ability (*Realist Social Theory* 254–93). These elements align with social ontology as I've defined it: persons are the foundational structures, which are related especially to persons' material being; agents, obviously, constitute society's agential stratum; and actors operate with an eye toward the discourses about their roles and activities. The images that Lakoff and Johnson present (self as object, location, essence, and/or person) pertain to the basic structure, personhood. Agency concerns people's power to exist, be affected, choose, and act within the networks of social relationships and institutional structures. It is shaped by people's concepts of the individual self and its relationships with other people, with particular social groups, and with society as a whole; that is, by concepts of self (which are socially and culturally variable), as distinct from the sense of self. Last, the self as actor, as one who performs social roles, acts in part according to discourses—images, models or stereotypes of their roles. Those discourses are clearly social constructs, such as the norm of the "good mother" or the movie character-types that may unconsciously or even consciously guide people's behavioral styles and activities. But such role-images are also more particular and localized than concepts of self, because they attach to specific positioned practices.

I've emphasized the variety of the metaphors of selfhood, but some of the most fundamental image schemas concern the relationship between the agent who thinks and acts, and the world around her. The resulting concepts of agency frame epistemological and ontological assumptions. For instance, as I showed during my discussion of medieval theatre, during the Middle Ages agents were generally conceptualized as moral types. This view was associated with the idea that people are ranked within a hierarchy of dependence and quality that culminates in the absolute perfection and self-sufficiency of God. Rank—outwardly and publicly recognized—defined a person's quality. In contrast, the characteristically European (and later, American) notion of individualism that arose during the Renaissance and crystalized around 1700 posited a more-or-less horizontal relationship among people, asserting their fundamental independence and equality. On this view, people are essentially isolated individuals whose social relationships are exterior accessories to their existence (everyone their own Robinson Crusoe). Their value or quality may be reflected in their public accoutrements, but ultimately belongs to their inner moral worth, as we will see in my analysis of eighteenth century theatre. Agency is located in or derived from the individual's internal development and psychological response: the self is constituted by subjectivity, psychodynamics, inner depth. Our true selves are hidden deep within us.

As these examples show, different concepts of self are grounded on a number of image schemas describing the ontology of agency. Among them are containment, outside/inside, and connected/separate. Modern individualism elaborates upon the idea of the "essential" self through images of containment (isolation, inner depth, internal development)—more specifically, of being self-contained. But what is contained is one's *self*: this is different from the notion of a body possessing a soul, which is associated with an exterior divinity.

Metaphors of selfhood are always numerous, but societies tend to make one concept of agency dominate. Different sorts of practices converge in that concept's favor. For example, modern individualism has been attributed to the increasing division of labor under capitalism. However, the division of labor by itself would more likely foster a group identity than individualism (Goody 14). More plausibly, individualism arises from economic competition—but there are different forms of individualism, and competition often promotes an extroversion at odds with psychological depth (*Death of a Salesman* is practically a commentary on this point). There must be other forces behind the sense of interiority characterizing post-Renaissance individualism.

That interiority derives largely from communication practices; specifically, from print culture. By the twelfth century, silent reading had become customary in the clerical realm, and by the fourteenth, increasingly among aristocrats as well. It enabled greater privacy of thought and emotion, encouraging everything from intellectual independence and potentially heresy, to intensified devotion and spirituality as the reader sought inner communion with divinity within herself, to sexual fantasy (Saenger 399–405, 410–14; Stock 16–18). With printing, silent reading spread throughout society. The reader came to view the world from isolation, whether from a personal perspective into a world of private sensibilities and interpersonal interactions, or from an abstract, Archimedean viewpoint examining the natural world of objects. An individual's viewpoint thus formed the basis for interpreting the world and imposing some sort of order upon it. The private, solitary reader, denuded of sociality, became the model of the knowing Subject.

Concepts of self necessarily affect the way agents act, and their vision of the kinds of action available to them. The embodied practices of communication generate image schemas that deeply shape societal concepts of agency. Anchoring those practices are the material elements through which communication is produced (writing, speaking) and received (reading, listening). Communication practices establish epistemologies, which in turn construct concepts of the agent. The concepts become habituated in people's consciousness, their bodies, and their behaviors. Concepts of agency, then, are not simply ideologies in a functionalist sense, nor epiphenomena of economic relations, nor discourses unfettered by social and material conditions. They arise principally through embodied experiences of communication, which contribute to the experience of agency and selfhood, and provide foundations for (in this example) individualistic and psychologically oriented relations with the world.

The existential encounter with the world, which initiates both the recognition of mind-independent reality and the reflexivity founding the sense of self, does not leave the self static: as encounter succeeds encounter, the mind constantly discovers new things and revises old ideas, so that the self is inherently processual (a point that conjoins Peirce's concept of infinite semiosis with his argument that the self is a sign). Hence we think about self and identity in terms of narrative. Although narrative is not the same as plot and not all theatre involves plot, nevertheless narrative in theatrical performance is nearly ubiquitous—another example of the deep connection between theatre and agency. Since agents must engage with the world and make choices about how to interact with it, concepts of self involve strategies of thinking and acting. These take theatrical form as performance strategies.

4

Concepts of agency and performance strategies are not isolated or arbitrary cultural elements: they are related to other parts of the culture. Cognitive science challenges rationalistic concepts of culture, which emphasize the *logical* relations of consistency, inconsistency, or independence among ideas. That approach underestimates the important of *analogical* (often iconic) relations among ideas; more fundamentally, as we have seen, certain logical relations themselves have metaphoric foundations in image schemas gleaned from embodied relations with the world.

Just as image schemas provide a generative principle for systematizing a particular theory, they can serve similar functions in entire cultures, even though they seldom produce the same level of coherence. Cognitive science concretizes the concept of culture as a totality of ideas, values, beliefs, images, feelings, and attitudes that develops historically. Cultural systems are open, *partial* totalities. These possess not only an internal structure and necessary connections, but also external and contingent connections (Bhaskar, *Dialectic* 405). In cultural totalities, the body brings the outside in, via the image schemas formed through interactions with the world. Culture's connection to the body provides a constant touchstone across cultures: from a sensorimotor perspective, human bodies have trivial differences, and basic activities like moving, standing, pushing, eating, and feeling heat are identical among all peoples. But local, generational, sociological, and experiential commonalities provide other grounds from which cultures grow.

The principal internal connections within any cultural formation consist of logical relationships and analogical consistency (or their absence), but there are also historical ties (such as the Puritan heritage of the United States) and sociological relations (e.g., the way that members of a social group typically have similar tastes in music, movies and clothes, distinguishing them from other groups). Sociohistorical connections derive from contingent and causal relationships. Sociological connections may also utilize analogy: for instance, freedom from manual labor might be displayed analogically by refined (smooth and relaxed) bodily movements and gestures, abstract language, and so forth—issues extensively examined in Pierre Bourdieu's analyses of habitus, taste, and social distinction. Actors may take these different tendencies into account when they decide how a character should move, stand, and talk. But some experiences may be shared across society, such as driving or riding in a car. Thus cultural systems are structured totalities, but nonetheless flexible, porous, and dynamic, and image schemas provide many of the structuring principles.

In many totalities a part has disproportionate importance in the functioning of the whole, that is, one part is dominant (although circumstances may bring another part forward). Examples include the motor of a car, the mind in the body, the judge in a trial.[2] Within the cultural domain, particular images and metaphors may become dominant. For instance, as Bruce McConachie has shown, the image of containment was key in 1950s American culture.[3] This is a form of cultural hegemony, albeit a diffuse one. Particular metaphors' dominance may be evident in various ways, such as their presence within more complex metaphors, or their placement within crucial cultural products. The dominance of some set of image schemas naturally affects theatre and drama; however, dominance isn't absolute, alternatives may always be invoked.

A set of metaphors may become dominant for several reasons, but one is because cognition emerges from embodiment: major social structures and practices may involve sensorimotor and social experiences that generate key image schemas. The best-known theory of a dominant social structure is the marxist one of an economic base that conditions a political and ideological superstructure. The superstructures are relatively autonomous from the economic base. As I observed earlier, communication is relatively autonomous because on the one hand it produces meaning, and on the other it depends on the materiality and uses of the modes of communication. But these two sources don't have equal weight: the social use and development of the various means of communication—the communication framework—provides the conditions under which meaning is produced and understood. The communication framework plays the central role in organizing the cultural domain and establishing certain metaphors' dominance. It has this role not only because it produces and disseminates meaning, but also because the embodied practices involved in communicating (speaking, writing, painting, and so forth) generate many of a culture's basic image schemas and metaphors. Prominent metaphors arising from other social structures (such as politics, economics, or gender) do so within that overarching cultural context, or if you prefer, on top of the conceptual foundation produced by communication. Consequently, cultural change occurs in a stratified manner: upper levels can change without fundamentally altering lower ones (though perhaps introducing some adjustments), but when lower levels transform, upper ones are forced into major upheavals. Due to the communication framework's relative autonomy, radical economic change (for example) may affect a culture's key image schemas less than a revolution in communication. We will see this in the next chapter, as one of the forces behind metatheatricality.

Culture, then, is a partial totality, open to external forces and possessing a highly complex and dynamic internal structure. It is structured not only by logical relations, but even more by analogical relations, many of which have their basis in sensorimotor experience, and their underlying organization and heirarchization from various socially based activities—communication high among them. The network of logical and analogical relationships traversing a cultural formation is integral to performance strategies.[4]

5

Among the muddier topics in theatre and drama studies are the concepts of genre and style. Their conceptual boundaries are notoriously vague. However, even though genre and style are unavoidable concepts, there are also other ways to sort through the similarities and differences among plays and performances. The approach I will take here joins analysis of communication structures with the insights of cognitive science in order to distinguish types of theatre and drama in terms of discursive and performance strategies.

I put the terms "discursive" and "performance" together for several reasons. The understanding of discourse invoked here is a broad one, encompassing (among other things) the logical, analogical and emotive relations established among concepts and representations, and admitting all forms of representation (not just language). A discursive strategy is similar to an episteme, which in Foucault's analysis is embodied not only in theories and speculations, but also in processes, techniques, and effects, such as a painter's use of space, color, proportions, contours, and even gestures (*Archaeology* 193–94).

Performance strategies similarly concern the entire arena of materials and techniques that playwrights, actors, directors, designers, managers and other theatre personnel use or assume when constructing plays. They include performance space, dramatic action, characterization, acting, scenery, sound, stage/audience dynamics, expected audience behavioral norms, performance time, pre- and post-performance discourse, and so forth. Although the elements can't all be controlled by the people involved, within a single production and often across many productions throughout a culture, the elements tend to cohere into a more-or-less integrated system governed by a set of image schemas and metaphors.

Unlike Foucault's epistemes, discursive and performance strategies have clear ties to social structures and forces. They necessarily bear the marks of the dynamics from which they emerge and upon which conditions they operate. "Strategy" here means an approach, practice, or method adopted within particular conditions, resources and assumptions that limit options: it is *not* a choice made with an utterly free hand. There are various alternatives in any context, but always under constraints. Discourse and performance strategies may differ because the production of (say) novels, philosophy, and plays each involves specific conditions and relations that alter the available strategies. Nevertheless, they face many similar social conditions and imperatives. Discursive and performance strategies consequently tend to share many concepts, methods, and historical trajectories.

Agency is a core element of what theatre is "about." Characters, as fictive agents, typically strive to solve problems, satisfy a need, ward off some danger, face a challenge, or in some other way remove impediments or fulfill desires. To do so, they adopt certain strategies, or at least ad hoc tactics. Performers, directors and other theatre artists likewise seek to solve problems, though their problems are usually very different: how best to interpret a script, how to make the transition from page to stage, how to communicate with their prospective audience, how to make optimal use of their financial, material, and organizational resources, and so forth. They too employ various strategies to achieve their ends. Not all of these strategies directly pertain to the performance itself, but the ones that do usually focus on the performance's intelligibility, audience appeal, and artistic success. Toward these ends, performance strategies involve selecting and organizing image schemas. And since some schemas derive from experiences with fundamental social relationships (or the institutions through which such relationships are maintained) or play an exceptional role in reproducing or transforming social relations, a few image schemas may in effect become the premises behind performance strategies.

For an example of how a small set of image schemas structures performance strategies, I will consider the "sentimental" dramaturgy of early eighteenth-century England. At the time, theatre buildings divided their audiences into a pit, a horseshoe of boxes, and galleries rising above them, with chandeliers lighting the entire interior; the acting area included a forestage. Thus the auditorium created a sense of collective observation while demarcating social stratification. The back half of the stage contained wing flats and shutters for perspective scenery. Before England's civil war, double-casting was commonplace; but when the theatres reopened in 1660, productions of new plays largely ended this practice, and actors played one and only one role in each play. Beginning in the early eighteenth century, theatre men like Richard Steele and Colley Cibber increasingly enjoined actors to speak the script, the whole script, and nothing but the script.[5] The acting style itself was organized around gestures and "points," that is, gestural moments and tableaux encapsulating pinnacles of dramatic tension or expression; a considerable amount of critical writing at the time emphasized and elaborated on performers' gestural skills.

Starting in the 1690s, dramatic genres developed in which characters (increasingly from the merchant class) offered a new standard of behavior to the audience. Rather than worry about the exact definitions and boundaries of the genres, my attention is on the dramaturgical strategies and motifs that developed during this period, whatever the precise genre. Playwrights were becoming less interested in characters' wit and extrinsic behavior: their attention was moving toward the characters' judgment, self-awareness, inward struggles, and intrinsic merit. Pathetic incidents and meditative moments provided opportunities for exploring characters' inner qualities. Asides and soliloquies revealed less about plot and more about character; the audience ultimately reacted to and judged (or were encouraged to judge) the characters by the exposure of their inner moral worth rather than by their actions. The combination of heartfelt emotion with judgment is the essence of the "sentimental response," the hallmark of sentimental dramaturgy, which in one form or another was one of the major approaches taken by new plays throughout the eighteenth century and influenced melodrama and later forms.[6]

Agency, then, was increasingly understood not outwardly, in terms of its relation to the social and religious order of things, but inwardly, in terms of cognition and emotion, and especially as the personal development and waywardness that identifies an individual as "unique." The change is reflected in the development of the word "psychology," which according to the *Oxford English Dictionary* appeared in the 1650s, when it referred to doctrines about the soul; in 1680 it still had that meaning, but by 1748 it was defined as theories of the mind.

Audiences interpreted performance and its context in conjunction with various discourses which operated not just within the theatre space, but rather as general attitudes and assumptions—cultural commonplaces, as it were, which were regularly articulated in guides to behavior and in important mainstream periodicals such as *The Tatler* (published 1709–11) and *The Spectator* (1711–12). Those two papers, especially the latter, were hugely popular and remain critically lauded today for their brilliance, their genial urbanity, and their role in creating civil society. They lie at the intersection of the changes in print culture and the changes in theatre, and not just because both were edited and in good part written by Richard Steele, whose play *The Conscious Lovers* (1722) set the standard for drama during the early eighteenth century. From today's perspective it is difficult to grasp why the play was so popular for decades, but most likely it stems from the confluence of three things: its main characters' embodiment of certain ideals; the type of emotions it elicited; and its deep dependence on acting, which had a style lost on us now. All three factors bore connections to the dynamics of the new journalistic print culture. *The Tatler* and *The Spectator* introduced crucial innovations in print culture, paid significant attention to theatre, and formulated concepts and discursive strategies which enabled *The Conscious Lovers* to bring the nascent sentimental dramaturgy to maturity.

The Tatler and *The Spectator* took as one of their core themes the idea that family and friends formed circles of affection, in which the individual could retreat and disclose his or her inward self—a view closely connected to the sentimental response. The club or coffeehouse, which *The Tatler* often invoked as sources of "news," and which *The Spectator* recalled in its imaginary Spectator Club, suggested a milieu of urbane sociality and membership—an intimate, benevolent community. Among family and friends, critical or satiric laughter could not be allowed, for it would create division and ill-feeling: it was one's duty to bring ease and pleasure to the rest of one's community.[7] Moreover, at least in principle, everyone could join its community. In the papers' ideology, true distinction lay in behavior, thoughts, and sentiments, not in social class (*Tatler* no. 69).

The significance of behavior was reflected in the behavior manuals of the time. From today's perspective, behavior manuals were remarkably specific and formalized: along with offering advice on how to respond to, say, haughtiness, they instructed their readers in the correct postures and gestures for taking one's leave, expressing anger, feeling perplexed, and so on. Strikingly, these guides frequently described gesture as purer and loftier than the spoken word. Such views persistently appear in discussions of acting as well. For example, Steele—no fan of opera—praised the operatic castrato Nicolini for his gestural skills, and the actor Barton Booth evidently had similar talents. The underlying concept was that, whether on stage or in everyday life, gestures and facial expressions were necessary and immediate representations of a person's feelings, thoughts, and even intrinsic merit.[8]

6

The hallmarks of the early eighteenth-century theatre—the role of sentiment in dramaturgy and audience response, the turn toward characters' inwardness and psychology, the intimate community, the emphasis on gesture—cohere as an overall performance strategy built on various image schemas that arose from the print culture of the time. Many of those image schemas are essentially epistemological. Understanding this requires a departure from the usual paths of cognitive science, which emphasize the image schemas we glean from *direct* experience (practical knowledge). But clearly we do not obtain most of our knowledge *about* the world (discursive knowledge) that way. Few people travel around the world to learn if it is spherical, dig up bones to convince themselves of the theory of evolution, or locate records to see if Shakespeare ever existed. Instead, we listen to other people, read books, watch television, surf the Web; and conversely, to provide knowledge to others, we rely mainly on speaking, writing, and drawing. We provide and depend upon indirect, reported experience and knowledge. And just as image schemas emerge from direct experience, they are also generated through indirect experience, albeit in a different manner. The image schemas arise not primarily from discursive knowledge itself, but rather from the embodied practice most closely connected to the process of obtaining discursive knowledge: communication. Because such image schemas concern the process of obtaining discursive knowledge, they have a reflexive role in the further development of knowledge. In short, they theorize epistemology.

As print culture developed, texts took an increasingly dominant function in the everyday operations of life, administration, law, leisure, and so on. A key indicator of the shift can be found in jurisprudence: the validity of legal claims increasingly depended on documentary evidence. To a degree far surpassing late medieval purposes, truth was now to be found in texts. This "origin" of truth was considerably broader than the truth accorded to the Bible. During the Middle Ages and into the Renaissance, the truth of the Bible, Augustine and Aristotle derived from the authority of their authorship, which was bestowed on them by God or the accolades of generations. Of course, that view of books never vanished, even if it was not always attached to the Bible. However, by the early eighteenth century the truth borne by writings resided in their very textuality. People relied on documents to ascertain agreements, establish precedents, determine sources, provide evidence, offer best examples, and serve similar veridical activities. The emulation of classical writers' styles is another instance of the new weight given to textuality.

Language in general tended to be epitomized by its written form. This contributed to a new emphasis on vision as the source of knowledge. Not only did vision become more crucial to thought, but its qualities altered. Within oral and manuscript cultures, visual imagery necessarily took a mnemonic role, invested in physical symbols, emblems, allegorical personifications, and the pictorial works of the Art of Memory. Acts of imagination secured memory. But in print cultures, visualization's mnemonic role became unnecessary. Visual images had fewer accretions of allegorical or figural material; the result was a much more "literal" or naturalistic style of viewing. "Literal viewing" was conventional, since it was predicated on specific social practices and relationships. But the Enlightenment convention dispensed with communal and even individual mnemonic symbolism and introduced individual judgment as the crux of interpretation. Imagery was replaced by pictures. In other words, the advent of literal viewing led to the depiction of appearance rather than (figural) meaning. In theatrical staging, verisimilitude became a goal.

The use of oral/aural versus visual materials, and the reorientation of the source of knowledge from the one to the other, primarily concern the production process (as a moment in the communication cycle); however, the materials used for communication have quite different capacities and limitations and consequently require different methods of preservation. During this period there were also major changes in how the modes of communication were utilized. The roles and relationships of speech and writing within the communication framework of early eighteenth-century England consequently generated concepts and discursive strategies at odds with those of medieval times.

The semiological unit. In the Middle Ages, a semiotic chain referred writing to speech, spoken words to things or mental images, and the latter to ideas—a chain that was established at one end by the use of writing as an mnemonic aid for speaking, and at the other end by orality's construction of physical symbols. The chain could be reversed, culminating in the Bible as the text that could guarantee truth. The semiotic chain finally broke down during the Enlightenment. It was replaced by the semiological unit, consisting solely of a material form conventionally associated with a concept: in today's terms, a signifier and a signified. For instance, Locke (the leading English philosopher of the time, and founder of empiricism) maintained that articulate sounds were "*Signs of internal Conceptions*" and stood "as marks for the *Ideas* within his own Mind"; the mark and the concept are tied only "*by a perfectly arbitrary Imposition*" (Locke §3.1.2, §3.2.8; his italics), that is, by social convention.[9] This concept of the sign, made even more cognitivist by Saussure, continues to thrive.

The simplified unit of word and idea resulted from the restructuring of the communication framework. The subordination of orality meant that texts only secondarily prompted speech, and physical symbols linking objects to ideas were no longer needed mnemonically. Thus both ends of the semiotic chain broke off. The increasing availability of texts meant that there was also little need for an Art of Memory. Furthermore, as reading and writing spread, they increasingly isolated the reader and writer with the text, while the printed text lacked material connections to both its author and its referents. Thus printed writing appeared more autonomous and self-enclosed than speech. However, where the Bible had been a compendium of the universe, the printed text's author was human, not divine, and reference between word and idea was established through convention, not by natural or supernatural order. The chain of signifiers became a closed circuit consisting only of the text and the mind that understood or composed it. The outcome was a binary sign structure, a signifier and a signified, and the chief mental operation was to accommodate them to each other. The written word was no longer a signature of things, no longer inscribed in the nature of Nature; it transformed into a neutral, nearly invisible conduit of thought as it was conducted inside a single mind or expressed to others.[10] The token of writing's ascendancy was that it displaced itself.

Directivity. Contracts, manuals, and similar texts had long directed action or guided thought. By the late seventeenth century, the utilization of texts as directives extended beyond a text's meaningful content, to its very source of availability. It was not just a matter of acting or thinking according to a text's guidance: writing itself was the manner in which ideas came to the mind. Locke constantly described the formation of ideas in terms of writing and printing. In arguing against the notion of innate ideas, he asserted that simply informing a person of the presence of "native Inscriptions" (§1.2.7) did not "print them clearer in the Mind, than Nature did" (§1.2.21). On the contrary, all ideas come from sensation and reflection, and a person "has *not any* Idea *in his Mind, but what one of these two has imprinted*" (Locke §2.1.6).[11] That sentence is as good an expression of the perception criterion of reality—empiricism's foundation stone—as one is likely to find from that time. Perception itself is conceptualized as a kind of printing process, in which the external world acts as a scribe upon the body, and the body as a scribe or printer upon the mind. In Joseph Addison's words, "Aristotle tells us, that the World is a Copy or Transcript of those Ideas which are in the Mind of the first Being; and that those Ideas which are in the Mind of Man, are a Transcript of the World: To this we may add, that Words are the Transcript of those Ideas which are in the Mind of Man, and that Writing or Printing are the Transcript of Words" (*Spectator* no. 166). Thus writing became a model for epistemology, due to writing's visual nature and its manner of linking the material and the mental. The model derived from practical experience and awareness that the source of knowledge was writing. It was, in fact, an image schema.

Textual space. Both the "marginalization" of orality and the directive utilization of writing led to a semiology in which signs refer only to ideas in the mind that issues or receives them. That was one of the basic tenets underlying Enlightenment philosophy; the second consisted in a fundamental spatialization of reality, such that all things could be conceived in terms of distance and position, measurement and order (Cohen 43–77; Foucault, *Order of Things* 52–58; 78–124). The line and linearity (continuous movement along a path) became print culture's paradigmatic image schema for rational thought. Such linearization too had its foundations in the framework of communication.

It is important to understand how print culture generates linear thinking—and how it doesn't. According to Walter J. Ong, "Print situates words in space more relentlessly than writing ever did. Writing moves words from the sound world to a world of visual space, but print locks words into position in this space. Control of position is everything in print" (*Orality and*

Literacy 121). Ong offers several explanations why printing has a deeper spatial orientation than handwriting. First, the typographic composition process involves locking letters and words into positions in space. Second, printed texts appear far more even and regular than manuscripts do, thus offering a notion of repeatable exactitude. Third, textual reference systems—indexes, catalogs, and the like—disengage words or texts from their context and situate them within a continuous, sequentialized space (page number, shelf location, call number, and so forth) (*Orality and Literacy* 121–29).

Ong's first explanation is decidedly technologistic: somehow printing technology itself communicates meaning to people who never see it. His second idea is better, since it involves a process of reading and interpretation, but it ignores the social determinants of the reading process. Both theories are contradicted by the examples of East Asia: well before Gutenberg, printing was developed in China and movable type in Korea, but neither country is associated with a development of linear culture similar to that of post-Gutenberg Europe. His third reason, however, is more on target. Printing proliferated books, which were easily retained. That created problems, for once stored, books must be retrieved and language within them located. For two millennia the issue didn't exist and there was little interest in how to organize and store documents. But difficulties began to be felt within late manuscript culture, when scriptoria and copyists developed ways to produce books at a sometimes startling scale, and feelers toward the solutions began to appear as well—print technology *as such* was not the key issue (Febvre and Martin 18–22, 26–28; Eisenstein 11–15). The practical problem was solved by using writing's symbol system as a directive to analyze and organize the literature: indexes use the alphabet and page numbers to locate terms within a text, emphasizing the spatial character of a written work, and library catalogs place that text within a building's physical architecture of categories (say, astronomy on the third floor, literature on the first). Kernan attributes a similar importance to the library as a spatial "paradigm of knowledge" (246–58). Printing preserved ideas, and to make them quickly accessible, ordered lists of isolated terms direct the reader to a position within a textual space made of words or books. The directivity discussed earlier established printing as the source of knowable things; here, instead, the index and catalog direct actions and analyses that assume an ontology in which writing is a construction of visible marks locked into positions in space.

The very existence of ideas was conceptualized by analogy with writing. When Locke explained how all ideas are constituted out of simple ones, he suggested that this atomistic notion could be readily grasped

> if we consider how many Words may be made out of the various composition of 24 Letters; or if going one step farther, we will but reflect on the variety of

combinations may be made, with barely one of the above-mentioned *Ideas*, *viz*. Number, whose stock is inexhaustible, and truly infinite: And what a large and immense field, doth Extension alone afford the Mathematician? (Locke §2.7.10)

Simple ideas are the letters and numerals that combine into the "words," the complex ideas, and ultimately the propositions that comprise thought. Thus for Locke, writing was a model both for how we come to have ideas and for the way ideas themselves exist: the ontology of ideas was conceptualized through another image schema formed from the embodied activity of using texts.

Locke's atomistic analysis suggests the possibility of a vast table (a "field") charting all the possible combinations of simple ideas. It also suggests that this table could be completely and consistently ordered, for both letters and numbers have places within a fixed, unequivocal sequence that can be used to establish progression and hierarchy. Before printing, the alphabet was seldom used as a method for organizing words and ideas, and even in the early seventeenth century people had to be instructed in its use. But thereafter, alphabetization was more and more common, as was systematic pagination.[12] The dictionary (increasingly popular in the early eighteenth century) was organized on the basis of letters as atomic units, placed in a sequence of unit-combinations, *A* preceding *B*, *Aa* preceding *Ab* but both classified under *A*, and so on. The alphabet could thus present the possibility of, and offer a model for, securing knowledge within a comprehensive system providing sequence and subdivision, order and taxonomy. Encyclopedias tried to create this universal table, some using a taxonomy that attempted to mirror natural or logical divisions, others simply applying the alphabet to organize their material.[13] Locke's analogy between ideas and numbers further indicates not only that ideas could be ordered and measured, but that their relationships could be calculated. In various ways, then, letters and numerals provided image schemas for spatialized thought, and provided means whereby that space could by divided, ordered, and measured.

Consequently, linear thinking emerged not directly from physical or technological characteristics of the printed page, much less the printing press, but rather from the social primacy given to print and from the methods and experiences of accessing and using printed materials. Textual space, then, is constituted through image schemas born from the activity of obtaining knowledge from writing. It is only secondarily a physical space, a visual structure of words, pages, and volumes: more importantly, it is a conceptual space that locates, measures, and orders ideas in the mind.

The space of social performance. According to print culture, the mind operates within a textual space constituted by writing and universal among people. But if textuality is the universal, spoken words are the individual and particular.[14] Parallel to textual space is the space of social performance, in which speech and gesture mark the character of each person. Oral performance before others both identifies the qualities of the speaker (and his or her audience), and allocates to the speaker greater or lesser authority to address that audience. A major part of oral performance was skill in the art of conversation: indeed, Steele defined a gentleman as a "Man of Conversation" (*Tatler* no. 21). Social performance was constantly being molded by books on the Art of Speaking, conduct books, and periodicals (including, of course, *The Spectator*). Speech and writing were to guide each other. Steele warned that conversation should not seem learned, whereas writing should be somewhat conversational. He also compared men's and women's skill in talk: "You see in no Place of Conversation the Perfection of Speech so much as in an accomplish'd Woman. Whether it be, that there is a Partiality irresistible when we judge of that Sex, or whatever it is, you may observe a wonderful Freedom in their Utterance, and an easy Flow of Words, without being distracted (as we often are who read much) in the Choice of Dictions and Phrases" (*Tatler* no. 62).

As Steele's distinction emphasizes, the space of social performance was internally divided by gender. Women were marked (whether by nature, training, or men's perceptions) as more skilled in spoken communication, while men read too much to be orally fluent. Textuality meant abstraction and impersonality, speech the opposite. The performance of self was construed as primarily an oral activity, and women as more strongly attuned to interpersonal speech. The gender division in the space of social performance was connected to print culture itself: "During the eighteenth century, as upper- and middle-class Englishwomen increasingly began to participate in the public realm of print culture, the representational practices of that culture were steadily enclosing them within the private sphere of the home" (Kathryn Shevelow, qtd. in Freeman 67).

Gender division was related to the division between the private sphere and the public sphere, which emerged during the late seventeenth and early eighteenth century. Elizabeth L. Eisenstein finds that printing encouraged a sharper division between public and private (133, 424–31). The demarcation between the two realms was promoted by the fact that the printed text was produced for a mass public, yet was consumed privately through silent reading. The book-driven differentiation between public and private spheres was intensified by the rise of periodical publication, as we will see.

Silent reading is linked to a further tenet of empiricism: that individual experience belongs at the center of methodology. Silent reading founds a polarity between individual and society: publication and silent reading helped constitute the public/private split, replacing an individual's direct, personal ties to others with an abstract imagined community. The polarity could be inverted, making the social more important; such appears to have occurred in mid to late eighteenth-century language theory, when the national and sociohistorical character of language came to the forefront yet individual expression became language's principle function. Indeed, the very individualism fomented by texts encouraged a new valuation of speech as representing underlying feelings.

Individual and society were nonetheless connected, specifically by language. For Locke, "Speech [is] the great Bond that holds Society together, and the common Conduit, whereby the improvements of Knowledge are conveyed from one Man, and one Generation to another" (§3.9.1). Thus language has to be gauged against a social standard. Words must be meaningful to others or they will fail to communicate. While empiricists claimed only individual experience could establish ideas, only social custom could secure words as a medium of exchange.

Underlying the methodological individualism of eighteenth-century thought, at the heart of the individual/society dichotomy, is a radical, unalloyed anthropocentrism; an anthropocentrism that, being internally divided by gender, is also an androcentrism. Within it, the natural world exists merely as a thing to be observed, dissected, exploited. It does not secure meaning; far less can it embody meaning and form a continuous semiotic universe like that of the Middle Ages. Thought and knowledge (including ideas of God) are absolutely contained within the perimeters of human capability. In the early eighteenth century words represented ideas within human minds, and by the late eighteenth century they expressed human emotions, desires, and psychology, but they did not refer to a mind-independent reality. Both early and late eighteenth-century thought presupposed the centrality of human experience.

The image schemas I have considered so far were produced by print culture generally. However, as I've emphasized, communication practices affect thought not simply through the effects of a technology, but also through how the technology is used and developed, and the roles that it plays within a society. Changes may arise when the social utilization of a communication technology alters, even though the technology itself does not.

That is exactly what we find in the early eighteenth century. The production, distribution, and consumption of printed matter was undergoing a crucial shift: during its first 250 years the printing press was used principally for books and broadsheets, but at the turn of the eighteenth century, the demands of the mercantile class and improvements in transportation made regular periodical publication economically and logistically sustainable for the first time. Journalistic print culture was born, eventually bringing major social transformations in its wake—the result not of a technological revolution (the printing press remained exactly the same), but a revolution in the social use of a well-established technology. Book culture continued unscathed and even benefitted from the rise of the periodical press, but new image schemas and new inflections of old schemas entered cultural dynamics. The new features include several that I described as part of early eighteenth-century "sentimental" performance strategies: an emphasis on pathos and inward struggles; the revelatory gesture; the reflexive perception underlying the sentimental response; the intimate and benevolent community.

The key pragmatic distinction between books and periodicals lies in their methods of distribution. Periodicals are distributed rapidly across a geographical region (often a city), and are also distributed across time (such as daily or weekly). Books were usually bought and read one person at a time without any coordination; the periodical press, however, was the first mass medium, and it faced certain challenges in making that mass into a public. For their economic survival, publishers had to find ways to maintain the periodical's identity and create a unified readership: unified across space, joining readers under one common umbrella; and unified across time, preventing each evanescent issue from acting as a wholly discrete publication. The most common strategy was to adopt a subject of recurring interest (for instance, business reports, advances in the natural sciences, scandals, and high society), and within that scope include a potpourri or "mosaic" of items, as if to present a snapshot or cross-section of the ever-changing present—so to speak, a slice of life.

The needs of the periodical and the needs of its readers produced several social and cultural changes which sometimes conflicted but generally cohered. Central among them was the "imagined community," which according to Benedict Anderson's analysis emerged from the "extraordinary mass ceremony" of newspaper consumption:

> It is performed in silent privacy, in the lair of the skull. Yet each communicant is well aware that the ceremony he performs is being replicated simultaneously by thousands (or millions) of others of whose existence he is confident, yet of whose identity he has not the slightest notion. Furthermore, this ceremony is incessantly repeated at daily or half-daily intervals throughout the calendar. What more vivid figure for the secular, historically clocked, imagined community can be envisioned? (Anderson 35)

Thus Addison would "recommend these my Speculations to all well regulated Families, that set apart an Hour in every Morning for Tea and Bread and Butter; and would earnestly advise them for their Good to order this Paper to be punctually served up, and to be looked upon as a Part of the Tea Equipage" (*Spectator* no. 10). *The Tatler*, *The Spectator* and other periodicals were of course frequently read aloud in coffeehouses rather than in silent privacy, but this was not a real barrier to the formation of imagined communities: as Jürgen Habermas observes, the coffeehouses were already so numerous that contact among them could only be maintained through a journal (42); conversely, papers like *The Tatler* and *The Spectator*, with their eyes trained squarely on the space of social performance, made it possible for the coffeehouses' patrons to feel part of an imagined community by reading aloud. Like many routines, especially those concerned with communication, regular periodical reading became an image schema, soon elaborated in cognitive frameworks which provided the conceptual foundations for social and theatrical practices.

The formation of privatized readers, already under way in simple book culture, accelerated with the periodical press, which also provided the readers with a new means of communicating with each other. The result was a special type of imagined community: the public sphere. Habermas holds that the public sphere arose "as an expansion and at the same time completion of the intimate sphere of the conjugal family" (50). His claim is somewhat incomplete, since by his own account the coffeehouses played a crucial role. Nevertheless both the home (especially the salon) and the coffeehouse were spaces of social performance, where speech and behavior were encouraged and regulated by the articles that *The Tatler* and *The Spectator* offered to the "public."

The Tatler and *The Spectator* established precedent-setting strategies for securing readership which profoundly shaped journalistic print culture. The two journals simultaneously used the coffeehouse for settings and subjects, and emphasized the ideology that family and friends formed circles of affection allowing personal self-disclosure. But the journals also strove to generate a *dynamic* sense of community between the readers and the journal by giving a special salience to letters to the editor. About half of *The Spectator*'s issues included correspondence, and some issues consisted of nothing but readers' letters. These letters of personal opinion or experience could expand on topics recently considered, or send the editors into a new direction; they could reply to the essays, or to other letters; the editors could incorporate the letters in various ways, and even directly respond to them. Letters came from all sorts of people, and many were personally revealing or even confessional in nature. The letters played a key role in the development of the public sphere; but in addition their private character was deeply connected to the development of personal interiority, standing more or less mid-way between the two spheres. The letters made the public presentation of the private person fundamental to social interchange, while giving the public a new concept of the private. They were, in a way, fragments of autobiography, and notably, the letters retained significant proximity to speech. Michael Ketcham observes that the sheer variety of viewpoints in these letters itself modeled a tolerant community (Ketcham 11, 125–32; Mackie; Polly; Bannet; Habermas 42, 48–50).

Thus through both discursive and pragmatic means, *The Tatler* and *The Spectator* fostered a sense that within their pages an intimate community came to life, and offered their readers the opportunity to enter their social and emotional circles.[15] The periodicals were preoccupied with observing people's behaviors and manners, and through letters to the editor, readers and writers observed each other, both of them subject to social judgments and understandings. The reader had an emotional response, a reflection prompted by a perception. However, perception (as reading) was the key source of knowledge; perception (as writing) printed upon the mind; one's own mind had then to be read, generating an emotion response that was written upon the body and in gesture; and so the sequence continues. Thus we arrive at the cycle of sentimental response—the emotions and behavior of one person produce sympathetic feelings in the observer, and the reflex of sentiment reflect the observer's inward self.[16]

Circulating throughout these varied discursive strategies, then, are a few basic tenets generated by print culture: knowledge comes from "reading the signs," an image schema generalized to mean perception (especially vision); words are atomistic units that in the aggregate represent the mind, but must form linearly ordered and internally consistent sequences to do so; the logic (grammar) of such ordering is public and universal, even if minds are fundamentally private; and by reading one another through newspapers and other periodicals, these private minds founded an imaginary community. Connecting all of these ideas is an underlying methodological individualism, paradigmatically based on the image of a solitary, silent reader.

7

The communication framework generates image schemas which establish epistemological and ontological assumptions. These in turn are reembodied in performance, both in the theatrical practices and in the dramatic text. Thus, underlying early eighteenth-century performance strategies and the ideologies that shaped them is a handful of image schemas and metaphors. Their generative powers can be found at work in Steele's *The Conscious Lovers*.

The play's main plot (adapted from Terence's *Andria*) concerns Bevil Jr., who is in love with Indiana, a destitute virgin of unknown parentage who he rescued from a dire fate in France and brought to London, along with her caretaker aunt Isabella. But Bevil Jr. cannot marry Indiana: his aristocratic father Sir John Bevil has arranged for him to marry Lucinda, daughter to the wealthy merchant Sealand. Sealand, however, has caught wind of Bevil Jr.'s attention to Indiana and now opposes the match. Bevil Jr., attempting to be honorable toward Indiana yet obedient to his father, is effectively immobilized until the final scene, when Indiana is discovered to be Sealand's long-lost daughter. A secondary plot presents the efforts of Bevil Jr.'s friend Myrtle, who loves Lucinda, to stave off his rivals. One rival is Cimberton (a relative of Lucinda's stepmother), who arrives to look over Lucinda. Myrtle comes to believe that Bevil is preparing to marry Lucinda as his father desires. In response, Myrtle challenges his friend to a duel. Bevil Jr. resolves their conflict by proving that neither he nor Lucinda wish the marriage to go through. Finally, a tertiary story shows the playful amour of Tom and Phillis, two servants. The turning points of the play all center around sentiments, perceived dangers to sentiments, and self-examinations on sentiments.

John Loftis notes that two things most the play set apart from its antecedents, announcing the arrival of "sentimental comedy," and also raising the most controversy. The use of sentiment was not one of them, for Colley Cibber and others had already injected sentiment into comedy. What distinguished *The Conscious Lovers* was, first, its introduction of pathetic incident into comedy; and second, its use of admirable, exemplary characters (Loftis, *Steele* 196).

Consistent with *The Spectator*'s ideology (born to sustain the periodical), Steele's use of pathetic incident met several goals: to conjoin the group cohesion of comedy not with expulsion of aberrant characters but with the intimacy of the benevolent circle; to pair the social judgment of comedy with sentiment; and to reveal depth of character, the inside within the exterior, to the public view. Earlier sentimental comedies depended on breaches of morality and last-act repentances, or occasionally having a character be deceived through four acts and finally learn the truth in the fifth. By replacing such reversals with pathetic incident, nearly all of Steele's characters could be honorable and praiseworthy.

Similar goals lie behind the meditative moments of the play, especially the scene in which Bevil Jr. first appears, reading an essay by Addison inviting a "long view" of eternity and the human lifespan within it. It is dramatically appropriate because Bevil Jr. must prepare himself for a difficult day. But theatrically, the scene presents the audience with a frozen gesture from which it can read young Bevil's character.

Character, in fact, is what *The Conscious Lovers* is principally about. The use of sentiments, introspective asides, and pathos allow ample opportunity to develop the character's moral virtues, inward development, and intrinsic merits. For example, Isabella's asides introduce psychological motivation for her enmity toward men. But the idea that a stage persona could and should be exemplary (Bevil Jr. describes himself as "one who takes more delight in

Reflections, than in Sensations": II.iii.130–31), and that such a construct would have a salutary effect on the audience, derives from the anthropocentrism pervading print culture, more directly from Steele's work on the journals, and in particular from his exploration of the theory of sentiment in the context of forming an intimate community.

Despite the characters' exemplary quality, several engage in disguises and dissimulation. Bevil Jr. hides his feelings from both his father and Indiana, and acts as though he will actually marry Lucinda, which he uneasily describes as "honest Dissimulation" (I.ii.15). His father's servant Humphrey helps Bevil Jr. keep up the deception, while fishing for information from him about Indiana to bring to Sir John. Sealand pretends to deliver a bill to Indiana in order to meet her, and upon his visit, Isabella recognizes Sealand but hides the fact that she is his sister. Most theatrically, Myrtle gets into costume to interfere with Cimberton's designs upon Lucinda. But his imposture has curiously little actual influence over the subsequent action, as it stops nothing, causes no confusions, and reveals no information. In Shakespeare's plays, masquerade is often a strategy for revealing a truth. In Restoration intrigue comedies, disguises serve to manipulate and control other characters. But the goal of disguise in *The Conscious Lovers* is entirely different. They aim neither to manipulate, nor to hide, nor to reveal. Their purpose is to stall action, and more, to protect—protecting not so much the dissimulator, as those nearest to him. Dissimulation maintains the benevolent community.

The introduction of pathetic incident and exemplary characters shapes the comedy in *The Conscious Lovers*. Three types of comedy occur. First there is the "Joy too exquisite for Laughter" that Steele writes of in the preface to the printed text, pertaining especially to Bevil Jr.'s transformation of a challenge to a duel with his friend into a renewal of their affection, and Indiana's reunion her father: in these scenes laughter would interfere with the audience's sentimental response. In contrast, some characters are satirized largely for their "affectation founded on an assumption of superiority" (Loftis, *Comedy* 84), helping to exclude those who would disrupt the intimate community by importing status. Finally, there is the lover's comedy between two low characters; they may not be exemplary, but neither are they destructive, so there is no harm in having genuine laughter, particularly as we laugh with (not at) the young lovers. In all three cases, intimate community—the space of social performance—is paramount.

Pathetic incident, exemplary character, protective deception, and warmhearted laughter—key performance strategies in *The Conscious Lovers*—all aim toward creating and maintaining an intimate, benevolent circle in which self-revelation and gentle correction may safely occur. This circle is the preeminent space of social performance. The image schema was developed as part of periodicals' strategy to maintain their economic viability, but had much larger social and cultural effects.

8

Alongside the dramatic text, the most crucial parts of a performance strategy are acting and stage settings.[17] Perspective scenery was used throughout most of the "Age of Empiricism." Illusionism in art and scientific accuracy in drawing have previously been attributed to print culture, particularly the dissemination of engravings. Eisenstein, for example, argues that the availability of exactly repeated prints made it possible for researchers to compare illustrations with their models in nature and correct the renderings (Eisenstein 252–69; see also Peters, *Congreve* 133–34). Perhaps so, but it does not explain how perspectival verisimilitude became a goal or why certain techniques and not others were used to achieve it. The artistic strategy is better explained by cognitive aspects of print culture. "Literal viewing" encouraged the depiction of appearance rather than (allegorical) meaning. If the semiological unit posited a sign stripped of its collective symbolic associations, then those would also have to be excised from representation to facilitate individual interpretation. The imagistic and conceptual underpinnings of textual space would require that an artistic representation impress its viewers' minds with the same idea as its model, and therefore look as identical to that model as possible. Finally, the geometry of perspective and the superimposition of divisible grids used to paint landscapes implemented the protocols of linearity and measurement, in contrast to the "eyeball" estimates of perspective sometimes employed previously.

A crucial element of eighteenth-century theatre is gesture. Throughout his plays Steele insists on the language of gestures, expressions, what can be read from them, how they can be imitated or mocked. In *The Funeral*, for example, an undertaker carefully arranges his paid mourners' expressions, a widow names and enacts various ways of looking at acquaintances (there is a similar moment in *The Tender Husband*), and the gestures of the two young women are constantly described. During *The Conscious Lovers* II.ii, a sonata is played while Indiana and Bevil Jr. exchange modest but passionate glances. The entire moment rests on the effectiveness of the protagonists' gestural language.

The concepts and meanings behind the theatrical emphasis upon gesture can be gleaned from Steele's frequently commentaries about gesture. He constantly sounded the same note, whether referring to gesture on stage or in everyday life. "Our Thoughts are ever in our Features" (*Tatler* no. 182); "every Thought is attended with Consciousness and Representativeness.... This Act of the Mind discovers it self in Gesture" (*Spectator* no. 38). When discussing oratory and acting, Steele consistently focused on gesture and the visual representation of the passions, writing that "he who hears *Demosthenes* only, loses much the better Part of the Oration" (*Tatler* no. 66). Skillful expression thus includes skillful bodily action. In several papers Steele emphasized the important of dance as training the body to move and gesture gracefully (see for example *Spectator* nos. 66, 334, 370). Steele's ideas were widely shared. Charles Gildon, for one, argued that "the Passions and Habits of the Mind discover themselves in our Looks, Actions and Gestures," and emphasized that "on the Stage, where the Passions are chiefly in View, the best *Speaking*, destitute of *Action* and *Gesture* (the Life of all Speaking) proves but a heavy, dull, and dead Discourse" (41, 51). The best paid (and presumably most popular) performer of 1709 was an opera singer, the Italian castrato Nicolini, who was praised for his gestural skills (Roach, "Cavalieri Nicolini" 189–205). Likewise, Barton Booth, who created the role of Bevil Jr., was lauded for his grace and grandeur (Victor 32–33; *Spectator* no. 518).[18]

For Steele, gestures were signs of emotion and character. This correlation already had a venerable history, reaching all the way to classical oratorical writing. The idea's importance is demonstrated by *The Spectator*'s practice. The papers' social observations scrutinized the behaviors, particularly the gestures, of the people observed, concentrating not on the gestures' outward forms but rather on their ability to disclose the mind, so that one may "calculate" the intrinsic merit of a person in the space of social performance.[19] As Michael Ketcham expresses it, *The Spectator* "resolves itself into a succession of scenes, a shadow play of gestures in the theater of the world, where words may be spoken but where the drama is in the accompanying action" (30). *The Conscious Lovers* likewise articulates its action around a series of tableaux or "points": Bevil Jr. reading, he and Indiana slyly gazing at each other as a sonata plays, Bevil Jr. recollecting himself during his argument with Myrtle, Indiana safe in her father's arms.

Gesture was a medium of social exchange—"the Commerce of Discourse," Steele called it (*Spectator* no. 4). The journals articulated social exchange in two ways: through letters of personal opinion and experience printed as part of a dialogue; and through the theory of gesture which reveals the inward mind, to which the observer responds in turn. Both techniques made the public presentation of the private person fundamental to social exchange: they cross the divide between private and public. As a result the journal can be seen as a "group confessional form." Within the journal's pages, reader and writer observe each other and are observed. The spectator's sympathetic reading of social performance derived from the process of judgment. In this world of observation and exchange, both observer and observed were subject to social judgments and understandings, assessments and measures. As Addison put it, the "Fraternity of Spectators" consists of "every one that considers the World as a Theatre, and desires to form a right Judgment of those who are the Actors on it" (*Spectator* no. 10). On its surface, Addison's metaphor simply recalls the classical commonplace of the world as a stage. However, here spectatorship does not strive to recognize moral types. Rather, the spectator has to penetrate the outer surface and read the inner sentiments of the person viewed; trace the connections linking person to circumstances; or consider the spectator's own participation and understanding. By interpreting gestures, the spectator creates a framework of comparisons for measuring gratification, satisfaction, or pleasure (Ketcham 28, 38–42, 52–53). For *The Spectator*, gesture reveals the person's self-image; but we respond to this gesture with an emotion, and that emotion stirs a gesture from us, hence revealing our own self-images. This again is the theory of sentiment; we see it dramatized in *The Conscious Lovers*' tableaux, which rest on the characters' moments of self-reflection and sensitivity.

The source of these views of gesture ran deep. Gesture had connections to seventeenth- and eighteenth-century thought on language itself. It was recognized as a means for teaching language to the deaf and dumb, and commentaries on the effectiveness of gesture frequently praised it in terms of its ability to speak to the deaf or its derivation from the language of the mute. In fact it was thought to be a universal language. For example, John Hughes wrote in *Spectator* no. 541 that "Action is a kind of Universal Tongue" (see also Knowlton 495–508). Gesture could speak universally because it conjoined mind and body in a sign. This was the age when, through a Cartesian conception of the body as a sort of hydraulic machine, the passions were assigned specific expressions that were classified and codified into ideal and universal forms.[20]

The human body was, in fact, the linchpin of the era's performance strategies, yoking together scenic background, dramatic action, and theatrical performance. Medieval performance strategies, in contrast, at most reduplicated the image of the body onto various macrocosmic and microcosmic levels, for the "central" role was played by God and manifested throughout Creation. Human flesh was significant analogically or symbolically, but its material reality was relatively unimportant. For Lockean empiricism, however, the material body was the perimeter where sensation entered (leading to perception and experience) and where reflection returned thought to itself.[21] It is the formative principle of anthropocentrism.

The passions and their respective gestures were codified throughout the eighteenth century. For example, James Burgh's *The Art of Speaking* (which appeared in 1761 and was frequently reprinted thereafter) contained a catalog of what Burgh considered the principal passions and their physical signs. Here is a typical example:

> *Perplexity*, or anxiety, which is always attended with some degree of fear and uneasiness, *draws* all the parts of the *body together*; *gathers* up the *arms* upon

the *breast*, unless one hand covers the *eyes*, or rubs the *forehead*; *draws down* the *eyebrows*; *hangs* the *head* upon the breast, *casts down* the eyes, shuts and *pinches* the *eyelids close*; *shuts* the *mouth*, and *pinches* the *lips* close, or *bites* them. Suddenly the whole *body* is vehemently *agitated*. The person *walks* about *busily*; *stops* abruptly. (19–20)

Burgh advised his readers that "It is to be remembered, that the *action*, in expressing the various humours and passions, for which I have here given rules, is to be suited to the *age, sex, condition* and *circumstances* of the character" (33). In directing his readers to adapt what he has written, Burgh called his catalog "rules": his descriptions were also prescriptions, textual directives for action. His book instantiates the eighteenth century directivity of writing.

Burgh illustrated the passions' manifestation and employment through a sequence of "lessons" consisting of excerpts from plays and poems, which he annotated to indicate the passion that suited each passage. Burgh chose several scenes from Steele's plays, three from *The Conscious Lovers* alone. He rendered part of the argument between Myrtle and Bevil Jr. in this manner:

Complaisance.	Bev. Sir, I *have received* a *letter* from you in a very *unusual style*. But, as I am *conscious* (1) of the *integrity* of my behaviour with respect to you, and intend that *every thing* in *this matter*, shall be your *own seeking*, I shall *understand nothing* but what you are pleased to *confirm face* to *face*. You are therefore to take it for *granted* that I have *forgot* the contents of your *epistle*.
Anger.	Myrt. Your *cool behaviour*, Mr. Bevil, is agreeable to the *unworthy use*, you have made of my *simplicity* and *frankness* to you. And I see, your *moderation* tends to your *own* advantage, not *mine*; to your own *safety*, not to *justice* for the *wrongs* you have done your *friend*.
Offence.	Bev. My *own safety*! Mr. Myrtle?
Reproach.	Myrt. Your *own safety*, Mr. Bevil.

(1)—"*conscious* of the *integrity*," &c. may be expressed with the right hand laid upon the breast. (Burgh 116)

In principle, one could look up each passion in Burgh's catalog and discover the proper way to enact each speech. Through his marginalia Burgh composed a sort of emotional "score" from which any competent orator might reproduce the ideal representation—a rather literal "performance text." His work harmonizes with Steele's frequent assertions that every thought has an immediate expression in gesture (see Roach, *Player's Passion* 76–78; Roach, "Power's Body" 111–13).

The actor's "points" concretize Locke's concept of time: duration was spatialized, linear, homogeneous, and evenly subdivided (§2.14–15). Time was atomistic, consisting of frozen, divided but successive moments, akin to the print-based concept of (textual) space in which all complex units can be broken down into simple, elemental units. Locke's analysis of time suggests a sequence of fleeting still-lifes, held just long enough to impress the mind with their ideas. Thus actors' "points" are points in time, as though the era's oratorical handbooks' grids containing illustrations of various gestures were rearranged to follow an expressive or logical sequence such as Burgh's, one gesture following another, like letters spelling out a word. Gestures themselves became a kind of printing, a visible writing with the body, involving momentary positions locked in space.

Joseph Roach, in fact, calls Burgh's marginalia of gestures a "subtext" ("Power's Body" 111), a suggestive phrase for them, for *The Conscious Lovers* presents characters who were incessantly riddled by their own scruples and self-examinations. Such subtextual thoughts and emotions were expressed gesturally, as when Bevil Jr. and Indiana exchange glances during the sonata. But the notion of subtext must be taken further. Discussions of gesture constantly circled around a basic equation: gesture was a form of writing. Gesture, like writing, was opposed to the voice; it held positions in a spatial frame, like letters on a page; it revealed the inner self to the public eye just as writing did. Occasionally this equation became explicit. Steele connected gesture and writing to explain why he urged that every gentleman be trained in movement and dance:

> When we read we do it without any exerted Act of Memory that presents the Shape of the Letters; but Habit makes us do it mechanically without staying, like Children, to recollect and join those Letters. A Man who has not had the Regard of his Gesture in any part of his Education, will find himself unable to act with Freedom before new Company, as a Child that is but learning would be to read without Hesitation. (*Spectator* no. 334)

Steele draws an analogy between gestures and individual letters, and equates facility at transforming text into utterance with the capacity to turn the space of social performance into a realm of ease and companionability. Both skills require the inculcation of habit, which in Peirce's analysis is a sign's ultimate logical interpretant. The sign in this case is an image schema of "gesture is writing." And like fluently reading a text aloud, executing ingrained and habituated gestures presented the appearance of spontaneity.

But the goal of that education in manners was *apparent* spontaneity, not the real thing. Just as the text lay submerged under an actor or orator's voice, the notation of movement—the inscription of gesture within memory—was to be immersed below the liquid surface of the well-wrought turn. To be sure, the cultivation of well-crafted "spontaneity" has a long history; the difference is that now its pursuit was under the directivity of writing. And again, writing effectively erased itself. The dialectic between mechanism and organism arising not long after Steele thus was an argument over ways to read the action of writing with invisible ink. The passionate logic of movement parallels the rational logic of letters, as universal methods of inscription.

With gesture thus equivalent to writing and in a sense underwritten by it, it makes sense to call Burgh's annotations a subtext. The subtext unmasks the inner workings of the characters portrayed by the text. Such action makes textuality gestural, just as gestures are textual. Indeed, texts are a specific kind of gesture: when we meet Bevil Jr., he is reading Addison's "Vision of Mirza," which prompts him to say, "Such an Author consulted in a Morning, sets the Spirit for the Vicissitudes of the Day, better than the Glass does a Man's Person" (*Conscious Lovers* I.ii.2–4). The "mirror" trope reappears in act IV: Bevil Jr. ends the argument with Myrtle by showing him a letter he received from Lucinda demonstrating that neither of them wishes the marriage. As Myrtle reads the letter, Bevil Jr. speaks aside to tell us, "When he is thoroughly mortify'd, and Shame has got the better of Jealousie, when he has seen himself throughly, he will deserve to be assisted towards obtaining *Lucinda*" (IV.i.181–84). For Steele, texts are mirrors; gesturally, they reflect the human character back to itself. In doing so they allow the reader to establish or reestablish his or her inner character and outward, social performance. Still further, Bevil Jr. watches Myrtle read and forms a response to him, judging his merits and his own relation to them. In other words, Steele actually stages the theory of sentiment through dramatic action.

Gesture became for the eighteenth century the remains of an orality valorized yet silenced by the supremacy of textuality. Speech, which once was a form of communication involving the entire body, split into a spoken part and a visual part; and many thinkers threw away what seemed the worser part of it, to live the purer with the other half. But the equations of writing and gesture derive from a yet deeper equivalency, for dramatic characters were not just portrayed by texts: they were purely and completely textual. And they were textual not merely because they were fictions wrought by an author, but also because they shared in a metaphor that defined human beings: in the late seventeenth and early eighteenth century, and into even our own day, discourse drew a fundamental equation between people and texts.

That equation appears throughout Locke's *Essay*, particularly in his depiction of the mind at birth as "white Paper, void of all Characters, without any *Ideas*" (§2.1.2); it is on this blank sheet that sensation and reflection write their texts. The idea—the projection of image schemas of textuality to create the metaphor "the mind is writing"—was a turn-of-the-century commonplace. To Roger L'Estrange, "*Children* are but *Blank Paper*...and it is much in the Power of the first Comer, to Write Saint or Devil upon't" (sig. A1ᵛ). William Congreve used the metaphor in his plays: in *Love For Love*, Valentine tells Angelica, "You are all white, a sheet of lovely spotless Paper, when you first are Born; but you are to be scrawl'd and blotted by every Goose's Quill" (IV.i.637–39); and in *The Double-Dealer*, Lady Plyant complains, "Have I, I say, preserv'd myself, like a fair Sheet of Paper, for you to make a Blot upon?" (II.i.259–60). Addison expressed the notion in a decidedly Lockean tone, describing "the Blanks of Society, as being altogether unfurnish'd with Ideas" (*Spectator* no. 10). Steele himself wrote, "It is incredible to think how empty I have in this Time observ'd some Part of the Species to be, what mere Blanks they are when they first come abroad in the Morning, how utterly they are at a Stand till they are set going by some Paragraph in a News-Paper" (*Spectator* no. 4).[22]

Thereafter, commentary regularly used the author's character to validate the text, while the text received the character of the author: the text was personified and embodied consciousness (see Kelly 19–23). Such texts became quasi-autobiographical, in an age when biography and autobiography (the writing-out of one's life, person as text) achieved popularity. This equivalency is latent in the idea of the "author," whose existence and identity take objective form in the shape of texts, and whose name often stands as a metonymy for those books: "read Locke." Authors occupy positions in their own space of social performance: inside or outside the canon (see also Kernan 71–75, 158–63).

In this manner, both living and fictional people become "characters." Likewise, according to the *Oxford English Dictionary*, during the mid-1600s the meaning of *character* began to shift from the established senses of a written mark or description, to a newer sense of a human personality. The condensation of a person with his or her literary portrait into a "character" goes hand in hand with the anthropocentrism of print culture, signaled dramaturgically by the emphasis on character over plot in plays like *The Conscious Lovers*. And if texts and people are equated, then individuals too are correctable, society itself is capable of reform—merely, as it were, by changing the script.

The equation of person and writing establishes a notion of theatricality in which the spectator reads the text and subtext of characters' actions while being inscribed by those actions and responding with passions leading to gestures and discourse that reflect one's own character—in short, the "sentimental" dynamic. In theatre, the spaces of social performance (stage and auditorium) are also textual spaces, and *vice versa*. Theatre thus plays a special role in correcting society as a place of mutual reinscription.

Bevil Jr. is Steele's exemplary character, the person-text all other person-texts should copy. Perceptive, sensitive, reflective, and yet a charming and witty man of conversation, he is the epitome of the fine gentleman. He is also a "man of letters," as revealed by his first appearance on stage, reading Addison. For Steele and the early eighteenth century, ultimately every man is a man of letters; every letter is a gesture revealing character; gestures are movements inscribed and locked in space like printed words; space is the mental vision or physical theatre, centered around the human spectator, in which things appear in order to be measured and positioned; things are measured and positioned since humans experience them as the basis of ideas, and so they must be arranged in their logical order and proper syntax, creating a "Scene of *Ideas*"; and "because the Scene of *Ideas* that makes one Man's Thoughts, cannot be laid open to the immediate view of another, nor laid up anywhere but in the Memory, a no very sure Repository: Therefore to communicate our Thoughts to one another, as well as record them for our own use, Signs of our *Ideas* are also necessary" (Locke, *Essay* §4.21.4), according to the visual, typographical, theatrical philosophy of a man of letters Locked on stage.

That mass of metaphors defining cognition, gesture, and sentiment in terms of writing was born from the dynamics of early eighteenth-century England's dominant communication framework. The communication framework altered with the rise of periodical publication and cannot be reduced to its technology. At the structural level, it conditioned and enabled agents' activities. On that foundation agents organized civil society, a (masculinized) public sphere, and (feminized) private sphere, and along with them created imagined and intimate communities. Their communication practices generated an image schema of textuality as the model of human thought and selfhood at society's discursive level. All of these converged to shape agency and concepts of agency. Although some of these were new at the time, and some of them would fade away, they did not manifest themselves simply due to the vicissitudes of intellectual or cultural fashion. Underlying causal forces were at work.

All sorts of forces could affect performance strategies. The communication framework analyzed above was only the dominant one: there were others, associated with different economic positions, educational levels, and many other factors, and the relationships between frameworks could shift. Since conditions constantly altered, and since people outside the dominant culture could push for admittance or be adopted into it, forms of performance with less absolute commitment to text such as pantomime and burlesque could pose challenges to the theatre of the upper classes. There is always flux surrounding performance strategies. These slow pressures could push a secondary metaphor to the top, until they caused a sea change. Thus the theory of sentiments bore a seed of expressivism that eventually bore fruit as Romanticism; in fact Steele and Addison have been called early Romanticists (Graham 79). But that was just the inversion of the dominant metaphors. As mentioned earlier, some image schemas allow for reversals, opposite perspectives, and similar alternative formations; I will discuss an example next.

9

I will leap now to the latter phases of the "Age of Empiricism," the period beginning in the late nineteenth century and continuing to the mid-twentieth. Something curious happened in Continental drama when that period began, as these examples show:

A Doll's House (1879)	*When We Dead Awaken* (1899)
Miss Julie (1888)	*A Dream Play* (1902)
The Weavers (1892)	*The Sunken Bell* (1896)

In this group, the plays in the left-hand column are "naturalist"; those on the right, "symbolist" (one might want to say, proto-expressionist). The plays on top row are both by Ibsen; the two in the middle were written by Strindberg; and the bottom pair are by Hauptmann. Whatever their reasons, three major playwrights shifted between major dramatic styles, and while playwrights certainly influenced one another, there are more fundamental questions.

The issue I am considering here isn't about these plays specifically, but instead the relationship between these two genres, naturalism and symbolism. Why would playwrights find it so easy to "switch poles," as it were? Playwrights try different genres, but why specifically these two, which were new to dramatic history and were purportedly at odds, even though they could also be found cohabitating? Why not instead alternate with sensational melodramas and boulevard farces? Were they perhaps connected as performance strategies? These questions are not even restricted to drama, for similar flips occurred in other realms, such as philosophy (earlier versus later Ludwig Wittgenstein) and fiction (James Joyce's objective distanciation in *Dubliners* and his stream-of-consciousness tactics in *Ulysses* and *Finnegan's Wake*). When a variety of major dramatists, novelists, and philosophers switch between the same pair of approaches, one must wonder what produced these genres and tied them together as "logical" alternatives.

Émile Zola's *Naturalism in the Theatre* (1881) most famously stated naturalism's premises. Conjoining ideas of scientific accuracy, historicism, and more-or-less evolutionary notions of genesis and decline, he argued that naturalist drama was the only kind appropriate to his era. "We are an age of method, of experimental science; our primary need is for precise analysis.... Most of all we would need to intensify the illusion in reconstructing the environments, less for their picturesque qualities than for dramatic utility. The environment must determine the character" (Zola 361, 369; see also Schumacher 71–72, 152). In a word, Zola based naturalist theatre on positivism, a philosophy officially founded about thirty years before. Just a few years after Zola's essay was published, André Antoine began staging plays along the same naturalistic lines. The box set and imaginary fourth wall were born.

Positivism was empiricism's successor. The basic dynamics of print culture from which empiricism was born continued well into the twentieth century, and in most respects are with us still (although print culture is increasingly embattled). The positivist philosophical family has frequently been opposed by the relativist family of philosophies, but as I showed in chapter 1, they nevertheless share many of the same ontological and epistemological assumptions.

Two of these assumptions affected theatre particularly clearly, bringing with them many corollaries. One was the perception criterion of reality, with its strong objective/subjective distinction. Positivists adopt the objectivist view; their opponents reverse the perspective from the objective to the subjective, from outer experience to inner experience, from the absolute to the relative, from things to their signs. Such were symbolist drama's declared goals. According to Jean Moréas's "Symbolist Manifesto" (1886), symbolism "will build its work of *subjective deformation*, strong in this axiom: that art can find in *objectivity* only a simple and succinct point of departure" (Caws 51; Moréas's italics). The inversion was made possible by the individualistic anthropocentrism underlying the perception criterion. In Romantic drama, the subjectivized version of the perception criterion was not very pronounced, mainly appearing in the portrayal of mood. But a century later, shortly after naturalist theatre staked its ground on the power of external things (heredity and environment), symbolism pursued the power of symbols. Its symbols, however, were not established by tradition: they were formulated by the individual playwright for a single play, in order to encapsulate some spiritual or ethical idea or the distortions wrought by a particular psychic state. The symbolists relocated truth from the outer to the inner world, and also from the natural and material to the ideal and supernatural, treating the individual psyche as the door to the universal. As Pierre Quillard wrote in two 1891 declarations of symbolist ideas, "The human voice is a precious instrument: it vibrates in the soul of each spectator"; the illusions of material decor "are useless in 'dream' works, that is to say, in works of *real truth*.... [V]erse is freed to fulfill its essential and exclusive function: the lyrical expression of the characters' souls." Most specifically, "words will conjure up in every soul a personal, private image, which will clash with the crude stage representation" (Schumacher 87, 90; Quillard's italics).

A second concept that relativist philosophies share with positivism is the division of cultural spaces. The textual "logic" of print culture created a sense of a linear, universal space in which all minds operate—or strictly speaking, all male minds, for in contrast spoken words belonged to the feminine realm of the personal and the particular. Orality characterized the space of social performance, the sphere of intimacy and individuality—the circle of family, friends, and female care. Toward the end of the eighteenth century these ideas, taken a bit further and shifted from inner moral worth to inner spirit, formed the basis for the Romantics' theory of language as the expression of identity. Because oral culture was subordinated in print culture, for some intellectuals it thereby gained all the allure of the exotic. Thus we find the Romantics' fascination with folk life, ancient tales, and the Middle Ages. A century later the symbolists likewise were enraptured by the vocality of lyrics, the spiritual realm, and abstract personifications (such as Death) reminiscent of medieval drama. Along with the focus on the oral and personal came the sentimental response, which has remained a staple of drama ever since, particularly in melodrama and domestic tragedy. However, symbolism reconstructed the sentimental response as the lyrical expression of the individual soul.

But the Romantic and symbolist fascination with some of oral culture's expressive elements incorporated little of its epistemics. Instead their advocates emphasized the irrational, that is, what escaped the intensely textualized logic of empiricist reason, particularly the emotions. Selfhood was fused with the affects and with expressiveness. Indeed, the capacity for emotion displaced reason as the essence of humanity, as what unites all people, transcending every narrower division. In linguistic theory too, language was understood not so much as representing ideas as expressing and eliciting emotions, and vocal sound gained a new value as the basic carrier of meaning (Cohen 78–136; Voloshinov 48–52).

Cultural forces born of the communication framework encouraged this alteration (and alternation) by generating arrays of polarities, paradoxes, and fissures. Journalistic print culture contrasted with book culture in important respects. The conceptual space that book culture had developed was a grid arraying all things into objective and external relations. Yet its sociocultural space was deeply private and focused on inner development. Its founding image remained the solitary reader. The reader was consequently set in opposition to a regimented external world (possibly as its "best" observer). In contrast, popular journalism's sociocultural space was founded on the image of the imaginary community in which individuals were united by their locations within a readership. Since journals had to secure their readership over time, time became a medium through which the imaginary community developed yet sustained its identity. According to these conceptual presuppositions, ideas and values were innate not to individuals, but to collectivities, in such forms as the "national spirit" and its historical heritage. The resulting conceptual space consisted of an inward-looking whole composed of assorted parts, possessing a central essence or ideal that was manifested or expressed through its periphery. Each part had a function with regard to the whole; space was subjective and relative. Because journalistic print culture emphasized collectivity, it was a major force in the creation of the public sphere in which the latest news, policies, and discoveries could be scrutinized and objectivity sought. At the same time, since every reader was fundamentally equivalent, an opposition between the individual and society emerged here as well (with the individual as perhaps society's victim).

The differences between book and journalistic culture made it easy to switch perspectives on fundamental tenets of print culture, such as the perception criterion of reality and the relationship between textual space and the space of social performance. Oscillation between genres, and especially between naturalism and symbolism, becomes intellectually coherent in this light. But as the book and journalistic print cultures also have their own options for perspective switches, other oppositions could arise as well.

The coexistence of book and journalistic print cultures thus infused society with a variety of dualities and opposing perspectives, and to a greater or lesser extent people could combine them as they saw fit (always, of course, under given social conditions and pressures). Thus bourgeois realism, naturalism, psychological realism, psychically oriented symbolism, and politicized expressionism could all be made possible by the same basic image schemas and their cultural elaborations. By about 1925, however, personal psychology, emotions, and sex settled as the core themes, and psychological realism in some form became the norm.

"Realism" in this discussion is strictly an aesthetic term referring to the effort to create the appearance of reality—it is not the properly philosophical concept, much less the philosophy of critical realism. The relationship between aesthetic and philosophical realisms is too large a topic to be thoroughly addressed here; one need only recognize that the similitudes of medieval theatre were grounded in medieval philosophical realism to see the difficulty. In theatre studies, however, there is a pernicious tendency to muddy the distinction, most evident when naturalism is called "realism," a misconception exacerbated by descriptions of Bertolt Brecht (who opposed naturalism) as an opponent of realism. Naturalist theatre adheres to positivist philosophy; the latter is realist insofar as it upholds the existence of the world outside the mind, but insofar as it gives credence only to perceptions or observations and rejects ontology, it is decidedly irrealist. Naturalist theatre seeks the *appearance* of reality because from the positivist perspective, appearances are in effect the *only* reality. To conflate aesthetic naturalism with realism (and then to attack this falsified realism) is at best poorly informed; in some cases it is a tendentious sleight of hand. As for Brecht, to deny his realism is to ignore what he wrote. He insisted upon realism, and defined it as "laying bare society's causal network" and "emphasizing the dynamics of development" (109)—a stance that is in line with critical and other postpositivist realisms. I should add, however, that although "naturalist" and "Brechtian" theatre identify certain aesthetic and intellectual goals, they neither define nor guarantee the artistic quality, entertainment value, or political impact of any particular play or its performance. Nor, obviously, must a play be performed according to the philosophical assumptions that went into writing it.

Positivism and naturalism emerged during a period of increasing upheaval in society and economics, and also in communication. Starting in the mid-nineteenth century, the Western world experienced successive and continuing waves of innovation in communication technologies: telegraph, typewriter, radio, sound recording, motion picture, telephone, television, computer network. These injected all sorts of new dynamics into the communication framework, producing various ruptures in the dominant cultural paradigms. So far the upshot theatrically has been a broad theatrical eclecticism that has dominated the stage since the 1940s—though in general, some form of psychological realism prevailed, and prevails still.[23] There has scarcely been time for a new framework of communication to stabilize, much less establish a new set of fundamental image schemas for knowledge: at that level, Western societies are still essentially print cultures.

10

To close my discussion of the "Age of Empiricism," I will look at one of Bruce McConachie's investigations of the image schemas behind 1950s American theatre. As he observes, certain images schemas and metaphors dominate or maintain cultural hegemony during historical periods. His example is Michael Gazzo's *A Hatful of Rain*, on Broadway during 1955–56. McConachie holds that during the 1950s, the image schema of "containment" was key ("Doing Things" 584–86, 593–94). Having proposed containment as the primary metaphor, McConachie uses it to investigate the production's theatrical spatiality, narrative, and acting.

A Hatful of Rain focuses on Johnny, a Korean War vet whose life has taken a downward turn through heroin addiction. Though harassed by drug pushers, he attempts to kick the habit and restore his family ties; but in the end his wife must call the police to take him to the hospital. McConachie finds signs in the play reviews that several aspects of the play aroused anxiety about gender roles, while related elements hinted at fears of "subversion from within"; the two dangers were frequently associated in Cold War discourse. "Subversion" invokes the containment image, in this case of an inner essence (588–91). The containment schema also shaped the performance given by Ben Gazzara, the actor who played Johnny. Gazzara's Johnny was a man who was still decent and good on the inside, but who had taken the outer shape of a "Monster Addict" (in McConachie's phrase) which threatened to overwhelm him. Further, Method acting such as Gazzara's was itself built around the image of an inner self struggling to break free and sometimes bursting explosively into the light (591–93). Finally, the play ran in a typical proscenium theatre; the "fourth-wall" configuration of that stage is clearly an instance of containment. McConachie notes that the schemas of "center-periphery" and "near-far" organize the space as well.

In addition to the containment schema, McConachie proposes that the original Broadway audience responded to the performance via what Lakoff and Johnson call "advisory projection." Advisory projection is one way in which people put themselves in another's shoes, exemplified by phrases like "If I were you, I'd do X" and "Don't do that!" The alternative is "empathic projection," in which one adopts the other's viewpoint or experience, as in "I see why you feel that way" or "I can imagine how you feel." Although he only identifies evidence for advisory projection, McConachie does not rule out the possibility of empathic projection in proscenium theatres (McConachie, "Doing Things," 586–88; Lakoff and Johnson, *Philosophy* 281). Elsewhere I have suggested instead that in an effective 1950s mainstream production like *A Hatful of Rain*, it seems likely that the production would systematically encourage audiences to feel both advisory and empathic projection, albeit not necessarily in equal measure (Nellhaus, "Critical Realism").

I think it is no accident that McConachie alights on projection for analyzing audience response. The prototype of projection is a relationship between two people, but it can be scaled up: it is a specifically *social* image schema. The two projection schemas provide ways to manage the discursive relationships between Self and Other (in whatever way the latter are defined), which belong to the agential level of social ontology. Significantly, the Self/Other relationship is directional: Person A's relationship to Person B, and Person B's relationship to Person A. Further, as I observed earlier, images of Self and Other are indexical (in Peirce's sense)—they point to agents' location in the system of positioned practices and in social space generally.

As an elaboration of an image schema, the critical word in the phrase "Person A's relationship to Person B" is *to*, and typically the image underlying "to" is the arrow (A → B, B → A). In other words, projection (as the term itself suggests) is structured by the image schema of movement along a path. Empathic projection is essentially retrospective, interpreting where someone is "coming from"; advisory projection is prospective, suggesting what steps someone should take next. Thus the two types of projection are flip sides of the source-path-goal image schema. Interestingly, the source-path-goal schema also gives these projections an epistemic character: the complementarity between empathic (retrospective) and advisory (prospective) projection correlates with the critical realist distinction between epistemic relativism (recognizing that all theories are sociohistorically produced) and judgmental rationality (asserting grounds for recommending one theory rather than another).[24]

In demonstrating the coherence of the space, narrative, and acting of *A Hatful of Rain*, a coherence built around the image schema of containment and prevailing far beyond that one play, McConachie approaches the concept of a performance strategy. But more accurately we should call it a performance sub-strategy, for what McConachie demonstrates is how image schemas can be deployed within (or on top of) a larger system of schemas with a deeper structural basis. His analysis addresses a higher, more transient level of cultural activity than the one I've been examining.

Print culture fostered a strong objective/subjective division. The division was embodied theatrically in a variety of ways, increasingly to generate subjective perception. For example, the late nineteenth-century rearrangement of seating into the fan-shaped auditorium gave the entire audience a more or less straight-on view of the stage, and the shift from wings and grooves to three-dimensional sets (which never suffered from distorted perspective or outright fragmentation) meant that everyone's vantage point was roughly as good as everyone else's, and no one possessed a uniquely privileged position. Further, with the audience in darkness, only the privatized experience remained.

Likewise, during the nineteenth century, individualism gained an increasingly psychological character. Around 1900 it was conjoined with an extended containment schema to produce the notions of psychological layers, an unconscious buried in the nether reaches of the mind (a mind within a mind), and a deep (and deeply sexualized) self associated with Freud, ideas which were widely popularized in 1950s America. As McConachie observes, *A Hatful of Rain* strove to "plumb the depths of Johnny's psychology," and the real sources of Johnny's problems "are mired in the search for the mother he never had and the Oedipal rage he still feels toward his father" ("Doing Things," 589). One can see here the fusion of certain image schemas regarding the sense of self (inner essence versus outer person; self as location) with an image schema deployed by sociopolitical concerns (containment).

Still further, early eighteenth-century print culture introduced sentimental forms of comedy and drama. Sentiment touched Romantic drama, but mainly fed into various types of melodrama, which also often invoked the primacy of individualism. The essential dynamic of sentimental response (seeing behavior, judging character, and responding with spontaneous feeling) is in fact still very alive, most powerfully in tear-jerkers but in many other dramatic genres as well (although perhaps more now in film and television than on stage). The sense of psychological interiority born with the sentimental response is even more deeply embedded in modern drama—the sentimental response constituted the first effort at psychological realism. With the rise of true psychological realism, motivation, processes, and experience—the subjective realm—took center stage. From there it was but a short step to psychologically symbolist drama, expressionist theatre, surrealist performances, Pirandellian enigmas on sanity/insanity and illusion/reality, memory plays and the like, performed alongside the ever-dominant objective or naturalist form of psychological realism. Nor was it hard to patch elements from several of these styles into a single play. Thus a small set of image schemas permitted a wide assortment of permutations that nevertheless always converged on the concept of individual subjectivity and psychological truth. The schema complex of the deep self lay the foundation for numerous performance sub-strategies, one of which was mainstream Broadway in the 1950s.

The social forces that generated subjectivization in the performance on stage also produced it in the audience. As I will argue in the next chapter, theatre operates as a model of social agency. In the twentieth century agency was (for many, still is) defined as the Subject, a being primarily constituted through (or as) psychological depth. Audience response formed on that basis: as an emergent entity, theatrical performance has powers that can affect its audience members and in principle can even alter their concept of agency, but it emerges on the condition of the agent-form that already exists. Theatre has to work with what's already there.

The dynamic of spectatorial reflexivity involving a notion of individual inwardness was probably first articulated in the theory of sentiment, in which the meaning of an outward appearance lay in the observer's inner response. A roughly similar dynamic of reflexivity and dialectical perspective-switching operated in twentieth-century mainstream performance, but now the self had been configured with embedded interiorities: deepest of all, a seething morass of passions battling with an ethical veneer to escape, within a Subject seated in the dark with his or her own locally true perspective. This theatre's reflexivity involved empathy and judgment toward Self as well as Other; that is, both empathic and advisory projections. In, say, medieval allegorical drama, advisory projection almost certainly dominated, but its target was the agent as moral species. In a 1950s Broadway show like *A Hatful of Rain*, the tension between the two sorts of projection, the combination or alternation between them, the constant inward and outward transgression of the containment barrier, probably supplied a considerable part of a production's gripping quality.

Significantly, as McConachie notes, Method actors were often considered self-involved ("Doing Things," 593). Their heightened narcissism may have been real or reputation, but some degree of self-absorption was virtually inevitable given the sort of agency dominant at that time. For the audience too, the performance afforded an opportunity for self-involvement to the degree that empathy—seeing from the Other's perspective—can serve as a reflection of and attempt to fill one's own hollowed-out self. There was effectively a gap within agency itself, stipulated by its multiple interiorities, the disjunction required by the containment schema. In post-war America, agency was its own problem, "solved" by becoming ever-inward. The performance strategies of the time modeled it because that is what theatrical performance does; aimed to solve it because that is what agency does; and tried to do so by reinforcing it, even glorifying it, because social dynamics—the communication framework high among them—established that Subjectivity is what agency is.

11

Performance strategies are rooted in embodiment, through the emergence of image schemas in general, and communication practices in particular. Lakoff and Johnson emphasize the massive role of our subconscious and practical knowledge born out of embodied experience and taking cognitive form as image schemas. However, most of our discursive knowledge (propositional knowledge about the world) comes not from embodied experience, but rather from communication. Communication practices generate their own image schemas. At the same time they corral the primary image schemas into some sort of arrangement: discursive knowledge is an emergent semiotic system. In other words, changes in communication frameworks not only introduce new metaphors, but also reorganize the roles played by older and in some cases quite basic metaphors. Much as emergent systems do generally, the higher-level social structure for communication sets the conditions for the operation of older and lower-level cognitive structures through which we interact with the world—it poses the questions which we strive to answer by marshaling existing experience-based metaphors and developing new ones. Models of agency are in part strategies for answering those questions. And performance strategies, especially approaches to acting and characterization, provide models of agency.

The communication framework involves embodied experiences with the material world (including technologies) and social relationships. The image schemas it generates explain several matters in theatre history: the formation of the dominant performance strategies of a particular period; why some artistic options are explored but not others; why "opposed" artistic options may be explored at the same time by the same people; how audiences made sense of performances and understood them as communicating something about the world; and why performance strategies remain relatively stable for a time and then undergo major, even drastic, transformations.

Performance strategies are inherently relational and dynamic, and they are intimately linked both to philosophy and to concepts of agency. Ultimately they concern the constitution and exercise of agency; agents devise strategies to achieve certain goals, solve certain problems, and answer certain questions about what it is to be an agent. A single set of image schemas can lay the basis for several performance strategies. Thus, as we saw, naturalism, symbolism, and expressionism in drama employ different approaches to staging and characterization, yet assume essentially the same concept of agency. Such variety is possible because the conditions for action always underdetermine the actions undertaken. Though social structures place often enormous pressures on people to act in certain ways, options and choices always remain: people are not mere "bearers" of social relations, marionettes manipulated by social forces, or for that matter utterances spoken by discourse. They are real agents who make real decisions which have real consequences that differ from what would have resulted from another choice.

The concept of performance strategies allows one to see the common threads among divergent approaches, and to locate coherence (or noncoherence) among different elements such as acting, staging, narrative, costuming and so forth not simply on a thematic level, but on an underlying conceptual level that becomes embedded even with the actor's body. Some of the variety-in-commonality exists because reversals and perspective switches enable a single set of conceptual components to establish differing (complementary) dramaturgies. Many image schemas allow such perspective switches, such as between the container and the thing contained. Reversals of this sort arise from sensorimotor experiences with real objects, and belong to their real entailments. Conversely, the metaphorical implications or applications of image schemas may make sense of realities. Unlike the concepts of genre and style, performance strategies are founded in sociohistorical relations, resources, dynamics, and processes which emphasize or provide the sensorimotor and social experiences that play a key role in organizing that society's ideas and art. Further, performance strategies reflect the choices that people make within their social conditions. Thus the concept of performance strategies concerns connections between structures, agents, and discourses—the whole of social ontology, which includes the body itself.

Genre is basically a formal, categorical, or stylistic notion. It functions on the discursive level alone, without any necessary connection to people's actions, much less social dynamics. The concept of performance strategies cuts across genre distinctions while linking them to the rest of reality. That said, the concept of performance strategies doesn't necessarily serve every research question: it is "scalable," in the sense that it allows broader or finer levels of sub-strategies, but it may or may not be effective for understanding (say) the nature of comedy. Only further efforts to analyze theatre in terms of performance strategies will prove the extent of its applicability. In the meantime, the notion of genre remains useful, at least for indicating a loose "family resemblance" among plays or approaches to performance, even though in the end it may not be a real analytical tool.

CHAPTER 4

SOCIAL ONTOLOGY, (META)THEATRICALITY, AND THE HISTORY OF COMMUNICATION

ANALYSES OF PLAYS-WITHIN-PLAYS AND OTHER TYPES OF THEATRICAL self-reflexivity—in a word, metatheatricality—have been problematic. Many tread no further than categorization. Efforts at explanation usually find it in stylistic techniques or universal technologies, begging questions of metatheatricality's historical emergence and functions. In particular, they often fail to investigate its connections to social dynamics. In chapter 1 I outlined a social ontology consisting of social structures, agents, and discourses which provided the basis of my historical analysis in which agents, faced with various social structures like print capitalism, developed strategies for economic and cultural success that generated unforeseeable discursive and performance strategies. Here I will show that analyzing theatrical performance in terms of that social ontology leads to a social definition of theatre; and that theatre's relationship to one structure, the communication framework, explains how metatheatricality emerges out of an interaction between the structure of theatrical performance and larger social forces. Just as this chapter's title echoes the title of the first, so too do many of the first chapter's themes resound here.

1

For some writers, metatheatricality is just a device which takes various forms and can be used in various ways. For instance, both Dieter Mehl and Richard Hornby devise categories of metatheatricality. Mehl examines specifically the play-within-the-play during the English Renaissance, distinguishing between a play performed by a company of actors, a play performed by the main play's characters, the framed play, and so on. Hornby takes a broader historical and formal view and offers a whole taxonomy of metatheatricality: the play-within-the-play, the ceremony within the play, role-playing within the role, reference to literature or real life, self-reference, and relativized or problematized perception. His discussion sometimes narrowly concentrates on the formal and the literary, and his idea of metatheatricality as a matter of perception is overly vague, but his taxonomy is reasonably comprehensive nevertheless.

Still treating metatheatricality as an aesthetic device, Richard Nelson conducts a functional analysis of metatheatricality, specifically the play-within-the-play, and presents a more or less historical view of its changes. The functions he describes include the play as mirror, magic, mask, game, confessional, lie, clinic, life, and maze. *The Spanish Tragedy* and *Hamlet* offer examples of the inner play as stratagem; *Bartholomew Fair* and *The Knight of the Burning Pestle* provide instances of the play as game; Dumas's *Kean* and Scribe and Legouvé's *Adrienne Lecouvreur* are confessional, and so forth. Nelson doesn't claim this is an exhaustive list, and some examples involve implicit, not explicit, plays-within-plays; but at points he suggests larger functional groupings which have shifting importance across history. During the sixteenth and seventeenth centuries, and to some extent the eighteenth, metatheatricality mainly concerned plot and served primarily strategic ends: the play-within-the-play occurred to elicit information, entertain, provide an opportunity for action (such as revenge), instill wonder, deceive, and so forth. Then, starting in the eighteenth century, metatheatrical performance strategies began to concentrate on character and perform expressive functions. A play about an actor would reveal his or her personality—the performance of selfhood—especially as that character's on-stage and off-stage lives intersected; often a play-within-the-play occurs simply as an episode in the actor's life. Throughout the nineteenth century the play-within is intended "not to effect but to affect, not to implement an action but to express a being" (Nelson 89–90). Similarly, plays about theatre or the theatrical profession often give an image of the world backstage, with whatever illusions, inspiration, ignominy, or in-jokes might arise. The primary goal of this "professional" mode of metatheatricality is not to affect a fictional audience on stage (if any there be), but rather the real audience in the auditorium, whose knowledgeability and values make them complicit both theatrically and ideologically. Katherine Newey describes many examples of "professional" metatheatricality in nineteenth-century melodrama, and she links the practice to the anxieties over identity wrought by capitalism (a valid but incomplete argument). While the representation of theatre as a profession and an art appears sporadically in earlier eras, in the nineteenth century it became the emergent norm of metatheatricality, a norm which continues to be quite powerful.

Metatheatricality as a character's agential stratagem and as an illumination of a profession are not metatheatricality's only possible functions (the twentieth century brought other options), nor are they mutually exclusive (eighteenth-century plays about theatre often mix the two). However, the functional analysis of metatheatricality highlights its historical transitions, albeit in Nelson's case without providing much explanation for those changes. These discussions are quite valuable, but their findings must be incorporated within a properly explanatory analysis.

Lionel Abel and Judd Hubert take a difference tack, defining "metatheatre" as a dramatic genre which does not necessarily involve plays-within-plays or other sorts of direct theatrical self-reflexions, but instead has characters engage at a more discursive level in their own dramatization, acting as playwrights, directors and/or actors within the play.[1] The idea is broader than role-playing within the role, encompassing more or less any sort of self-awareness—it is affiliated, in fact, with the idea that life itself is already fundamentally theatrical. For Abel, "metatheatre" ("metadrama" might be a more appropriate term) arises because metatheatrical playwrights are themselves self-conscious. It appears that for Abel, metatheatre is historically coterminous with modern, possessive, self-willed individualism—a crucial aspect of Western culture since the late sixteenth century (see Nellhaus, "Self-Possessed Jonson"). His position not only concerns individualism, but also (like the previous ones) adopts it ontologically and methodologically, in this case in an expressivist cast akin to professional metatheatricality.

According to a third line of thought, theatrical self-reflexivity has few or no historical boundaries. Instead it results from the very nature of art, or in some versions, from the nature of discourse. The Russian formalists adopted that position: for Victor Shklovsky, artistry was a matter of revealing aesthetic devices, and Boris Tomashevsky drew an explicit parallel between that activity and the play-within-a-play. This understanding of self-reflexivity perhaps has been taken farthest by Derrida, for whom self-reference is an inherent part of writing. He asks, for instance, why Plato and other writers so often condemn writing in writing, and he concludes that "This 'contradiction,' which is nothing other than the relation-to-self of diction as it opposes itself to scription,... is not contingent. In order to convince ourselves of this, it would already suffice to note that what seems to inaugurate itself in Western literature with Plato will not fail to re-edit itself at least in Rousseau, and then in Saussure."[2] For Derrida, the relation of writing to itself is always the same, serves identical functions in all periods, always producing a phonocentric antagonism toward writing in writing itself. Despite recognizing that discourse and representation are social forms, these positions tend to place them ultimately outside human control, even to the point of asserting that they control *us*. In some versions, language, or discourse constitute society *in toto*, and there may be little we can do to change it.

A variant of the "essential metatheatricality" thesis is William Egginton's argument that theatre—by which he means strictly post-medieval stage performance—is intrinsically metatheatrical. For him, medieval forms of performance were not theatre but spectacle or ceremony, and consequently could not be metatheatrical. In the Middle Ages, performance occurred in a space that was always full of meanings, whereas modern performance involves an abstract "empty" space literally or imaginatively framed and set off from its context, within which the actor constitutes the dramatic character by presenting a similarly framed image. Implicitly, one frame can contain another. The argument is peculiarly circular: the historical limit he places around theatre is akin to saying that the Middle Ages had no books because they weren't printed. He defines theatre in such a way that only one era can have it.

However, the main problem for Egginton's argument, and also for notions of metatheatricality as characters' self-dramatization and theories of self-reference as necessary to art, is that metatheatricality does not appear with the same frequency in all periods, and its uses or functions change as well. The clearest type of metatheatricality, the play-within-the-play, burst forth in the late 1500s—but (*pace* Egginton) *Mankind*, *Wisdom* and *Fulgens and Lucres* provide incipient examples from a century earlier, and there are touches of it in the Wakefield, Coventry, and (as we saw) York Cycle (Wiles; Debax; Furnish). And they do so without evincing the individualistic consciousness that (as Abel and Egginton have it) should characterize metatheatricality. Likewise, if metatheatricality truly were based on the phonocentrism of writing, metatheatricality should appear more-or-less evenly whenever and wherever theatre appeared, but it doesn't. Metatheatricality's historicity raises questions of the relationship of theatricality and metatheatricality to society, and of the structure underlying theatrical practice which leads it at times to become markedly metatheatrical. The alternatives are either a flattened history without change, or one that presents stylistic changes as essentially arbitrary or voluntaristic, implicitly underestimating agents' powers. In both cases the world consists of only one ontological level: the psychological and semiological, the life of the mind. Recognizing a complex, multileveled universe requires an ontology permitting depth. Metatheatricality is a performance strategy that arises out of the dynamics of certain structural relationships. Key among them are the communication framework, and the embodied agent whose practices play a prime role in the emergence of knowledge.

2

Let me briefly consider an example of metatheatrical activity. One of the richest periods of metatheatricality was the Renaissance, and one of the most metatheatrical playwrights was Ben Jonson. Most of Jonson's comedies, including all the major ones, incorporate theatricality as a central motif. *Volpone* casts himself in several roles, such as the marketplace charlatan and the dying magnifico. The swindlers of *The Alchemist* play even more parts. *Epicoene* reveals the title character as a boy masquerading as a woman. *Bartholomew Fair* starts with a contract between dramatist and audience, and ends with a puppet show. Many more examples could be offered. Even within English Renaissance drama, Jonson's insistent metatheatricality, the sheer weight that he gives it within his dramaturgy, is exceptional. Though often laced with antitheatrical sentiment, in Jonson's plays metatheatricality rises to the point of method.

Jonson's plays have other features closely related to his representations of theatricality. Not only does theatricality appear within his plays, Jonson does as well: in several plays (such as *Every Man Out of His Humour*, *Bartholomew Fair*, and *The New Inn*) he includes a character who is much like himself (see Riggs 59–60; Helgerson 132–39; and Leggatt chap. 6). Jonson's strong self-presence also appears in the way his plays were published. At a time when plays were considered a "low" form of entertainment, when a gentleman seldom admitted to writing and still less to writing for money, in 1616 Jonson audaciously printed his plays and verse under his own name and entitled this collection his *Works*, pronouncing himself an author. In the plays' prefaces and prologues, he presented himself through his opinions. Jonson also corrected page proofs and in other ways designated his writing for publication. All in all, his use of and control over print was unprecedented, and played a notable role in the formation of modern authorship.

Such attention to the dissemination of his writing is a symptom of Jonson's concern with language and representation, which appears throughout his writings and his attention to publication. On the one hand, Jonson saw himself as introducing an artistic discipline and verisimilitude—even a veracity—hitherto unknown in English drama. On the other hand, his attentions over language and representation are riddled by deep suspicions. Jonson's discomfort with representation is vividly manifested by many of his theatrical and antitheatrical motifs. Characters in disguise (such as Volpone and Epicoene) are the occasion for Jonson's reveling and reviling, revealing in the finale a "true" character underneath. In his commonplace book,

Jonson attacked mimesis itself as inherently dangerous (Jonson 8.1093–98). Stanley Fish finds that Jonson's poems are self-referential in order to free themselves of representation (34–35); arguably, his plays reflexively represent theatricality in order to attack the theatricality of representation itself.

The character of Jonsonian metatheatricality can be clarified further by comparing it to strategies of self-reflexion in medieval literature and Shakespeare. Judson Allen contrasts the latter two in a highly suggestive way. Medieval poetry and its interpretation, he argues, operate by "a continual process of looking in and looking back—looking at a text itself, and then looking for some external similar which will furnish the explanation" (150). Medieval texts invoke the external world as their referent, double, and completion. Conversely, the sensate world finds its models and explanations in texts. For instance, the York Cycle's pageant of *The Entry into Jerusalem* conspicuously mirrors royal entries, while the latter secured their legitimacy with images drawn from history, allegory and the Bible. But *King Lear* (like other Renaissance texts) offers parallels for the main plot within the play itself, such as by drawing similarities between Lear and Gloucester, and between Lear and the storm: "everything past the literal sense is in the [play], explicit in the shape of events or implicit in the coherences and parallels which the [play] itself creates."[3] Thus Renaissance literature is far more self-contained than its medieval counterparts, which must be completed by referring to an external analogue.

In both cases the texts use a system of doubling to construct meaning, above and beyond immediate referentiality. Medieval writing doubled the literal meaning of the text with a figural meaning whose locus was outside the text, in the natural, cultural, or moral world: text and macrocosm completed each other to provide explanation and signification. Medieval theatre's performance strategies were likewise built upon similitudes and related tropes, such as allegorical characters, biblical figures and fulfillments, and trade symbolism. As meanings and references multiplied, texts and performances were the subject of interrogation and dialogic interpretation. The doubling of the literal plane by figural analogues continued in Shakespeare's time, but within the text itself, through subplots, correlates in nature, and other devices; the text was becoming a discursive microcosm, needing only internal relations for explanation and interpretation.

Jonson generally eschewed the mirroring of nature and action, plot and subplot: he preferred to have the play's literal meaning doubled not by a figural meaning, nor by internal analogues, but instead by the play's own manner of producing literal meaning—that is, by its being theatrical. Not only are all the play's relations internal representationally, they are internal performatively: the representations on stage parallel the process of representing on stage. Thus, for example, the actor playing Volpone is doubled by Volpone enacting a dying man; the wits of *Epicoene* devise plots and scripts for other characters; the real audience is mirrored by an on-stage audience in *The Staple of News*; a sort of miniature playhouse appears in *Bartholomew Fair*. Virtually the only microcosmic doubling in Jonsonian theatre is that of theatre itself.

Systems of doubling can be combined—for example, *Hamlet* has both the doubling of human catastrophes by disturbances in nature, and "The Murder of Gonzago," a play-within-a-play. Likewise, Jonson readily utilizes direct address to the audience and emblematic characterizations when it suits him. Yet what distinguishes Jonsonian metatheatricality from previous forms is its degree of internality and self-consciousness. The fact that such different conceptual and performance strategies were not considered mutually exclusive was not simply a matter of their coexistence, nor really of their compatibility. The social relations of the period gave writers and artists investments in both discursive strategies, so that despite whatever discursive conflicts might erupt, they were often imbricated within each other, even used to support each other, in a kind of generative tension that (in England) only eased in the latter seventeenth century.

The implications of Jonsonian metatheatricality go beyond questions of self-consciousness, to include the representation of theatre within Jonson's plays, the more figurative plays-within-plays staged by individual characters, representations of Jonson's person, and conflicts over representation itself, including its relation to the external world. This sketch should indicate the complex range of issues and strategies to which metatheatricality may be related. Three major questions arise: how to explain the prominence and character of metatheatricality in the English Renaissance; how to explain the particularly insistent theatrical and personal self-reflexiveness in Jonson's work specifically; and what these things tell us about metatheatricality in general, and the relation between theatrical performance and society.

3

Explaining metatheatricality requires an ontological analysis of theatrical performance, and a historical examination of the connection between changes in social structures (particularly communication frameworks) and changes in performance strategies. Analysis of theatre and society must be in terms of their ontology—the nature and structure of their existence—because they involve not only concepts and representations and inter-agential activity, but also underlying social and cultural forces which change and generate change.

As I showed in chapter 1, social ontology consists fundamentally of three levels. I will review them briefly because some of their features will become central for the discussion that follows. Social structures are relationships that involve (depend on, utilize, distribute, et cetera) material resources, whether physical or human. They condition, constrain, but also enable and motivate agents' activities; they establish the possibilities of action, or more precisely, the system of social positions and the practices they make possible (positioned practices). However, because social structures are relationships, connections to material resources have conceptual aspects, such as "owning," "renting," and "sharing." Moreover, concepts are embedded in material products themselves, such as in their design and production. Consequently social structures must be understood as being simultaneously material, sociological, and meaningful—but with the greatest weight on their material aspect.

Agents can be individuals, who always occupy various social positions (such as teacher, parent, employee) and engage in various activities and practices. Agents can also be organized groups (such as a football team, a business, a labor union, or a university), called "corporate agents." The internal structure of a corporate agent need not be harmonious, nor in fact are individuals necessarily willing members of the corporate agent. (Groups that are simply categories—like the homeless, the retired, or the wealthy—are not corporate agents: their main agency is through the uncoordinated but aggregate effects of individual agencies.) Agents are central to society because neither social structures nor meaning-systems would have come into existence without them. Like structures, agents have material, sociological, and meaningful aspects, but their sociological dimension is primary: their positions and powers within various social relationships, and the interests such positions establish, must be considered agents' foremost social attributes.

One of agents' basic capacities is their awareness of their actions and the results of those actions. This allows them to act in pursuit of particular results. However, the awareness and monitoring of one's actions can itself be monitored: by "monitoring the monitoring" of their actions, agents generate understandings of what they do, producing the meaning-systems which influence their intentions and the actions which result. Put differently, we are not only aware of what we do, but we can also be aware that we are aware: consequently we can account for our actions, and plan for them as well. This capacity for reflexive self-monitoring is a crucial constituent of human agency, and is intimately connected to the possession of a sign system. Language is the most obvious sign system, but it is far from the only one (Bhaskar, *Possibility of Naturalism* 35, 81–82; Harré and Secord 88–99).

That brings us to society's discursive level. It encompasses not just discursive practices in a general sense, but also specific discursive products, such as theories, novels, plays, concertos, dances, and sculptures—anything which is primarily communicative or expressive. Discourses, far from being solely linguistic, are built with icons, indexes, and symbols, elaborated in the form of analogical, expressive, and logical articulations. Through them agents understand their actions and the surrounding circumstances, and which guide or motivate their subsequent actions. However, while discursive practices primarily involve meanings, ideas, images, and values, they too have their sociological and material aspects. Discourses involve interactions between individuals or groups, since they require an audience, though that may be oneself; and as I have emphasized throughout, they require physical activities such as the production of sounds, marks on a page, or paint smears on canvas. The materiality of discursive practice is not trivial: in everyday life as well as in the arts, the qualities of the material used contributes to meaning and impact. Discourses are produced not only through connections among meanings, but also through practical activities. For that reason discourse and communication are not equivalent. Insofar as communication consists of meanings, it is governed by and produced through analogical, expressive, and logical signification. But insofar as communication is a material practice, it occurs through the social organization and development of material practices such as speech, handwriting, printing, or electronics: modes of communication, which are social structures that condition agents' activities as fundamentally as economics and gender.

Communication is a productive practice. Since communication produces various effects, including meanings and interpersonal or social relations, one can accomplish things by communicating, or as J. L. Austin put it, "do things with words": every speech act, and communication in general, is performative.[4] Verbal performatives and stage performance have a number of things in common. The most important here is that both pertain to the production of meaningful—in Peirce's terms, significate—effects. They concern *production* because they generate something new, an array of meanings, emotions and sensations in an audience; they concern *effects* because no speech act and no performance can be considered performed unless it achieves some effect upon that audience—even if not the one intended.[5] Thus performance is (among other things) a productive practice that aims to produce meaningful effects. This description is intentionally broad, because there are many types of performance, and because the concept of performance crosses both discursive and nondiscursive practices. These in fact intersect in certain ways—discursive practices affect nondiscursive practices and vice versa, because each possesses material, sociological, and meaningful aspects. Thus the production of meaningful effects is only one of the ways in which theatre and communication possess a common performative structure. That commonality will play an essential role in explaining metatheatricality.

4

The "Prague school" semiologist Jiři Veltrusky shed considerable light on theatre's ontological structure when he distinguished between the "acting event," consisting of the conventions and relationships governing the interactions between performers and audience members; and the "enacted event," the story represented or narrated by the performers—the interactions between the characters that they perform. As Veltrusky observes, the difference between these two planes can be blurred, and some genres of performance make a point of blurring the distinction. Nevertheless the two are analytically distinct: the blurring effect derives from close interplay between the two levels, not from an actual disappearance of their difference (577–78).

However, theatrical performance possesses a third plane which Veltrusky does not consider, consisting of the complex network of ideas, impulses and imagery which direct, are transformatively concretized in, and/or emerge out of the enacted event. The "performance score" used to produce actions and characterizations may be a traditional playtext, but it might be simply a scenario, or even a mere attitude or image. Bert States expressed the idea nicely: "even in most forms of improvisational theatre the actor is performing only what he has, in Hamlet's phrase, 'set down' for himself to improvise.... From the phenomenological standpoint, the text is not a prior document: it is the animating current to which that actor submits his body and refines himself into an illusionary being" (128). Noël Carroll uses the phrase "performance plan" for the same idea (106–12). Thus *in performance* a script is not something previous, but rather happens concurrently, as an ongoing process of interpretation (in Peirce's sense of the unceasing semiosis producing ever more developed and determinate interpretants). Moreover, it is not the same as a "text," since rather than supplying the literal contents of the performance, it provides one basis for the performer's and audience's interpretive activity. For that matter, the audience's own experiences and expectations (of genre, casting, and so forth) provide another set of scripts to be applied, continuously interpreted and perhaps controverted during performance during which the performance itself serves as yet another script. Both the performers and the audience seize scripts as material to be worked upon. The traditional playtext is paradigmatic of the scriptive level, but as scripts in the theatre have always been, it may be cut, reorganized, refocused, and necessarily elaborated upon by the very process of performance, and even in the most conservative text-based performance, the playtext is never the *only* source of scriptive imagery, impulses and ideas—the actor's body is only the most obvious among many others. That said, the paradigm of the written play is crucial, since the transformation of dramatic text to live performance is not just the pragmatic norm but also the conceptual model for the production of all theatrical performance, with or without a playtext. One might even call the relationship an image schema. The third level of performance thus consists of "scripting" in a sense that applies even to the images and role-types involved in stage improvisation. It applies also to the audience's interpretive activity: for example, spectators may understand the movements of (say) geometric figures in an anthropomorphic way, that is, *narrativizing* their behaviors. We may, for convenience, refer to these levels as the theatrical, the dramatic, and the scriptive planes of performance (see also Nellhaus, "Performance" 6–7).

The three planes of performance parallel the three ontological strata of society. The theatrical level, which is a system of social relationships between performers, audience, and physical resources such as the theatre building and the stage, is akin to society's structural level; the characters enacting events on stage are agents of a sort; and the script is comparable to society's discursive level. In one sense this homology is unexceptional, because *all* practices involve structures, agents, and discourses. This is especially clear for collectively organized practices, that is, those of corporate agents, of which a theatre company is a type; from that perspective, performers are individual agents within a corporate agent, and the direct producers of its primary product, the drama (enacted event). Two of corporate agents' most important features are that they organize individuals toward some end, and articulate their interests, goals, or ideas (Archer, *Realist Social Theory* 185–86, 258–65). Thus a corporate agent possesses an *interior* structure/agent/discourse ontology, which consists of its organizational relations, the individuals it comprises (such as members or employees), and the discourses it produces for the outside public and for its internal culture. Organizations are in a sense miniature societies, with a local structure/agent/discourse ontology in the midst of society's structure/agent/discourse ontology; but unlike societies, organizations are agential in the sense that they can make decisions and act upon them.

However, there is a major difference between theatrical performance and society: the agents *in the drama* (the characters) are fictional, or if you will, virtual. Perhaps they behave much like real agents, and spectators may respond to them in similar ways, but they remain discursive, representational constructs which cannot, for example, make decisions within the theatrical organization. The introduction of virtual agents is one aspect of an ontological dislocation resulting from two distinctive elements of theatrical performance; and I must emphasize, here I am strictly discussing theatrical performance, not a generalized notion of performance or metaphorical uses of "theatre" to encompass sports or rituals, since ontologically those are different things. First, not only is every layer of society's

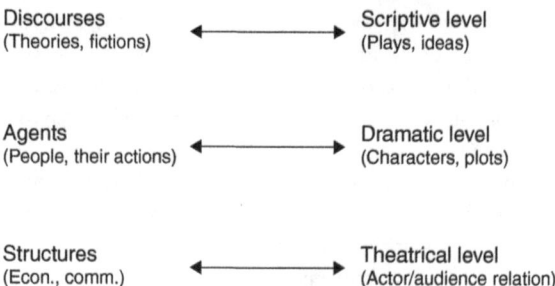

Figure 4.1 Theatrical Doubling (examples shown in parentheses).

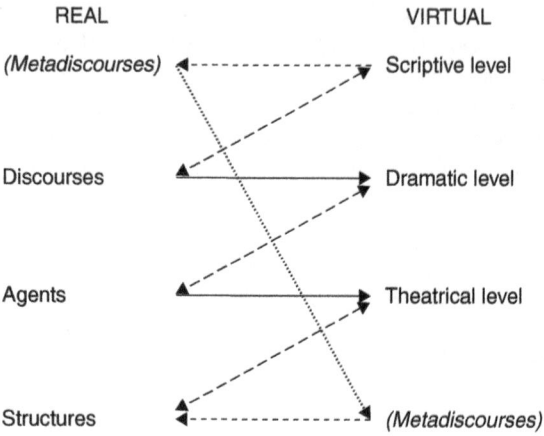

Figure 4.2 The Ontological Shift.

structure/agent/discourse ontology implicated in theatrical performance (as it is in any practice), every layer is doubled. (See figure 4.1.) Society's structural level is echoed in the theatrical dynamic; real agents find a counterpart in the drama's virtual agents (characters); the discursive level is reduplicated in the script. The last doubling is especially complex, for ordinary speech acts—performatives—already involve reflexive self-monitoring. The script, then, performs a monitoring of monitoring-of-monitoring: the performatives of the scriptive level govern and interpret the performatives of the dramatic level, forming a new, metadiscursive level of reflexivity. Theatrical performance thus consists of discursivized actions of producing discursivized actions, the enactment of enactment, the performance of performance.

The second element is that theatrical performance not only doubles social ontology, it also shifts or rotates it: an "ontological shift." (See figure 4.2.)

The theatrical structure is formed by real agents (actors and spectators); that is, agents take the role of structures. Within that structure, the virtual agents (characters) act; but they are fictive, the products of discourse—discourses take the role of agents. Structures are (re)presented by agents, and agents by representations. The ontological shift within theatrical performance explains how the virtual agents can sometimes displace the real agents (such as the seeming disappearance of an actor into her character): the real agents are in a social relation which positions them as part of performance's *structure*. (The displacement can even involve different bodies, as in puppetry.) But strictly speaking there is no ontological level beyond meaning and discourse; instead, the discursive level is doubled by becoming a system not just of signs, but signs of signs. (Again, discourse consists not just of verbal signs, but signs of any sort.) Due to the systemic nature of its signs-of-signs relation, theatrical performance bears a capacity to double the discursive level through a metadiscourse that theorizes the underlying conditions of human existence, in whatever manner those may be conceived: humans' relations with nature, with god(s), with each other, with their own selves, and so forth. In a sense, then, in theatrical performance (meta)discourses take the role of underlying structures, and structures form (meta)discourses. The circuit connecting metadiscursive activity to fundamental structures of human and social existence is completed by the audience, who (like the actors) occupy a structural position within theatrical performance, yet possess the power to respond intellectually, emotionally, and ethically to the drama enacted on stage. The audience is part of a "conscious social structure," or better, a virtual structure.

Theatrical performance doubles the social structure/agent/discourse framework *ontologically*, not substantively or mimetically. The theatrical level (that of performers, stage, and audience) reduplicates the structural level of society insofar as both are systems of social relationships establishing positioned practices. But the theatrical dynamic need not mirror the dominant social relationships, and in fact can differ from them sharply. For example, theatre need not take a commodity form despite prevailing capitalist relations, as in forum theatre (where spectators are also the actors) or free performances in the park. Likewise, the dramatic characters who pass before the spectators need not behave at all like contemporary people, or for that matter like human beings. Nor, finally, must the play's discursive content (and potentially its metadiscourse) be familiar, mimetic, realistic, acceptable, or even comprehensible. Theatre's key likeness to society is not a question of imitation or representation, but homology. Whether or not a theatre performance portrays a model of society, ontologically it *is* a model of society. The social situation alone—a performance event with a performed event governed by a performance score—makes it so. Naturalism and verisimilitude thus do not have any privileged capacity to address social reality, and can even obscure it by (say) effacing the stratified nature of social ontology. By the same token, stylization, strangeness, or even subversiveness in a performance need not limit its potential audience. Theatrical performance's doubling of society's ontology, which is necessary to all forms of theatre, is in principle enough to make it "speak" to anyone.

Theatre's structure as a doubling of social ontology emerges in other ways. In discussing the nature of society's structure/agent/discourse ontology, I emphasized that agents are the central element: structures and discourses *exist* only by virtue of agents' activities (especially what they have done in the past), and can continue or change only through agents' actions and inactions today. Yet agents can *act* in the present only on the basis of the structures and discourses given by the past, which provide the conditions and real possibilities for agents' activities. If society is understood simply as the structure/agent/discourse ontology, it will appear static; but once the special position of agency is clear, the ontological framework becomes dynamic and sociological analysis is immersed in history.

A similar dynamic exists in theatrical performance. Nothing happens without the characters' activities. One might say, in keeping with critical realism's causal criterion of reality, that action or acting upon is what identifies a stage figure as a character. (The point holds for characters who never appear on stage, Protopopov in *Three Sisters* for instance.) When they act, the changes that even the most non-human characters instigate become almost unavoidably narrativized, and their actions are accomplished on the basis of structural conditions and discursive directives established within the drama, howsoever they may be construed. The characters also act within the parameters of the theatre's underlying stage/audience relationship, and in relation to discourses existing outside the drama as well. With the virtual agents thus nestled dynamically within two types of structures and discourses, theatrical performance must be understood as being not just a model of society, but also and more specifically as a model of social agency.

This argument should not be misunderstood as enforcing a character-oriented concept of drama. Characters do not exist frozen in time: they only emerge by virtue of their emplotted activities. The connection between character and plot draws upon another aspect of theatre's ontological doubling. Theatrical performance involves corporate agency, insofar as a group of people work together to present a show; but often it also involves *virtual* corporate agency, in the sense that drama usually consists of the interactions of virtual agents toward some end (or at least some ending), not usually known to or intended by them of course, but the result of their actions nevertheless.[6] Depending on the play and the sociohistorical context, the characters may be (seen as) the masters of their actions. They may be subjects caught within an action driving them ineluctably forward and creating them as it presses onward. They may simply be ciphers if action and suspense are the only significant interest. The centrality of virtual agents within theatrical performance stems from their ontological position, not from the particularities of the play. Thus even the production of *rasas* depends on virtual agency as transformative praxis, or equally, transformative praxis as agency.

Theatrical performance doubles society's three ontological levels in a different semiotic mode at each level. The stage/audience relationship within theatrical performance, in all its institutional complexity, is a kind of image of the existence of social structures which enable and constrain agency—not an image of any particular social structure (though that may be the case), but of what it is to be a social structure, that is, a system of social relationships that hinge on material resources (such as the physical arrangement of a stage and auditorium) and establish a system of positioned practices (actors, spectators, directors and the like). Dramatic acting doubles agency by producing virtual agents, which are simultaneously products or causal effects of actual agency, causes of action in the dramas, and indexes of what it is to be an agent; that is, they point to agent forms or positions as defined within some society (as do methods of dramatic acting, and historical agency itself). For example, character names often indicate social class, ethnicity, moral type, profession, role, character traits, individuality and so forth (see Carlson 26–38). The indexical quality of virtual agents appears even when the characters act like no human ever has on earth: their nonhumanness is itself defined by some society, as one of its "negative images" of human agency. The script, for its part, constitutes an organization of and comment upon existing discourses—that is, the systems of conventionalized signs, each of which is a generality (for instance, the word "dog" applies to all dogs) that becomes incorporated through the script into a system of higher generalities: again, a system of signs of signs; again, generalities that concern the fundamental conditions of human existence.

Thus, the process of ontological doubling in theatrical performance involves the construction of an organized representation—in a broad sense, a sign—of each level of social ontology, by means of the next level up (structures by agents, agents by discourses, discourse by metadiscourse). But the sort of signs involved differs at each level. In fact they belong to Peirce's three classes of sign. The theatrical level is an icon of structures, the dramatic level involves characters and actions that are indexes of agency, and the scriptive level consists of symbols of discourse. Further, as I noted in chapter 1, the three levels of *society's* ontology (structure, agent, discourse) are related to each of the three types of Peircean sign (icon, index, symbol) respectively. (See figure 4.3.) Theatrical performance, as a double of social

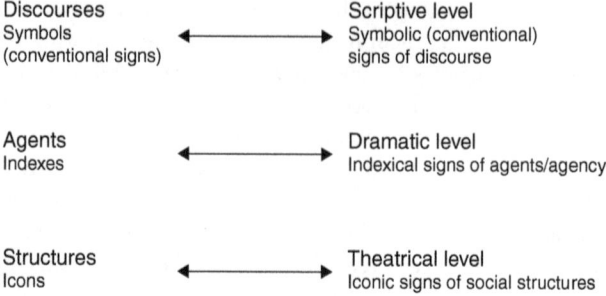

Figure 4.3 Theatrical Doubling as Semiosis.

ontology, models not only each of the latter's levels, but also the modes of semiosis embedded at each level. One may say not only that the scriptive level consists of signs of (conventional) signs, but also that the dramatic level consists of signs of agents (virtual agents) and the theatrical level consists of signs of structures (virtual structures). Theatrical performance, then, is a complex, partially embodied sign of society.

However, although the scriptive level symbolically represents (doubles) society's discursive level, the nature of the latter is a separate matter. Marvin Carlson has analyzed the multifaceted ways in which naturalist and other modern theatre forms introduce iconic imagery, such as actual tables, detailed verisimilarity in sets or even the use of extra-theatrical locations and so forth (75–91). At first blush his point may seem to contradict mine. However, he also mentions that "In more stylized theatres, most notably those of the classic Orient, symbolization replaces iconicity—a table represents a mountain; a flag, an army; a piece of cloth, a river" (76). So there are two dimensions to discursive doubling in performance. On the one hand, stage conventions (symbolic systems) are always most immediately in force. On the other, a society's dominant discursive strategy is normally extended to performance strategies: positivism and its concomitant perception criterion of reality steer naturalist theatre, bringing with it an intense focus on verisimilar iconicity; in contrast, figural thinking (the discourse of similitudes) guides medieval performance.

Interpreting theatrical performance as ontological doubling of society resolves problems that arise in alternative approaches. Some focus on repetition in time. For example, Richard Schechner, who adopts an anthropological perspective, argues that performance is "restored behavior" or "twice-behaved behavior." (The focus on behavior is curiously positivist.) Coming from a post-structuralist orientation, Judith Butler arrives at a similar conclusion, arguing that "performativity must be understood...as the reiterative and citational practice by which discourse produces the effects that it names.... [I]t is always a reiteration of a norm or set of norms."[7] The notion of performance as "temporal doubling" encounters difficulties in theorizing performance's transformative potential, innovation and immediacy, or even the influence of personal age upon a spectator's interpretations—all issues pertaining to change, which these other approaches typically convert into questions of difference (such as different combinations of given behaviors). The notion that performance is a repetition of the same generates a flat concept of (say) how directors cast actors, how actors articulate a text or embody a role, and how audiences receive a performance. "Temporal doubling" also tends to support mimeticism (both naturalistic and parodic) and/or ritualistic anti-rationalism. By grasping the repetition as not a temporal but an ontological aspect of performance, those problems do not arise.

Schechner and especially Butler misconstrue the function of the "citing" or "reiteration" that necessarily occurs in performance. Discourse is performative, and it involves citation and citationality; but the reason discourse is performative it not that is citational. Performatives and performance are citational because they are semiosic, and more specifically because discourse works with *conventionalized* signs. Conventionalization occurs through repetition. That's part of the mechanism that enables language. But iteration or restoration of behavior is not what makes it performative. "Performativity" is a discursive power to reproduce or transform a social relationship or circumstance through a production of meaning. It is an act of *agency*. (This is not to say that agency always places primacy on meaning.) And without a satisfactory account of agency, a theory of theatrical performance is necessarily unsatisfactory, and indeed, misses the point. Agency is crucial to what theatre is, what it does, and why anyone should care or even enjoy it. For the exercise of embodied agency—flawed, foolish, klutzy, arrogant, vulnerable, ecstatic, horrific, compassionate, confused, wry, empty, blocked, denied, and all other ways and circumstances in which we act—are core to the being and pleasures of theatre. I should emphasize, however, that this is a matter of agency, not a universalized notion of the human condition (though there are similarities). Agency is always structured and situated within structures; it is socially and historically variable. On this view of performance, discourse is *real*, in the critical realist causal sense. It has powers to cause people to think, feel, and imagine; and it is susceptible to its audience's misinterpretations, counterinterpretations, criticisms, and inattentions. And like any other power, discourse has its scope: social transformation may be accomplished in part through discourse, but that doesn't make society or its transformation simply or even principally a discursive matter.

Social actions do of course frequently repeat or invoke previous actions, and so accomplish similar acts that reproduce underlying social relations, but events are not (textual) citations. The post-structuralist effort to treat society and social conditions as textual or discursive (the "linguistic turn") is grounded in a fundamental philosophical error, of which Butler provides a notable example. Although she constructs her notion of "performativity" upon Derrida's analysis of speech act theory (*Limited Inc* 1–23), Derrida himself does not commit the mistake of collapsing performativity into citationality. In fact, he never refers to "performativity" at all, only to "performatives" and "performative utterances"—that is, speech acts themselves. (Interestingly, the phrase "speech acts" connects these two facets of language: speech as a system of signs, and acts as exertions of social agency.) Butler's confusion of discourse's social dynamic with its semiotic mechanism commits the linguistic fallacy (the assimilation of being into language), which is a variant of the epistemic fallacy (the definition of being in terms of knowledge) and a form of destratification. Once the social is equated with or viewed as wholly determined by discourse alone, the confusion between performativity and citationality is not only inescapable, but invisible.

More Aristotelian arguments maintain that theatre is fundamentally mimetic or representational. For Bruce Wilshire, for instance, "Theatre is...a perceptually induced mimetic phenomenon of participation" (26); likewise, Eli Rozik argues that "theatre is essentially representational" ("Theatre" 93). This notion of "experiential doubling" has the advantage of involving a specific social or discursive relationship between theatrical performance and social life. It also draws on the aspects of agency that make theatre appeal to its audiences, although these theories generally rely on ideas of individual selfhood and on a very loose, unstructured notion of society, and lack a concept of social agency (Wilshire is a case study). Moreover, cognitive science has provided substantial evidence that mimesis is integral to human socialization, maturation and cognition. But "theatre is mimesis" flounders on the role that representation, referentiality and iconicity play in *all* social practices. Further, it tends to privilege verisimilitude or aesthetic naturalism and mystify the non-empirical. Ontologically, however, not only is there a semiosic aspect to all social practices, but also semiosis undergoes an additional degree of reflexion in theatrical performance, which "imitates" society not necessarily through what it represents, but through how it is structured.

Finally, both the mimetic theory and the iteration theory admit only one ontological level, that of observable behaviors and environments (or in Butler's case, discourse). As I argued in chapter 1, such ontological monovalence—the recognition of only one level of reality—is a critical flaw shared by positivism and social constructionism.

My analysis is most akin to Augusto Boal's view that "Theatre is born when the human being discovers that it can observe itself.... On stage, we continue to see the world as we have always seen it, but now we also see it as others see it: we see ourselves as we see ourselves, *and* we see ourselves as we are seen." Also similar is his assertion that in theatre, two spaces—one real, the other fictive—occupy the same place at the same time. "We are here, seated in this very room, and at the same time we are in the castle of Elsinore" (13, 22–23, 26). It is perhaps no surprise that Boal expressed this view, since he was deeply committed to a social understanding of theatre and the use of theatre to advance agency. The key difference is that his analysis of reflexivity is essentialist; instead, theatrical reflexivity should be firmly planted within a theory of social dynamics.

To hazard another definition, then, theatrical performance is the production of societal reflexivity. Both terms should be glossed. On the one hand, *societal* reflexivity involves reflexivity at each level of social ontology—their doubling into the performance event, the performed event, and the performance score. Thus the structure of theatrical performance is a model of social ontology; the structure, but not necessarily its representations. However, the practice of societal reflexivity can only be performed by specific societies—specific in their history and geography as well as their social structures and culture. Consequently theatres must be understood institutionally, in terms of not just what they perform, but also their location, occasion, architectural arrangement, performance styles, and performer and audience social categories; all areas which can involve social struggles. (Social specificity will turn out to bear on metatheatricality.) By the same token, because theatrical performance is ontologically a model of social ontology, it can function as a "virtual public sphere" capable of presenting alternatives to the dominant social, political, and cultural order (see Kruger 11–17), but it almost inevitably offers representations of (part of) *some* society, whether or not it is one that has ever or could ever exist.

On the other hand, societal *reflexivity* involves communication, and so must be performative and dialogic. For that reason, the performers and the audience must *both* be aware of the reflexive character of the event, and both must recognize that the being who enacts the drama is a virtual agent (a character), not a real agent (a person), and so govern their social relationship to that being accordingly. Situations in which someone "puts on an act" for unsuspecting witnesses, observes people in life as unwitting actors, and similar permutations might be described as theatrical in a metaphoric sense, but not in an analytic sense. However, since the reflexivity of theatrical performance is societal, it constitutes a structural (not simply discursive) reflexivity involving all three ontological levels; and there is no reason why discourse must be the most important among them, or when it is, that the discourse need be abstract and intellectual rather than, say, affective or even sensualistic. Since the reflexivity of theatrical performance is "global," it can engage the audience on numerous levels—including the reflexive experience of enjoying themselves. From a formal semiotic perspective theatrical performance simply produces various signs and representations (or better, signs of signs), but from the standpoint of social ontology something far more complex takes place: theatre doubles society's overall ontological structure and creates a special sort of social agent who exists only virtually and only within the confines of the drama; and it produces intended and unintended cognitive, emotional and sensuous effects within the audience.

Theatrical performance's distinction from other performance genres cannot be adequately understood as the presence or absence of some element, because the basic elements—structures, agents, and discourses—are the same for all practices. What makes theatre unique is the set of *social relationships* it establishes among these basic elements: in particular, its doubling and "shifting" of social ontology. The definition of theatre belongs on ontological and sociological grounds, as critical realism understands them, and not on technical, formal, or experiential grounds. A definition of theatrical performance based on its social ontology is the only sort that can achieve an understanding equal to its complexity and richness. The point has two reflexions of its own. On the one hand, the fact that theatre doubles social ontology illuminates theatre's value for understanding society, for not only do theatrical performances often present images of a society (however ideological in character), its very ontology echoes society's. On the other, theatre's (doubled) embodiment of social ontology makes it an image of critical realism's theory of social ontology; and as we saw in chapter 1, because society is an emergent totality produced through agential reflexivity, social ontology parallels philosophical ontology itself (identified in critical realism as the domains of the real, the actual, and the semiosic), which makes theatrical performance a model of critical realist philosophy.

5

Theatrical performance possesses a special relationship not only to the ontological structure of society, but also in particular to communication practices. In very general terms, of course, theatrical performance is a type of communication, and communication is performative. But communication in the sense of discourse is crucial for the constitution and activity of agents; and the virtual agents (characters) in drama are discursive constructs. The reflexive dimension of discourse, as the monitoring of monitoring, is reduplicated within theatrical performance as the performance of performances, and still more so as the production of societal reflexivity. And on the practical level, theatrical performance often involves a complex relationship between speech and writing, a relationship that builds upon the complex relationship they have within most societies.

However, neither the use and function of a mode of communication nor the relationship among modes is stable. An existing mode of communication may be used by new people, utilized in a new way, lose its previous importance, and so forth; and a new mode of communication can be introduced. But after a revolution in the communication framework, the old modes of communication do not disappear. Instead they are relocalized, and generally relegated to a subordinate role. Which is not to say they are used less: they may in fact find new, previously unimaginable uses. For example, as print culture matured, whole new groups of people began to (hand-)write manuscripts and see them disseminated once they reached print. The effects of such changes in communication practices are profound, because as we have seen, the social organization of communication creates image schemas—generative principles which govern the production of concepts, and shape the basis of their validations. But when communication practices significantly alter, the old order of representation and conceptualization is put into question. A crisis in representation ensues.

This brings us back to the English Renaissance and the problem of Jonsonian metatheatricality. As many studies have attested, there was a crisis in representation in Renaissance England. One major cause was the rise of print culture, which produced disruptions within and departures from manuscript culture. In medieval manuscript culture, cultural dependence on orality strongly affected uses and understandings of texts, even while texts (especially the Bible) shaped oral culture. With expanded manuscript production and especially with the introduction of printing, slow transformations arose, mounting into a cultural breaking point around 1600. Writing could now be produced in two forms—handwritten and printed—and writing's relation to oral communication changed. Books and pamphlets became increasingly commonplace, they played an ever-broader role in culture and society, and the deepening cultural dependence upon them fostered a new standard of textual counterreference and systematicity. Educators relied on classical Roman authors to fill their textbooks, and as classical writings became more readily available, the humanists used textual evidence to discover the historicity and conventionality of language. The legal profession began to depend on the publication of case books that allowed citation of precedents. Protestants located their spiritual foundations in reading the Bible, grasping its words as literal truth, and using the text as the launching point for castigating the older, more orally and ritually based religiosity and for their own self-questioning and introspection.

Culture, then, became increasingly text-based. This was not solely a matter of print culture, since merchants and capitalists found the contract to be the essential model of social relations, and so the growing textual orientation in society arose because printing and capitalism went hand in hand: "print capitalism," in Benedict Anderson's phrase.[8]

The Renaissance crisis in representation can be understood as resulting from a conflict between the expansion of manuscript culture's old discursive products, and the introduction of print culture's new discursive process. For example, the massive growth in mystical and alchemical publications meditating on the similitudes between things was opposed by those advocating Baconian notions of scientific method and mathematically lucid writing based on a new role for linearity. But the dimensions of the Renaissance crisis in representation cannot be gauged simply in terms of the old versus the new, nor product versus process. The transformation in communication practices created a conflict between two discursive orders, two different ways to form and validate knowledge. The complex relations between old product and new process probably contributed to the fusions and confusions between contrasting or even contradictory epistemes. But such conflicts place a question mark over truth: an unavoidable uncertainty arises, an inadequacy or absence in knowledge which must somehow be enclosed (Reiss, *Tragedy and Truth* 11 and passim). "Enclosed," not "solved." Problems of this sort are not fixed, because the source of the problem—the presence of alternative modes of thought founded on differing communication practices—never actually goes away. And in this conflict, knowledge itself becomes a problem. Thus we find that Renaissance theorists of drama and poetry were preoccupied with issues of knowledge and truth, consequently reviving the Horatian call for instructive entertainments, and even arguing (as did the Renaissance Italian critic Lodovico Castelvetro) that writers must choose subjects and methods that pleased the uneducated. Whether as wisdom or ignorance, knowledge was the crux. This is the context for Jonson's constant concerns regarding language and representation, and his pursuit of a kind of truth-to-life in his drama.

The transition from a manuscript culture to a print culture generated specific pressures toward metatheatricality. The medieval strategy of doubling text and world, multiplying discourses' referential aspect, was part of seeing all things as signs authored by God. This strategy gave theatre enormous power, as its representations had direct applicability for interpreting the world at large; but by the same token the Church constrained the permissible interpretations. Print culture displaced the medieval discursive rules that asserted bonds between culture and nature with rules that asserted bonds within culture alone—that is, it replaced world-referentiality and external relations with conventionality and internal relations. That change was a corollary of emergent anthropocentrism, which as I showed arose from the dynamics of print culture; anthropocentrism was in fact one of print culture's earliest and most characteristic motifs. The Renaissance strategy of internal doubling emphasized discourses' formal construction and conventions, and their human authorship; interpretations of plays increasingly strove to reconstitute authorial intentions. Those developments turned plays into self-conscious artifacts of human creation and paved the way for authorship to become a prominent cultural function. Though the shift from external to internal relations occurred slowly and allowed for epistemic combinations, it ultimately provoked a crisis in the social relationship to representation, a crisis that highlighted discourses' internality, conventionality, and possession by a linguistic community; consequently, representation had to represent representation. The development of internal discursive relations forced a *theatrical* recognition of theatricality as a conventionalized, contingent mode of representation which offered truth through inner coherence. For this reason the focus on the problem of knowledge even oriented specific metatheatrical techniques: two major usages of the play-within-the-play were to represent the conflict between appearance and reality, and to offer a moral or allegorical exemplum (Mehl).

It is easy to see why Jonson was particularly ensnared by the crisis of representation, and as a result was frequently metatheatrical in his dramaturgy. His activity in editing and publishing his plays are just one aspect of his deep involvement in early print culture. His extraordinary scholarship, his reliance upon printed texts, made him question his knowledge and his theatre more than most—a questioning that consisted at core of demanding from each its textual validation, *Bartholomew Fair*'s "warrants." This authority was ultimately secured through the (implied or represented) presence of the author in the performance, declaring his possession of the text's meaning. Such possession was encouraged by capitalism but made possible by printing. As printing was one of the earliest capitalist enterprises, so too was the printed book one of the earliest mass-produced commodities. To have knowledge meant to have books on the shelf and in the head. Jonson thus printed his *Works* and inserted himself into his plays as evidence of his authority and mastery over his own meaning, the meanings he owned. Renaissance metatheatricality reduplicated the figure of the author, and no matter how jocularly or sneeringly Jonson depicted that author, the authorial presence was what mattered. The advent of the author function thus went hand in hand with the strategy of theatrical self-reflexion. And by doubling human products with a human process, Jonsonian metatheatricality effectively eliminated the lingering power of nature which oral culture posited. Creation was an act of authorship, and authorship an act of knowledge and power.[9]

6

In contrast to Derrida and Abel, I find that metatheatricality of the type appearing in the Renaissance results out of and is contingent upon social forces. Discursive reflexivity arose not because of the nature of writing's internal relation to speech or some other technological determination, or because of the arbitrary development of a style or genre, but primarily because the revolution in communication structures generated a need to reconceive discourse within discourse. The advent of print capitalism led to writers' political invocation of themselves as authorities—even incompetent authorities—over meanings, in circumstances where the new mode of communication made older strategies of discursive coherence and control uncertain or contested. The search for meaning through a text's internal relations and authorial intentions thereby imposed a new order of control over discourse and interpretation.

But that is only part of the explanation. So far I have restricted my discussion to the English Renaissance and pointed out some of the unique circumstances that fostered metatheatricality then. However, to gain a fuller grasp of the dynamics producing metatheatricality, we must consider other revolutions in communication, such as from an oral to a literate culture, and the introduction of journalistic print culture. Many of the problems that arose during the manuscript-to-print revolution of the Renaissance are features of all transformations in communication. In particular, they involve the emergence of a new discursive order, which in acute cases can conflict with the old, resulting in a crisis in representation marked by a gap or lack in knowledge that must somehow be contained.

A crisis in representation is also a crisis of agency: if discourse is crucial to the constitution of agency, a transformation of communication practices necessarily disrupts social understandings of agency and action as well as the structural conditions for action, thus posing the problem of what to do and how to speak—the problems which face Hamlet, who acts mad while trying to decide how to take action and how to justify that action and who finally ends in silence, and which also face Morose (in Jonson's *Epicoene*), who demands silence and comes to rue a decision made most carefully and rationally. In the twentieth century, Beckett, Handke and Artaud (among others) worked similar furrows. In short, slowly but surely, transformation at the structural level of communication induces crises at both the discursive and the agential levels.

That suggests some ways to refine the concept of performance, theatre, and metatheatricality. Discourses and social structures both depend on the exercise of agency—performance in everyday life, in the sense of conducting meaningful, real actions and interactions. At the same time, agents' activities involve discourse, especially their understanding of, reasons for, and comments upon their own activities in the world: reflexive (second-order) monitoring. Such discourse necessarily is itself performative: it produces meanings which alter social circumstances. Consequently, individual and group agency is constituted in part through discursive practices, as is the very concept and nature of agency within a given society; thus, for example, the differences between medieval and modern concepts of self.

But since discursive strategies are shaped by communication practices, changes in the communication framework disrupt the conduct of reflexive self-monitoring. That puts the concept and nature of agency into question: agents must then monitor the monitoring of monitoring, that is, be reflexive about reflexivity. This introduces not just performance in everyday life, but a theatricality of everyday life; but not theatre in everyday life, since the dislocation derived from the ontological shift—the creation of virtual agents recognized as such by the audience—does not occur. This theatricality within everyday life appears in forms such as Renaissance self-fashioning, or late-twentieth-century gender performativity and cultural "styling." Within theatre itself (as a model of social agency), the shifting of the communication framework generates the need for a third level of performativity, in which agents enact the enactment of agency. To fill that need, the structure/agent/discourse ontology, duplicated in the form of theatre, must be reduplicated yet again by way of theatrical self-reflexion. Metatheatricality, then, is a way to comprehend and perhaps resolve crises in agency, particularly when two (or more) models of agency are in contention.

The reduplication of the structure/agent/discourse ontology suggests a way to categorize types of metatheatricality on ontological rather than formal or functional grounds. Metatheatrical reflexivity at the structural level encompasses plays-within-plays, frame plays and similar embedded performances. At the agential level, metatheatricality entails characters who are actors, directors, playwrights, and so forth. Last, discursive metatheatricality consists of talk or images about theatre. The modes of metatheatricality can be combined or even blurred together, and the categorization has further aspects, but the distinctions will serve for now. In particular they indicate why the play-within-a-play (or its structural equivalents) is the paradigmatic form of metatheatricality: it reproduces theatre's entire ontological structure, and insofar as metatheatricality arises from changes in communication frameworks, the impact will be felt most strongly at performance's structural level.

Consequently one would expect plays-within-plays to crop up most during major alterations in the framework of communication (probably near the end, when cultural disruption is at its most intense). They are possible at other times because various sorts of social change can provoke similar, if less drastic, disruptions in the constitution of agency, and of course the strategy is always available in principle; but the need for theatrical self-reflexivity should be greatest during radical changes in communication practices. And with certain caveats, that seems to be the actual pattern. After the transition to print culture, data shows that in both relative and absolute terms, metatheatricality was most frequent during roughly 1590–1610, declining more or less steadily thereafter. In contrast, there were rather few plays-within-plays from the reopening of the theatres in 1660 to the end of the eighteenth century, a period when communication structures were fairly stable.[10] Unfortunately there are no figures for the nineteenth century, but I have seen nothing to suggest that there was any substantial increase. More significantly, as Jean-Christophe Agnew observes, "of the seventy or so plays that took theatre as their subject [between 1660 and 1737], none invoked the kind of epistemological or ontological anxiety that Elizabethan tragedy as a whole, and Shakespearean tragedy in particular, had invested in the trope of the *theatrum mundi*" (153), a comment that rings true as well for the subsequent century and a half. With the introduction of electric and electronic modes of communication in the late nineteenth century, epistemological and ontological (and existential) concerns once more rose uppermost in metatheatrical plays, such as Luigi Pirandello's *Six Characters in Search of an Author*, although such plays are more notable for their intensity than their frequency. But the emergence of those concerns may in fact be more telling than sheer numbers of plays, especially one theatre had become an industry.

If my historical inference is correct, then we should find performative self-reflexivity during the first communications revolution, the transition into literacy. However, classical Greek drama does not offer examples of metatheatricality in the form that we find in later epochs. Of course, that was the period in which theatre was invented, so to that degree it would scarcely be surprising if theatre was not yet grasped as a model for the structure of social agency. Yet if one considers what *had* been the core model for social agency, the form of metatheatricality possible for Greek performance quickly becomes apparent. Oral culture posited agency in humans' relationship with the gods, enacted through religious ritual, particularly of a communal sort. Such is the agency embodied in the tragic chorus, whose hymns and lamentations bear heavy traces of old ritual forms—the vehicle for the previous concept of agency—and whose effective dramatic role declined into decoration.

This difference in forms of theatrical self-reflexivity points to issues which deepen the historicity of metatheatricality. Ancient Greek religion and its rituals were themselves a historical form that emerged from a certain set of material and social conditions, most notably the society's dependence upon oral culture and hence upon embodied memory.[11] The rise of literacy within the ascendant mercantile and artisanal classes in Athens ruptured oral culture. The situation fused two different tendencies in conceptualizing agency into a tense, unstable, temporary, but also highly energizing compromise. On the one hand, oral culture posited ultimate agency among the gods, before whose interventions mortals were fundamentally helpless, aided only through religious rituals and support from a god. On the other hand, democratized literate culture tended to generate a notion of individual human will and responsibility, regulated by written laws and judgment in a court. Together, these two perspectives fused into a notion of human *participation* in the divinities' deeds—a notion exemplified in *Oedipus Tyrannos*. The epistemological crisis attending the communication revolution is apparent in *Oedipus Tyrannos* as well, in Oedipus's disastrously ignorant search for knowledge, and in the ironies and prevarications that pepper Euripides's plays. Theatrically, the religiously based concept of agency also fostered a representation of agents through masks, since their primary feature was not their inner depth but their external relations in terms of social status and divine (dis)favor; but the literate-based concept of agency motivated the creation of individualized protagonists and interlocutors—indeed, it stimulated the very notion of the actor on stage. The chorus in turn slowly lost its dramatic functions (Vernant and Vidal-Naquet; Schwartz 183–209; Ley 5–18). But the embedding of literate and oral concepts of agency also appears in Greek theatre's institutional structure, in which the theatre—a fundamentally *voluntarist* practice—occurred within the ritual context of the annual Festival of Dionysus; but interestingly, that festival was itself an invention, roughly coeval with tragedy. Thus were orality and literacy embedded within each other in classical Athens.

A similar argument holds for the change in the communication framework brought about by journalistic print capitalism during the early eighteenth century. I stated earlier that there were relatively few plays-within-plays during the eighteenth century, probably no more than forty between 1660 and 1800. Strikingly, about three fourths of them were "rehearsal" plays, the first and for decades best of which was the Duke of Buckingham's *The Rehearsal* (1671), performed only six times before 1700 but increasingly popular thereafter, until Sheridan's *The Critic* (1779) assumed its place as the best and most frequently performed of the genre.[12] One thing that differentiates rehearsal plays from Renaissance plays-within-plays is that the dramatic function of the latter is to affect the inner audience (for example, entertain, elucidate or elicit information, exact revenge), whereas the rehearsal play ridicules members of the theatre world, mainly writers and critics (including self-appointed critics), for the real audience's pleasure. While rehearsal plays are metatheatrical at the structural level, they are also metatheatrical at the agential level, which is their primary focus.

But plays-within-plays of whatever stripe weren't the only form of metatheatricality on the eighteenth-century stage: on the contrary, there were over one hundred plays that were "about" theatre or included commentary about theatre, without incorporating a play-within-a-play. They were metatheatrical on the agential or discursive level but not on the structural level. Some only touched on the subject briefly; others gave it their full attention, especially during the second half of the century, when plays on actors (and sometimes authors) flourished. Aside from a small flurry during the 1670s, plays with metatheatrical characters or commentary only appeared once every couple of years for the next three decades, but between 1717 and the Licensing Act of 1737 the average leapt to two per year, and crept up to three per year by the end of the century.[13]

The agential and discursive metatheatricality of these plays is significant in several respects. The eighteenth-century playhouse was a highly interactive place in which the spectators were often at least as much part of the show as whatever transpired on stage, and the actors were often quite happy to follow suit. But much of the metatheatrical material satirized spectatorial faults such as poor taste, ill-informed or arrogant criticism, rudeness, or outright disruptiveness. In other words, by criticizing certain characters, it aimed to regulate the audience's behavior and socialize it into more sophisticated and privatized spectatorship within the space of social performance—a struggle that continued for decades, often undermined by the actors themselves, but eventually successful (see also Straub 3–11). Long as it took, however, the theatrical strategy was a lesson in the "school for citizens," educating the audience toward their membership in the public sphere. Nevertheless, while resocializing the audience was a slow process, in a single stroke eighteenth-century metatheatrical criticism of the spectator's unreasoned behavior lodged the playhouse itself within the public sphere as a venue for social, cultural, and sometimes political critique. Eighteenth-century metatheatricality, then, played a role in the formation of a new type of individual social agent, the citizen, who was a new type of (partly corporate but primarily imagined) collective agent, the public.

Critical applications of "good taste" and reason (or an ideology of reason) to social interchange extended not just to the contested theatrical venue, but also to drama. Thus while a play set inside another play often depicts an old form of theatre or a poor performance (consistent with the effort to almost literally enclose the conflicts between old product and new process), in the eighteenth-century rehearsal play, the inner play is usually baffling and absurd, even incomprehensible; its perplexed observers' remarks on the inner play's inanity spotlights their status—and the audience's—as rational beings. Here the target is the reverse of the critique of spectatorial behavior: the author is the butt of the satire, the audience the locus of reason. The conflict between outer and inner play is not the new versus the old (in fact the inner play often satirized the pursuit of "novelty"), but the presence versus the absence of reason. In contrast, plays-within during the Renaissance were rarely if ever unintelligible: no matter how inexpert and silly one might imagine the "rude mechanicals" of *A Midsummer Night's Dream*, their play tells a coherent story.[14]

As I showed in the previous chapter, the ideology of reason was one side of the contradictory effects of printing's emergence as the paradigm of thought. Textuality defined rationality, and since the mind was a text, the "essence of man" was reason. Concomitantly the criterion of reality shifted from ontology (the medieval concept of real essences connected through similitudes) to epistemology in the form of empirical data or innate ideas. Thus as Lisa Freeman points out, "the driving force behind eighteenth-century plays about plays consisted not so much in a fear of ontological collapse as in a desire for epistemological authority" (49). Cultural programs such as Steele's strove to regulate audiences into rational behavior modeled on the idea of empirical, that is, passive, observation—Mr. Spectator, silent and unobtrusive, carefully reading the gestural language of the people before him.

Gestural expressions, "the mannerisms of public life" derived their importance in part from their function as "affective accommodations to the fundamental political, social, and economic settlements of eighteenth-century Britain," a way of negotiating place, power and perquisites within the new conditions of that world (Agnew 154–55). But as we've seen, the selection of gesture (rather than, say, ritually symbolic talismans) arose to a major extent from the dynamics of print culture. Gesture as the crux of social performance, the other side of print culture, shared with empiricism a strongly anthropocentric orientation. Its place as a currency of social exchange is responsible for the oft-attested theatricality of life in eighteenth-century London. In the open space of social performance as well as in the framed space of theatrical performance, gesture presented the articulation of character as a public presence. Consequently, "eighteenth-century theatre seems doubly reflexive, for it appears to have enacted an exhibitionist pattern of sociability that was already modeled on the stage," as Agnew remarks (154).

Inside that theatre, however, the audience constantly interacted with each other and with the actors. Freeman contends that eighteenth-century drama was "obsessed not with the tensions between interiority and exteriority but with the conflicting meaning of surfaces in themselves. On stage there was no public/private split; there was only public space and public displays" (27). As evidence of the absence of that split, she points to the audience's thorough awareness of dramatic narrative expectations, theatre managers' policies, actors' lines of business, and tastiest of all, the performer's personal lives (28–31, 37–39). But by her own account, audiences "were keenly aware of how public and private 'character' either converged or diverged in performance" (39). It seems doubtful that they could do so unless they were aware of the difference as they took pleasure in its violation, and there is significant evidence that audiences felt some anxiety about the issue (see Straub 13–14). Moreover, sentimental drama in particular emphasized the importance of discovering and exposing a character's inner moral worth. Rather than lacking a public/private split, then, it seems more likely that theatre in the eighteenth century was helping to create it, in part by what it staged, and in part by the social dynamics surrounding its staging. Whether by displaying a character's underlying worthiness or an actor's possible lack of it, the emergent bourgeois public sphere was busy carving out a private one.

7

The preceding discussion of classical Greek and eighteenth-century metatheatricality indicates three things. First, the relationship between the stage actor as real agent and the character as virtual agent is itself governed by a concept of agency: a discursive model that can become embedded in agents' practices and institutional arrangements, and may ultimately affect the very social structures from which the concepts originally emerged. The "movement" from structures through agents to discourses is succeeded by one from discourses through agents to structures, in multiple overlapping cycles that constitute the reflexive transformational process of human history. Hence the suggestion that metatheatricality may help to resolve crises in agency is more than notional: it is a palpable potentiality.

Second, concepts of agency arise on the basis of communication structures not alone, but in relationship to and conjunction with other structures, among them economics, politics and gender. These dynamics also condition the corporate agency of theatrical institutions. The specific circumstances under which societal reflexivity occurs (its time, place, methods, persons, and social relations) are consequently critical for the historical formation of metatheatricality.

Third, when the model of agency changes, so too must the nature and structure of metatheatricality. Thus the oxymoronic "rituals of individual will" recurring throughout classical Greek drama became self-reflexive through a ritual of individual will at another level. When the archaic ritual basis of the Furies' claim on a parricide is displaced by a human court in *The Oresteia*, the new quasi-ritual is invented at the behest and with the participation of a god. And the "little play" within *The Bacchae*, in which

Dionysus dresses up Pentheus to see and be the greatest performance of his life, similarly makes a human participate with a god in making a ritual out of his individual agency. In classical Greece, then, metatheatricality (if that is the best word here) consists of the individual ritualizations of ritualized individualities.

From this perspective it is clear that the need to contain absences in knowledge and govern ambiguities in interpretation need not be met in the way that it was during the Renaissance, by imposing the author as the source and final arbiter of meaning, and making the discourse's internal relations primary. That strategy was motivated in part by capitalism. Theatrical practice had become not merely voluntarist, but professional. Where classical Greek and, somewhat differently, medieval theatre were basically voluntarist institutions within ritual frameworks, most Renaissance theatre contained theocentric ritual within an anthropocentric institutional framework. Not only was ritual (and the ritual of individual will) interiorized, the will was as well. Henceforward characters would slowly gain inner psychological complexity and depth, which was largely a product of print culture. Casting moved toward a one-to-one relationship between actors and characters, giving character a more unitary representation. Agents' interiority opened the possibility of "metatheatre" as a genre of characters' self-dramatization. More importantly, however, theatre increasingly replaced the religious concerns pursued in mystery and morality plays with a representational focus, a shift that corresponded to the move from similitudes to verisimilitude. That too resulted from print culture—among other reasons, because beings and events once interpreted according to a natural and social order forged by God now increasingly had to be seen strictly through the eyes of an individual human. The theatrical representation of theatrical representation thus formed the play-within-the-play, allowing the source, center, and control of meaning to be situated within individual authorship.

Metatheatricality has essentially remained in this mode throughout print capitalism: in effect, an entrepreneurial representation of representational entrepreneurship. Thus we find the plays concerned with theatre as a profession and as a cultural agent, which has been the norm of metatheatricality from the eighteenth century to the present. The shifts in focus from the dramatist to the theatre institution to the actor do demarcate changes (perhaps encouraged by the advent of the star system, among other things), but they are shifts within the overall framework which makes metatheatricality concern the character of theatrical agents, whether they are corporate or individual—a concern that can even transfer the play-within to an offstage event. That concern is consistent with the era's empiricism and positivism, which conceived of reality in terms of discrete units acting under the compulsion of external (mechanistic) or internal (organic) laws of behavior, limiting the ontological gaze to the level of agents alone.[15] To that extent, the nineteenth century's plays about theatre are little different from its plays about stock speculation, prostitution, or poor-but-honest Irishwomen: theatre is just one in a field of individual and corporate agents.

8

During the massive changes in the communication framework of the sixteenth and seventeenth centuries, the play-within was often a stratagem chosen by a character in order to act, in contrast to an expression or instance of character. It was not something an agent does so much as a way of doing agency. As a result, the inner play generally had strong thematic and/or functional connections to the outer play, aiming to affect the onstage audience in some way. Such connections were nourished by the residual but still active medieval orientation toward external relations. Notably, the plays chosen as stratagems or entertainments, such as "The Murder of Gonzago" in *Hamlet* or *Bartholomew Fair*'s puppet-show, often involved a type of theatre that was outdated or disreputable, suggesting an effort to contain or supplant an old or problematic form of agency and its attendant discourse with a new form that the outer play already institutes.

At the beginning of the twentieth century, with communication practices in upheaval once more, plays-within-plays returned as a way to conduct agency within the drama. But another form of metatheatricality also became prominent: theatrical *self-presence*, in which theatre refers to its *present* performance. As Hornby notes, such self-referentiality has appeared most often during the same eras as the play-within-the-play, though it is even more uncommon (Hornby 114–17; the term "self-presence" is mine). But while it arises in various eras, I think it is no accident that Hornby's most extensive examples of self-presence come from the twentieth century: on the one hand, the technique extends the principle of internal relations yet one step further, in a manner consistent with the further sociological specialization and compartmentalization of artists and intellectuals, their concomitant instigation of competing avant-gardes, and the general acceptance of perception as the criterion of reality (most commonly in its subjective form); on the other hand, the increasingly obvious role of large sociopolitical forces in everyday life has attuned a segment of that group to questions of social and artistic process, which they incorporate into their own art.

Modern forms of self-presence once again make theatrical performance a method of doing agency. However, there are three basic ways in which theatre can refer to its own moment of performance, corresponding to its ontological levels and involving distinctive concepts of agency. The first refers to the theatre as an institution, a corporate agent possessing particular goals, strategies, resources and roles. Characters may refer to the conventions of theatrical performance, whether as drama or as professional activity, perhaps showing the events on stage to be mere dramatic illusions (that is, they have only a virtual existence), or conversely, maybe dramatizing the theatrical metaphor that all the world's a stage. This approach is a kind of offshoot from nineteenth-century plays-within-plays focusing on actors and dramatic art. It appears in Ibsen's *Peer Gynt*, when a character reassures the ne'er-do-well that he needn't worry since nobody ever dies in the middle of the last act (a moment which revives the theatrical gesture toward the author). The moments in Beckett's *Waiting for Godot* when characters appear to see the audience (such as "that bog," 10) or acknowledge the theatrical space ("End of the corridor, on the left," 24) fall into this category. Another example is Thornton Wilder's *Our Town*, with its stage manager conducting the theatrical representation of small-town scenes. Self-presence of this sort serves as a sort of knowing wink to the audience, ensuring its complicity.[16] It is essentially a further development of "professionalistic" metatheatricality.

An extreme instance of this first approach, bridging toward the second, occurs in Pirandello's "trilogy of theatre in theatre," especially *Six Characters*. In these plays, if the events in the inner play are mere dramatic illusions, so are those in the outer play and potentially in everyday life as well, and members of the audience are scarcely more substantial than characters who "literally" come to life in order to play out their drama. Identities are unstuck, but they are reduced to theatrical types and (melo)dramatic stereotypes, not dispersed altogether.

In its anthropocentrism, its focus upon perceptions and on regularities of behavior, and in other ways, "professionalistic" theatrical self-presence is fundamentally positivistic (even if the play as a whole isn't). Not surprisingly, the two other approaches have ties to forms of antipositivism. The second form of self-presence focuses on performance as discursive, a system of signs and representations referring in the end only to other signs and representations which (according to this view) constitute social life in an unending process of semiosis, without an underlying reality. Self-reference here is less a technique than a principle, an inevitability. Agency is dispersed into discourse: it is a cipher produced by and caught within discourse's self-weaving webs. This is the approach adopted in postmodernism, vividly exemplified by the music video of Björk's "Bachelorette," a *tour de force* of discursive self-presence in which Björk's character, digging in a forest, finds a blank book which begins to write itself, creating a narrative which she enacts as she reads. The book functions as a script, which Björk's character performs not just in the theatre of life, but when the book is turned into a Broadway show in which she performs, in theatrical restagings of those same events—unlike the traditional play-within-a-play, discursive self-presence incorporates itself not just generically, but *literally* (that is, as a reiteration or quotation), so that the inner play is largely identical to the outer play. In the "Bachelorette" video, when the recursive process reaches the point of theatre-within-theatre-within-theatre (within video), the performative cycle begins to unravel: the book erases itself while the inner theatres are consumed by the sinuous, mute greenery from which the entire sequence began, and just at the moment when, forced onward by its incessant discursive self-production, the performance would enter a still further level of self-reflexiveness, it crumbles into vegetation and in a sense (re)turns itself into a natural state.[17]

The sheer literalness of discursive self-presence can take the opposite path, not toward infinite recursions, but toward total reduction into the actors' and audience's consciousness of performance. Handke uses this tactic in *Offending the Audience*. The multiple layers of theatrical performance seem (but only seem) to collapse into present speech acts, as the speakers alternately characterize, curse, and compliment their audience. This theatrical implosion into what is actually present at the moment of performance might, aesthetically speaking, be called a style of ultra-naturalism.

Fascinating and suggestive as such performances are, discursive self-presence (like agential self-presence) treats agency as involving only one ontological level. Much more radically, however, theatrical self-presence can occur *performatively*, so that the production of meaningful effects refers to and hence reveals the production of meaningful effects (cf. Hornby 116). In this performance strategy, theatre refers to itself not so much as an agent or a discourse, but as a productive structure. More exactly, theatre's structure/agent/discourse ontology refers to and reveals itself as a structure/agent/discourse ontology, and it does so primarily through the activity of the actors and director (and need not conduct theatrical self-reference via the characters at all). The difference here is subtle but crucial: the performance refers to the theatre/drama/script structure of theatrical performance not institutionally—treating theatre as one agent among many—but *ontologically*, as a model of social agency itself. Agents are understood as being both distinct from and conditioned by preexisting structures and discourses, which then are reproduced and/or transformed as the (generally unintended) outcomes of agents' intentional and embodied activities. This form of self-presence expands the critical potential inherent in theatrical reflexiveness. Theatre becomes a mode of self-reflexivity not just about theatre, but about the very structure of society, suggesting its performative, transformative, and hence transformable nature.

The best-known proponent of self-referential metatheatricality of this type is Brecht. Reflexivity regarding social structures is the aim of his most crucial performance strategies, particularly estrangement and distanciated acting. The latter, for example, concerns the need to keep the actor from "disappearing" into the character, so that real agents in theatrical performance are not entirely displaced and hidden by virtual agents. Such distanciation contrasts with acting styles which aim for the disappearance of the actor within the character, the real agent within the virtual agent; a disappearance that is tantamount philosophically to the collapse of ontological strata into a single plane of perception. By keeping both sorts of agents evident, Brecht would reveal theatre's doubled structure/agent/discourse ontology. Since actors are not the only agents involved in theatrical performance, exposing theatre's structure/agent/discourse ontology exposes the role of the audience in that performance, inviting self-reflexivity on its part. Probably the most thorough-going effort along these lines remains Peter Weiss's *Marat/Sade*, which conjoins Brechtian self-referentiality with a play-within-a-play.

But Weiss's play also suggests the fragility of this strategy, which remains within the cultural and political structures of aesthetic autonomy and professionalism. The strategy unavoidably depends on voluntarist and individualist commitments by the performers (and the characters-as-performers, for the play-within) and by the audience, which ultimately are coordinated hierarchically in accordance with the script and an authorial or directorial intention. Should any of these commitments not be secured, the strategy generally fails.

Another form of theatre founded on roughly the same concept of agency removes this concern by abandoning the institution of professionalistic performance. In particular, it shatters the social and architectural division between actor and audience, turning all participants into "spect-actors" who may watch a scene and then assume a role within it, altering that character's actions. That is the basic approach of Boal's forum theatre, and of a whole strand of community-based performance in which a group of people utilize theatre directly as a way to reflect and potentially act upon situations in their own lives. The process fosters a dialogic reintegration of intellectual producers and recipients (and implicitly or explicitly, of mental and manual labor) and a reintegration of art with society, and so community-based performance constitutes a kind of anti-avant-garde.[18] In this type of performance, the inner play is a brief, "fictive" structure/agent/discourse ontology referring to the real structure in which the participants find themselves. Such performance involves self-presence in the sense that the participants reflect on their performances, but with an eye for its reflexion into performance in everyday life rather than professionalistic issues of doing theatre. It is self-referent insofar as it implicitly raises the question of the conditions and possibilities of enactment; it may even be said to position the real world as its outer stage. Interestingly, the metatheatrical moment I noted in the

York Cycle seems to be a similar instance of self-presence, albeit to religious rather than political ends.

The distinctions among the three modes of theatrical self-presence parallel the three categories of metatheatricality that I identified previously: structural, such as plays-within-plays; agential, involving actors, audiences, and the like among the characters; and discursive, in which characters talk about theatre. That differentiation too was established on ontological grounds. The difference between the two sets is ontological as well: it arises from the fact that theatrical performance doubles and "shifts" social ontology. As we saw, the shift involves the creation of virtual structures, agents, and discourses in contrast to the real ones. The distinction between the two classes of metatheatricality follows suit. The set I discussed earlier, which is "allotropic" since it refers to or presents theatricality other than itself, consists of reflexivity about theatre's virtual dimension; the forms of self-presence I have just described are "autotropic" because the performance refers to its own real structures, agents and discourses.

As did the play-within-a-play during the Renaissance, the various forms of theatrical self-presence focus upon a problem or fracture within knowledge (that is, within the dominant discursive order), and a need for a new order that can overcome that absence. Though space allows only a brief discussion, the basic contours of each conflict are clear.[19] The crisis during the Renaissance had as its background the late medieval discourse of patterning and similitudes (figural thinking) interpretable only by infusing any given discursive product with references to words and things outside it. This discursive order elaborated an ontology in the form of theocentrism and idealist (often mystical) metaphysics. In the Renaissance, against the revelation of truth through divine correspondences, there arose the possibility of human discovery of hidden truths via instrumental controls upon the empirical realm. The conflict between the two orders hinged on the nature and role of perception. During the struggle to make knowledge literally come to its senses, performance strategies sought the exposure of plots and the disclosure of mistaken identities, the shimmering peek-a-boo between putting on and pulling off masks and disguises, the play-within-a-play as a stratagem to release knowledge in its coy absence. In the end, the similitudes gave way to verisimilitude, external to internal relations, ontology to epistemology. The ultimate outcome of the struggle was a discourse of experimentalism and psychological verity in which, as Descartes asserted, only what was absolutely certain could be accepted as true. The different candidates for such certainty—empirical sense data, innate ideas, even sign systems—all circulated around one or another meaning of "perception." Perception became the litmus test of existence; at the most extreme, it was existence itself: *cogito ergo sum.*

In the twentieth century, the tables turned: the empirical realm was assumed, and the problem became the very relation between the *cogito* and the *sum*—that is, the relation not between perceptible appearance and reality, but between thought and material being. Such fractures in the epistemic legacy are everywhere. Positivism finds itself schizophrenically viewing agency as accountable for everything and/or capable of nothing; it makes experimentation the groundwork of science, yet it cannot adequately theorize the significance, implications or even intelligibility of that practice; despite according pride of place to causation, its notion of causality in fact treats "laws of nature" as though nature behaves according to laws of logic; despite seeming to insist adamantly on the existence of a reality outside the mind, it persistently conflates being with knowledge of being; and it surreptitiously generates a mitosis between itself and various subjectivisms, relativisms, idealisms and romanticisms which believe themselves to be its mortal enemy when in truth they are but its mirror images, its *doppelgängers*, its negatives. All of these cracks stem from a single fault line: the specter haunting epistemology is ontology.

Confronted by the patent inadequacy of positivism, the efforts to supplant it again revolve around problems of knowledge—this time, the relation between knowledge and existence, and the conditions of knowledge's possibility. That entails reflexivity within knowledge itself. We have seen the three major options within theatre. One approach, encompassing both the infinite regress of performance containing itself and its self-deconstruction, coils knowledge into its own circle so that it cannot escape, like a Möbius strip ever discovering itself on the other side of itself as it runs away toward itself: being collapses into knowledge of being. Other strategies, as in the Handke example, embark on the degree zero of performance that delimits knowledge into present actualities: the converse of the former approach, knowledge is compulsively determined by being.[20] In the final analysis, these approaches share empiricism's anthropocentric assumption that "Human discourse...is the measure of reality" (Reiss, *Discourse of Modernism* 362). Discourse captures the spectators within itself, because—or so that—it and they have noplace else to go, and all we can know is the discourse we already have.

But these are not the only alternatives to empiricism: the order of perception may be sundered by the *transformative process* through which we come to understand something. For the Brechtian actor and spectator, and still further, for the spect-actors of forum theatre, knowledge is never a given; it is a hard-won product that emerges through human efforts upon a world that resists the mind. This can only occur, however, if a stratified ontology is acknowledged as the condition on which knowledge has any possibility of emergence. Thought and being, epistemology and ontology, must be distinct, non-identical, irreducible. Knowledge is unable to provide its own truth through purely internal relations; it is fallible, contingent, tentative. It is a question mark in dialogue with existence.

For all these differences, however, the new self-referential performance strategies do have a commonality. Where the post-Renaissance era replaced medieval similitudes with verisimilitude, the recent modes of performance produce not verisimilitude, but rather perform homological *models* of existence. Endless self-reference, for example, enacts a discursivized universe. Moreover, the three models point to *social* elements (discourses, structures) as the cornerstones of society's existence and the touchstones for interpretation. We might describe these performance strategies as social modeling of societal models. But whereas Brecht and Boal are cognizant of their performative modeling and its assumptions and implications, postmodernist performance strategies can coherently sustain neither the significance nor the relevance of the modeling relations they embody, for a model (a Peircean icon) is necessarily a model of something else, a something else that motivates the model and enables us to understand things outside discourse. In other words, those strategies secrete an implicit ontology even if they explicitly repudiate any such thing. These latter modes of performance are ensnared in a performative contradiction.[21]

A final point about (meta)theatricality is spotlighted by the dynamics of community-based performance. As I observed earlier, agents are the central element of social ontology: nothing happens without their activity. Consequently the three levels of social ontology ceaselessly interact as people reproduce and transform them. The same holds true in theatrical performance: within an institution that forms a model of social agency, the theatrical, dramatic and scriptive levels necessarily interact with each other. The play-within-the-play as an agent's stratagem makes this especially clear, for it is crucial that the inner play elicits a response from the inner audience. Plays using that device emphasize the inner audience's behavior (as in *Hamlet*) or even their misbehavior (as in Jonson's *The Staple of News*). Likewise community-based performance rejects the notion of the audience as passive consumers, and instead seeks to recognize—indeed, maximize—their agency. In other words, it addresses the inner audience not solely as part of a virtual (theatrical) structure, the "conscious social structure" that I described before, but as agents.

It hardly seems coincidental that Brecht obtained some of his ideas from Piscator's work with motion pictures, wrote radio plays, and occasionally performed his own poetry; nor that Boal made some of his crucial innovations in the course of his involvement in a literacy campaign, that is, by working with modern oral cultures, and that his projects tend to deemphasize playtexts. It appears that the rise of new modes of communication, the reappropriation of older modes, and aspects of class-based political activism are involved in these theatrical innovations. How the new modes of communication may affect theatre is impossible to say, since so much will depend upon how we use and organize them. But in whatever way it develops, theatrical performance will continue to embody concepts of agency, and so to enact for society theories of society itself.

CONCLUSION

NEW MEDIA, OLD PROBLEMS

1

WE ARE NOW IN THE MIDST OF ANOTHER TRANSFORMATION IN communication structures. Or rather, a lengthy series of transformations. From radio in the late nineteenth century to social networking in the twenty-first, innovations in electronic means of communication have been relentless. Without question, they have brought significant social and cultural changes. Has the era of print culture ended—have we now entered the age of electronic culture?

I think the answer is, "Not yet." Print culture fully came into its own around a century and a half after the invention of the printing press, and there is no inherent reason electronic culture should mature far sooner (nor have we any idea what its maturity might look like). Although there is plenty of turmoil, one cannot assume that fundamental discursive changes will be the result. As I observed earlier, the sheer preponderance of a particular mode of communication has no obvious or inevitable bearing on its cultural role; otherwise we would still be living in an oral culture, although one with some textual options and accessories. In addition, people make choices which create unintended and unpredictable consequences. Nobody forced the Phoenicians to develop an alphabet, but once they did, it provided the basis for a variety of cultural possibilities and technical innovations that could scarcely be imagined three thousand years ago. We can't predict what innovations will arrive next, still less how any means of communication will be used.

That said, some of the anxieties around electronic media echo previous transformations in the communication framework (orality to literacy, manuscript to print). Postmodernist doubts and attacks on the very legitimacy of claiming knowledge recall the problematization of knowledge during the Renaissance. Once more we hear suspicion about the new medium's viability as a bearer of truth, and purist claims about the superiority of the old modes and the losses brought by the new. The privileging of speech (the living voice) over writing (the dead record of voice) expressed such anxiety in the past, and something very like it appears when performance theory privileges theatre (live performance) over film and television (recorded performance).

In *Liveness*, one of the most significant recent books on communication and performance, Philip Auslander rightly challenges the idea that "liveness" can really distinguish types of performance in a mediatized culture. Auslander thoroughly buries the advocates of liveness, and it is amusing that they take what for centuries writers and directors have sought to limit and control—straying from the text, the possibility of accidents, and improvisation generally—and turn it into the essence of theatre. But both he and the liveness advocates are wrestling with a difficult issue that arises from what may be an unprecedented situation in theatre history. Film, television and computers introduced forms of dramatic presentation that have much in common with theatre, but aren't exactly theatre. The problem is how to define their difference. Commonsense answers like "liveness" turn out in Auslander's hands to be not as viable as they appear; but neither is his rejoinder. A critique of his arguments will bear a more fruitful solution.

Auslander aims to unravel the logic of his targets, specifically the binary opposition between theatrical performance as live and evanescent, versus film and television as recorded and permanent. For example, in his crucial (but technologically deterministic) discussion of the constantly disappearing images scanned and then re-scanned onto a TV screen, he concludes, "the televisual image is not only a reproduction or repetition of a performance, but a performance in itself.... Both live performance and the performance of mediatization are predicated on disappearance" (*Liveness* 49, 50). Likewise, in "Humanoid Boogie," an article on robotic performance, Auslander criticizes the contrast between human and mechanical performance due to the requirement of routinized, exact replication: "[B]ecause the very concepts of 'performance' and 'performer' often entail the ability to reproduce the same effects on demand, they implicitly blur the distinctions between human beings and machines" (94). To be sure, Auslander does not contend that there are no differences whatsoever between theatre and television or between humans and machines: his purpose is to undercut these particular oppositions as workable foundations for performance theory.

However, all sorts of oppositions can be troubled, or troubled in different ways. For example, precisely what technologies count as means of recording? Auslander discounts writing as a form of recording: "Scripts are blueprints for performances, not recordings of them," he writes. "Written descriptions... are not direct transcriptions through which we can access the performance itself, as aural and visual recording media are." Following Roland Barthes's distinction between drawing and photography, Auslander argues that "whereas drawings, like writing, transforms performance, audio-visual technologies, like photography, record it" (*Liveness* 58).

A startling contrast! No matter how well achieved, recording necessarily transforms experience of performance, because it must frame it and force the viewer's attention in ways not possible in live performance. In a comment buried in a footnote, Auslander acknowledges as much; but nevertheless he asserts that recording media provide a special kind of access, on the grounds that unlike writing, "[electronic] recording media may be used to capture performance in real time" (*Liveness* 58n39). Actually, however, writing (particularly shorthand) *can* capture in real time. Some Renaissance scripts may have been transcribed from performance. Moreover, during several eras, such as the eighteenth century, most people read scripts in order to recall performances they had already attended. In other words, the script enabled them to "play back" the performance in their minds.[1] If writing can indeed be a recording/playback technology, then Auslander's argument that "live performance" as a concept could only arise with the advent of electronic recording collapses (*Liveness* 58–63). Finally, according to Auslander, "the televisual image is... a performance in itself" (*Liveness* 49); but in that case a video on a shelf is a blueprint for performance just as a script is—and cannot function any other way.

Auslander's challenge in "Humanoid Boogie" to the human/mechanical opposition sustains one of the very assumptions he thinks he critiques. He argues that while on the one hand robots do not possess humans' interpretive skills, on the other hand the history of the performing arts "yields examples in which human performers have been called upon to exercise their technical skills but not their interpretive skills" (91). Actors are expected to reproduce the same performance as exactly as possible night after night; orchestra musicians must play accurately and precisely according to the conductor's interpretation of the score, a situation in which the performers are "asked to cede a substantial part of their agency to someone else" (92). Consequently performance normally "blur[s] the distinctions between human beings and machines" (94). As Auslander points out, "the fact that much of the actual performing in conventional, Western genres is highly routine and 'machined' is often overlooked in favor of the individualistic, interpretive aspects of performance" (93).

The question concerns how we understand agency and creativity. Curiously, however, Auslander does nothing to challenge the individualistic nature of the human/machine distinction. On the contrary, he views the demands placed on the performer's technical skills as loss of agency. The agency in question is strictly individual: he never considers the possibility of collective effort through organized group (corporate) agency. Yet that is the norm: performance is ordinarily by a group. The larger the group, the more the group depends on each performer pulling her weight reliably, which allows every other performer to play their part as well; in most performing arts, when one performer upstages the others, usually the work as a whole suffers. For Auslander, one either possesses individual agency in art, or cedes agency and becomes machine-like. In reality the chief alternative to individual agency is to participate in a larger form of agency, so that ensemble performance becomes part of the artistry itself.

The upshot is that neither the oppositions that Auslander critiques nor his deconstructions of them are particularly useful in understanding theatre and how it differs from mediatized drama. They fail principally because of their constricted ontologies. In *Liveness* Auslander declares his opposition to ontology in a section that he bluntly titles "Against ontology." In doing so, he echoes a hostility to ontology that has long been a hallmark of both positivism and postmodernism.

But ontological grounds are exactly where the differences between theatre and mediatized drama lie. However, the ontological difference is not the polarity of live versus recorded. The difference is located in social ontology. Theatrical performance doubles the social ontology of structures, agents, and discourses through its theatrical, dramatic and scriptive levels. Due to that doubling, theatrical performance is a model of social ontology itself. We can compare other types of performance against that ontology.

Clearly mediatized performance possesses the "virtual" social ontology, that is, the theatrical, dramatic and scriptive levels: the film is projected in a movie theatre, the video is played in spaces like living rooms on a "home theatre"; mediatized performance has drama and characters (virtual agents); and it produces the virtual agency according to a script or scenario. Film and video are of course viewed within a real social structure, and they invoke numerous real discourses. But when they're being viewed, they lack real agents—embodied and intentional (reflexive) beings. It makes a difference that there's a physical body on stage, with a mind that is actively interpreting the script in order to perform it (see also Carroll 113–14). It also makes a difference that there is a real, physical audience, for the audience's own agency influences both the actors' performance and the audience's experience. The performer's interpretive activity includes her responses to the audience's responses. If real agents are present—able to interact, whether or not they actually do so in any obvious way—social ontology is doubled. Mediatized performance, lacking real agents, does not double social ontology.

For Auslander, "*reproduction* (recording) is the key issue" in the contrast between live and mediated performance (*Liveness* 57, his emphasis).

True, only recording technologies could enable an audience to watch a performance where, instead of seeing live actors (real agents), they saw only virtual agents, via the traces the actors left on film stock, magnetic tape or digital memory. But recording technology doesn't tell the whole story. For that one must look to what defines an activity as a performance, which resides in ontology. As far as the ontology of performance is concerned, if there is no possibility of interaction, it doesn't matter whether an image on a TV screen is recorded or live: mediatized performance presents virtual agents but not real agents, whereas theatrical performance has both. Mediatized performance is not theatre, even when performed live. On the other hand, the use of media doesn't necessarily make an event *not* theatre. Auslander mistakes this as well: "The spectator sitting in the back rows of a Rolling Stones or Bruce Springsteen concert or even a Bill Cosby stand-up comedy performance, is present at a live performance, but hardly participates in it as such since his/her main experience of the performance is to read it off a video monitor" (*Liveness* 25). But if the same person were watching through opera glasses, one would say nothing of the sort. Rather than be entranced by the technology, we should let social ontology be the guide. Spectators attend a show to be with others, perhaps including the performers themselves. But if they prefer to watch video monitors rather than the stage, they may be reflecting TV's social importance, or maybe they're just being practical. They are not necessarily establishing a different social ontology.

I do not want to exaggerate the implications of theatre's double social ontology. I would love to say that it makes theatre inherently subversive or radical, but the idea withstands neither historical nor philosophical scrutiny. Theatre has the deepest roots into social dynamics of any art, but that cuts two ways: it is also highly subject to economic, political, and ideological limitations and controls. The most one can argue is that its ontological doubling opens up certain possibilities for social critique in a performative mode which can cast light on social structures in ways that draw upon theatre's peculiarly social nature. These possibilities are unavailable to other sorts of performance—but the various types of mediatized performance (and for that matter, all arts) have their own possibilities for critique. As I observed in my discussion of Brecht and Boal, it is decidedly contingent whether those possibilities are ever realized. There are intrinsic political possibilities, but no ineluctable political effects.

Recording is important because mass (re)production for consumers is the basis for the entertainment industry's existence. Mass culture in turn creates the conditions in which, as Auslander observes, live music performances now imitate their recorded performance, in particular their music videos (*Liveness* 97–105). These are crucial matters for any analysis of contemporary culture. However, they concern the commodification of cultural creations, not the nature of mediatized performance as such.

Auslander's arguments for the primacy of the mediatized performance and for the mass production of theatre both rely upon the logic of imitation: the rock band's touring show tries to copy its music videos, the shows replicated from city to city all seek similarity, and Auslander describes play franchises as "mass production" by analogy to the large-scale duplication and distribution of recordings. Noël Carroll, commenting on this aspect of Auslander's argument, rightly points out that "these perceptual and functional congruencies are not ontologically bedrock" (118). Auslander is solely concerned with the ontology of perception. In terms of social ontology, imitative activities pertain to individual and corporate agents (such as consumers and media corporations) and how they behave. The underlying social structures are not part of his analysis—he destratifies social ontology.

The ontological distinction between theatrical performance and mediatized performance is not a polar opposition. On the contrary, it illuminates the "family resemblance" between these two modes of performance. They share many ontological features (most importantly, the dramatic level), even though they don't share all. There are several other family members. Puppetry is one: the puppet functions as a virtual agent, but its body and seeming intentionality substitute for those usually provided by a real agent (an actor). One might call it a "transferred" virtual agent (Goodall; see also Auslander, "Humanoid Boogie" 90).

Similarly, online roleplay games are essentially improvisational, participatory theatre performances using digital puppets. Players must (well, should) carefully distinguish between ontological levels. The scriptive level consists of a rough and ever-emergent storyline, driven forward by the players' chat and "emotes" (basically stage directions).[2] Each player creates one or more characters—virtual agents, in the computerized sense. But occasionally players have to interact at the real, theatrical level out of character, in order to (say) agree upon an attack or alert others to their absence while taking a phone call.

Another class of performance related to theatre is performance art, some types of which (in a sort of inversion of mediatized performance) present real agents but not virtual agents. For example, "Happenings" specifically avoid fictional frames and signs of signs. Chris Burden's *Shoot* (in which he was shot in the arm) is another performance without fictionality.

Ontologically, dance is similar to theatre in several ways, although its primary expressive register is the dancer's body, not language. Interestingly, it seems to have something akin to theatre's ability to focus on different ontological levels. It can emphasize virtual agency, such as in the narratives of classical ballet or in the appearances by spirits or ancestors in tribal dances.

It can limit fictionality and concentrate on agents' interactions through social dance. And it can strive to pare dance down to embodiment itself, as seen for instance in abstract dance and action dance. True, paring dance down to sheer embodiment is technically impossible, because movement naturally stimulates some degree of metaphoric thought in the audience (a neural fact), but this is scarcely a shortcoming; it probably contributes to the fluid way dance in general shifts between the ontological levels. The abstractness involved may even be a sort of metadiscourse.

Rather than construing performance genres as sharply categorical, an ontological analysis highlights areas of similarity as well as difference. However, by identifying the key distinction between theatre and other types of performance as their treatment of embodied intentional agency (whether real or virtual), it may seem that I'm remaining at the level of agents just as I say Auslander does. The difference is that in the critical realist view, agents do not simply interact, but rather interact under the conditions imposed by preexisting structures and discourses; and likewise, their activities not only affect each other (and themselves) as agents, but in the case of real agents, may also reproduce and transform those conditions. Hence when I speak of the presence of real agents in theatrical performance and their absence in mediatized performance, their presence or absence occurs within the entire totality of ontological strata, both real and virtual.

2

During my critique of Auslander's claim that musicians lose agency by playing in an orchestra, I said that the issue concerns how we understand agency and artistry. In this book I have paid considerable attention to agency, but only a little to matters of artistry. My principal goal has been to develop a historical argument about the relationship between theatre and communication practices; an extended discussion of aesthetics would require more space than I have available, and probably make the book ungainly. Even so, my argument does directly address one major topic in aesthetics by historicizing genres, not only in the sense of locating them within specific periods, places and cultures, but also by showing how they emerge in their particularity from the embodied character of communication, and theorizing communication as an underlying (and changing) social structure. Consequently the argument also illuminates aspects of how audiences understand and respond to theatre performances. However, I have restricted myself to only modest claims about my theory's ability to interpret individual plays and performances or even to define the range of viable interpretations; and for present purposes, I have steered clear of questions about aesthetic value judgments and most other topics in aesthetics. That is not to rule such matters out of court: the limits of my present argument are not the limits of its explanatory and interpretive possibilities, much less the limits of critical realism. Aesthetics has barely been broached within critical realism; but one does have to start somewhere.

I will however discuss audience experience a little more here, in terms of its connections to the ontologies of society and theatre. Since the playgoing experience is situated within society's structure/agent/discourse ontology, the same set of levels are present. Or rather, they're present twice, since theatre's ontological doubling of social ontology necessarily affects audience experience.

Structurally, the primary material element in audience experience is naturally the body. There is no question of the importance of direct and (more often) indirect embodied experiences in the theatre. Stage experiences run the gamut from passionate embraces to horrifying deaths, from graceful dexterity to pratfalls, from sexy looks to annoying voice, from marvelous special effects to imagined scenery, from the undercurrents of music to the smell of cigarettes. If it is true that "mirror neurons" enact people's activities in the observer's brain, so that when someone dances on stage, in a sense the spectator dances too, then the audience's indirect embodied experience is probably broader and deeper than one might have ever suspected. That would be one reason why people might flinch when a character is stabbed, or feel tears well up when a character is weeping. But it is not some Pavlovian response: plenty of counterforces can affect the spectator's reaction, such as their personal attitude or opinion, the actors' skills (or lack of them), and the dramatic genre. Audiences are quite capable of responding to a character's tearful wailing with amusement. (One thinks of Oscar Wilde's catty remark about a Dickens novel: "One must have a heart of stone to read the death of Little Nell without laughing.")

Social structures aren't simply relationships with material entities, although they entail them; economic, gender and communication structures are some of the most obvious ones shaping audience experience. Within theatrical performance itself, the principal structure is the playing space, including the organization of the seating or viewing area. The physical relationship between the audience area and the stage, and the organization of the audience area itself, can have significant effects on the audience's experience. The arrangements take physical form, but as with any structure they also have a social content: the separation of social classes in eighteenth-century theatres into pit, box and galleries entailed a different dynamic within the audience than the seemingly democratic arrangements of the subsequent era (setting aside the impact of seat prices), and that dynamic in turn affects the stage/audience relationship. Numerous performances during the second half of the twentieth century explored or exploited the effects of "democratic" and immersive seating arrangements, such as in Happenings, environmental seating, flexible stages and the revival of outdoor theatre. The physical arrangements are images—icons—of basic social relationships (typically economic or gender relations), and sometimes also of relationships with the natural world. Equally important is whether the audience watches the show in darkness or in light: observing other audience members is part of the theatre experience as well. It can even be the best part.

The social aspects of the performance space, while structural in terms of theatre's ontology, are agential in terms of general social ontology: the theatrical level is what I've called a "virtual" social structure. The fundamentally agential nature of the theatrical level is highlighted not only by intra-audience experience, but also by audiences' knowledge of and response to the performers in a show. Knowledge about the actors' personal lives was always a particularly significant part of theatre, but knowledge about actors' professional lives (such as the roles they've played before) is relevant as well. One can scarcely ignore such dynamics when considering what makes for an audience's experience, particular since they influence casting choices.

Likewise, ontological duality is central to the audience's involvement with characters' actions and circumstances. Although audiences know full well that characters are only (ontologically discursive) virtual agents, not actual ones, they often respond to the character in certain respects the way they would a person. The specific respects probably vary sociohistorically: it seems unlikely that modern responses to, say, Pilate in the York Cycle are quite like medieval spectators', as we tend to look for psychological motivations whereas they may have been more interested in the character's moral relationship with God; since the concepts of agency and selfhood through which we interpret characters' actions change, so too must audience involvement with the characters. On the other hand, while forms of agency change historically, many aspects of personhood do not. *Pace* relativist claims that cultures live in different universes, people do in fact have most things in common, including embodiment, general emotional spectrum, intellectual capacities, emotional ties, and a sense of self.

Thus regardless of the concepts of agency at work, advisory and empathic projections of the self onto the characters are probably always part of the audience's experience. As explained in chapter 3, advisory projection has the form, "If I were you, I'd do X" (or related expressions), whereas "I see why you feel that way" is an example of empathic projection. These projections can be shaped (or manipulated) by the performance, as McConachie's analysis of *A Hatful of Rain* shows. Although a play can call upon a single type of projection, I suspect that often the most compelling performances evoke both, pulling the audience first this way, then that, or even the two simultaneously. One can feel Romeo's love for Juliet and also want to yell at him to get out of her bedroom before all hell breaks loose, or laugh at Malvolio's ridiculous efforts to romance Olivia while feeling sorry for him because he's the butt of a cruel joke. Advisory and empathic projections are social relationships at the agential (interpersonal) level, which is why they can become deeply emotional or judgmental even though the audience is projecting onto virtual agents, not actual ones. Characters are indexes of various social and cultural positions, and our projections onto them are effectively indexes of our own.

The audience's advisory and empathic projections are social relationships in another sense too: theatrical performance is not self-contained, it is dialogic—it is a communication practice, and involves the audience as interlocutors. That is intrinsic to the ontological requirement that theatre (in contrast to, say, film) have real agents on stage. In chapter 3 I discussed how journalistic print culture formed communities, but the basic principle holds for any sort of communication: it builds affiliations among people, even abstract affiliations such as the imagined community of nationhood. It can also determine disaffiliations, the people one "won't talk with." These affiliations and disaffiliations contribute to the formation of social identities. And although to an important extent affiliations and disaffiliations are governed by structural constraints and enablements, they also rely on shared conceptions of self and shared meanings, which may override structural factors. The affiliations and disaffiliations that mark identity are *felt*.

Theatre, as a genre of communication, works upon people's feelings of affiliation and disaffiliation. The audience forms feelings of affiliation and disaffiliation not only with characters, but also with the characters' dramatic and environmental circumstances, and their relationship to the entire world. Affiliation does not require spectators to identify with any of the characters (though they may), but only to recognize and feel some types of commonality with them; disaffiliation of course does the opposite. There's no special *theatrical* reason why plays should aim for one rather than the other, although there may be other reasons. We can enjoy either. In doing so, however, we establish a "frontal" identity vis-à-vis the drama: we are defined by how we respond to the staged events. Moreover, usually audiences consist not of solitary individuals, but a group, and its members respond to the performance partly also in relationships of affiliation and disaffiliation with each other, producing a "lateral" sense of identity. The result might be one of intense community (what Victor Turner called *communitas*; 45–52), but generally it's simply one of shared experience—which might even be one of shared disappointment. Or more precisely, audiences imagine (correctly or not) that they shared an experience with others. And again, there's no reason everyone should feel they share in that experience. A lateral dimension of identity arises in any case. In short, through these feelings of affiliation and disaffiliation, audiences experience themselves as agents.

Although virtual agents homologically represent actual social agents, they are of course largely discursive constructs, since their characteristics, activities and circumstances are governed by a script (broadly defined). They and all other features of the performance are signs of signs. The signs that institute language, which forms the core of society's discursive stratum, are social conventions—in Peircean terms, symbols—and they are further structured through theatrical conventions. However, the ontological duality of theatre's scriptive level is of a different order than that of the theatrical and dramatic levels. The theatrical level represents social structures but is in fact created by agents. The dramatic level represents society's agential stratum, but it's a discursive product. The scriptive level represents the discursive level of social ontology, but in reality it's produced by... and here the parallels cease.

Or do they? The "ontological shift" that constitutes theatre enables the emergence of a governing metadiscourse that is really a metaphysics about the nature and value of relationships between people, between people and nature, between people and the divine, between the voices within their own psyches, and many other potential designations of fundamental realities in human life: in short, a meditation on agency, conducted through embodied metaphors. Such metaphysical considerations are not the preserve of serious or tragic drama alone: comedies can implicitly articulate a philosophy as well, and romances of all sorts can be joyful celebrations of life. Certainly not every play expands in this manner, not every audience member will follow where it tries to lead, and not every play that does so is a good one; but when it succeeds, theatre reaches through history to become philosophy. Although literature of every genre can entertain such ideas, what is unique to theatre is that its ontological shift involves a reflexivity that reverses what we saw in metatheatricality—by extrapolating a level of reality "below" society, theatrical performance can shift one's understanding of social ontology in a way that casts everyday life into a theatrical frame. All the world becomes a stage.

The various levels present not a set of inert elements, but rather a highly dynamic system in which the different aspects interact, perhaps one being foremost (such as, say, embodied responses in entertainment-oriented spectacles), or perhaps all of them thoroughly intertwined (for instance, Konstantin's presentation of the eponymous seagull in Chekhov's play, with its embodied, interpersonal and symbolic aspects). The doubling of social ontology is unique to theatre, and consequently so is the confluence of pleasures theatre can provide. The presence of all three types of signs—icon, index, and symbol—enriches the aesthetic possibilities of theatrical performance. Whether any particular performance fulfills these possibilities depends on a host of circumstances, but critical realism identifies the underlying structures that generate those possibilities and condition their actual realization. Although these notes scarcely exhaust the issues involved in audience response and aesthetics, they should indicate some of the starting points for a critical realist analysis.

3

Theatre began in ancient Greece, and so too did antitheatricality. Plato expelled the poets and playwrights from his utopian Republic. For centuries, Christianity, Judaism, and Islam, religions for which Scriptures were of the essence, all excoriated theatrical performance (which nevertheless occurred in some form or other, even if on the cultural periphery). Actors in particular were often condemned to society's lowest orders, not just in Europe but also throughout Asia, from India to China. If writing is so fundamental to theatre, why would antitheatricality be so prevalent? The history of antitheatricality would seem to contradict my argument that writing played a significant role in the emergence of theatre as a specific form of performance.

There are three replies to this objection. First, I have not argued that writing caused theatre in any mechanical way, but rather that it established a conceptual space which made theatre possible, intelligible and even desirable (even if not to everyone). Theatre was not, however, inevitable. Second, there is no reason to assume that writing's cultural role should enable only one outcome, theatre: on the contrary, another possible outcome of literacy is phonocentrism, which asserts that speech is authentic and imbued with presence, whereas writing is secondary and vitiated by the speaker's absence (as my discussion of the space of social performance showed). In societies riddled with divisions by social and economic class, sex, and positions within the communication framework, it would be strange if there *weren't* various and conflicting outcomes. Third, because the impact of literacy may take multiple forms depending on any number of social and historical factors, antitheatricality might result from factors not pertaining to theatre as such, and perhaps not even deriving from the relationship between orality and literacy.

As Jonas Barish's survey of antitheatricality suggests, antitheatrical critiques frequently advocate (or at least long for) a purity from the material world. Nearly all of the opponents of theatre that he surveys—Plato, the pre-Reformation Christian patriarchs, the Puritan polemicists of Elizabethan England, Jean-Jacques Rousseau, the Romantics—are philosophical idealists of one stripe or another. Not all idealists deprecate theatre, of course, but relatively few materialists do, or with anything like the fury and loathing the idealists express. For some idealists, ideality exists outside the mind (such as

Forms or God) and the material world is but its shadow, whereas others deny that anything is mind-independent and accept only the contents of the mind as truly real. But in either case idealists are in some respect irrealist. Theatre would therefore present a double threat: a threat to idealism because it is necessarily and often exuberantly committed to both the performer's and the audience's embodiment; and a threat to irrealism because, as I've suggested, theatrical performance is an embodiment of philosophical realism.[3]

Idealism is decidedly the more prominent basis of antitheatricalism. There are many roots of idealism, not all of them relevant here, but one is the social division between intellectual and manual work, which is simultaneously an economic relationship and a relationship within the communication framework. In many instances, idealism defends intellectual dominance and/or the offices of the dominant ideology, legitimizing the authority and existence of a category of educated people (priests, experts and so forth) who interpret the world for others. The economic facet concerns decision making—who sets the goals, methods, and rules under which others labor—and it soon becomes a class distinction. (Eventually distinctions arise within intellectual labor as well.) Separated from the embodiment necessitated by manual labor, intellectual labor views itself as independent of the material world. Manual labor and materiality itself become disdained. This is reflected for example in the history of writing itself: in manuscript culture, the "author" of a text usually dictated it to a scribe, whose work was often considered lowly and demeaning. The scribe's material product was honored, but as the bearer of the author's ideas.

The scorn dripped upon actors is often on the same terms. It is possible for the antitheatricalist to hold the playwright's words aloft, while vilifying the actor, who sullies with his or her very existence (the attitude in, say, Imperial Rome): from the perspective of both idealism and the upper classes' (mental labor's) superiority over manual work, this is no contradiction. At most the actor should simply speak the words, performing the manual labor of utterance. The actor is all the worse because acting exhibits the material body for the audience, particularly the passions that wrack that body. All vices and sins come trailing after, and also the seeming conflict between the antitheatricalist's claim that when the actor plays someone villainous, he or she is learning or becoming evil, but if the actor plays a saint, the performance is a fraud (see Barish 274–75). In other cases the theatre is scorned as a whole for being impure and immoral, often on the grounds that it stirs up emotions and enjoyment of display—that is, because theatricality calls upon the body and its material being. Theatre infects the audience with its sinfulness; it corrupts the author's pure poetry and the ideal of sincere speech.

The other charge most often leveled against theatre is that it trades in imitation. The issue here is more deeply philosophical. As an idealist, Plato argued that everyday objects are already imitations of ideal Forms, placing theatre's imitations *two* steps away from ideal reality. Moreover, an imitation is necessarily not the true original, and the Platonic antitheatricalist construes the fictions that theatre produces as falsehoods and lies. Here antitheatricalism attacks theatre on ontological and epistemological grounds. The philosophical basis of the assault is idealism's ontological monovalence. For Plato, only ideal Forms are real, and there can be only one modality of truth: these rule out any possible value in theatrical performance, with its irredeemable materiality and fictionality. Although Plato is realist regarding ideal Forms, he denies the reality of the perceptible world: his ontological monovalence conjoins idealism with irrealism. Ontological monovalence can undermine the ability to recognize theatre's events and agents as both actual and virtual, leading to a literal reading of performance. Jonson memorably satirized such incapacity in *Bartholomew Fair*—during a play-within-a-play no less— when his Puritan caricature accuses a puppet of moral abomination because it is an actor, and actors cross-dress, whereupon the puppet lifts its apparel to reveal its nothing. But the more typical flattened comprehension casts and castigates theatre's virtual realm as a falsehood, untrue to reality; actually it is a fiction, an ontologically different reality.

Irrealism also appears in social constructionism, according to which the things we say "exist" are actually social conventions, human constructs—a view that slides into idealism when conventions are taken as essentially discursive and thus little other than ideas. Social constructionism has an ambivalent relationship with theatre, and so a mixed record on acceptance or opposition to theatricality: its proponents may simultaneously exploit theatrical metaphors for their theories of the production of social appearances or citations without an underlying being, yet also want little or nothing to do with actual theatre (Erving Goffman and Judith Butler are notable examples[4]). Plays may adopt idealist and irrealist positions, but theatrical performance can not: ontological stratification is part of its very existence. Unlike the appearance/reality duality in Platonic idealism, in which the real must be found in intellectual abstractions, the reality behind theatrical appearance is evident in the actor's craft. Audiences *know* that the actor isn't the character, that the actor produces the character. Theatre's doubling of social ontology on the one hand produces signs of signs, the appearances which offend the Platonist as falsities empty of reality; and on the other hand prevents completely collapsing the actor into just another fictive character, which may irritate the social constructionist because theatrical performance *fails* to turn all levels of reality into empty falsities—theatre isn't devoid of underlying realities *enough*. There is a theatrical counterpart in the efforts to completely eliminate characters in hopes of achieving a de-fictionalized but nevertheless performed "encounter" between actor and audience. The strategy collapses theatre's ontology down to raw materiality, but basically to the same antitheatrical Platonic tune: rid theatre of its lies.

Philosophical idealism is not the sole source of antitheatricalism, not all philosophical idealists are foes of the actor and the stage, and not all antitheatricalists are philosophically idealist. For example, Oscar Wilde was clearly pro-theatrical but also (in his characteristically perverse way) idealist, declaring that Life imitates Art, and sounding remarkably like a social constructionist when he asserts that we perceive the world only under the terms established before us by Art (see Barish 360, and in general 350–99).

Nevertheless there is a strong connection between philosophical idealism and the antitheatrical prejudice. And idealism stems from a basic fault line, the social division between intellectual and manual work, which is partly founded and maintained through the organization of cultural production—that is, through one part of the communication framework. Thus theatre scholars must consider how we contribute to digging our own graves. We have the most to lose from philosophies that split mind and body. We delude ourselves that we understand and defend performance better when we slide into the warm, comfortable bath of relativism inherent in social constructionism. We may not be unable to undo the division between mental and manual labor, but we should be under a moral and political imperative to oppose it, starting with the philosophical idealism and irrealism that reject the fundamental nature of theatre.

4

> My aim is not to prove that I've been right, but to find out whether or not I have been.
>
> Galileo, in Bertolt Brecht, *Life of Galileo* (69)

Communication frameworks involve activities that are simultaneously sociological, conceptual and material, and because it involves embodied practices, communication produces image schemas that provide the primary conceptual structures of discourse and performance. I ground this argument philosophically in critical realism, one aspect of which is a commitment to fallibilism. Almost certainly I'm wrong about one thing or another, but that is simply the nature of the beast: although my argument meets critical realist criteria, it might nevertheless provide a faulty analysis of theatre and its history. But far from being the pursuit of absolute certainty, critical realist analyses strive for the more modest goal of a little less ignorance. For critical realism, knowledge is a continuing project, not a final statement. Nevertheless critical realism provides a stronger philosophical basis for historiography than either positivism or social constructionism.

Social constructionism construes knowledge as merely a discursive construct without real contact with the world outside discourse. Basically knowledge is a matter of opinion. But if yours is but one opinion among many, there's no particular reason to listen to you; if there is no truth, there is no worthwhile purpose to theatre scholarship. But if error is possible, then so too are knowledge and truth, without the least need for scare quotes. And theatre scholars should advocate for the possibility of knowledge, for otherwise we encourage the dismissal of our work, when we could provide true insight into society, culture and entertainment. Theatre appears to be all about producing appearances, spectacular displays, fascinating surfaces; but its real mode of existence, its performative process, is all about depth and the operation of underlying structures. Understanding theatrical performance, then, requires abandoning the generally prevailing view that experiences, surfaces, or representations occupy the whole of what exists; that "to be is to be perceived"; that all is just a show.

Like Brecht, theatre's historians and theorists cannot get along without using one or two sciences. Knowledge of society's ontological stratification into structures, agents, and discourses, knowledge about the interaction between these levels, knowledge of specific social structures, and knowledge about the embodiment of the mind provide theatre scholars with crucial tools for understanding the nature and development of performance. In particular, a critical realist analysis connects the historical transformations of theatrical practice to changes in underlying social structures. In doing so, it introduces new ways to define theatre itself. Significantly, although my analysis of social ontology is implied by social theories that are generally accepted in critical realist circles, it doesn't come from there: its roots lie in my research into the history and nature of theatre. Philosophy, history and theatre been in dialogue throughout this book, and perhaps theatre communicated a thing or two to philosophy and history.

Notes

Introduction

1. The fact that borrowed concepts can sometimes bring insights induces Mary Fulbrook to offer a more favorable assessment of eclectic approaches, which she calls "magpie theories" (47–48). Sociologically, theory "migration" is also a normal process, as marginalized thinkers within a field break out of its confines and seek fresh ideas—or greener pastures—elsewhere (Archer, *Culture and Agency* 213–26). However, their success in founding a new paradigm depends precisely on the paradigm's logical coherence and factual consistency. My point is not that intellectual borrowing is bad: it is that in the long run and often the short run, incoherence is bad.
2. E.g., McConachie, "Postpositivist," "Reading Context," and "Cultural Hegemony"; Davis, "Questions"; and Hays.

1 Philosophy, History, Theatre

1. See Foucault, e.g., *Archaeology* 31–34, 38, 46, 186–92; *Order of Things* 217–20, 236–40, 248–49; *History of Sexuality* 40–49, 97–102. See also Kuhn; Lovell 14–17; Keat and Urry 46–65.
2. See the critique in Bhaskar, *Realist Theory of Science* 16, 26, 28, 36–40, 44, 56–59, 163, 241–43; and Bhaskar, *Possibility of Naturalism* 133. The term "epistemic fallacy" is his. The ontological and epistemological privileging of observation language is also discussed by Keat and Urry 19–20, 37.
3. Some social constructionists appeal to the orthodox "Copenhagen Interpretation" of quantum mechanics to buttress their argument (e.g., Bank, "Theatre Historian" and "Time"; Kobialka, "Inbetweenness" and "Theatre History"). The "Copenhagen Interpretation" itself is scarcely unassailable, and its positivism is well recognized (e.g., A. Fine; Norris, *Quantum Theory*). For a fuller critique see Nellhaus, "Science, History, Theater."
4. On the history of the term "realism," see Williams, *Keywords*.
5. There are various terms as well as theories. "Postpositivist realism" is Mohanty's term; Lakoff and Johnson advocate "embodied realism." Lovell refers to "realism," as do Keat and Urry until their postscript, when they propose "theoretical realism." Williams (*Keywords*) suggests that realism in the sense I am using

now goes under the name of *materialism*, although this term too has an involved history and a problematic range of meanings. The various strands of contemporary realism seem to have developed largely unaware of each other; nevertheless there is broad agreement on the major tenets, if not on certain details. But some sort of adjective should qualify "realism," since positivism and platonism are realist insofar as they maintain that a world exists outside the mind.

6. Critical realism has evolved in various ways. It began as a philosophy concerning the natural sciences, and soon expanded to cover the social sciences. In 1993 Bhaskar introduced dialectics into critical realism, which proved somewhat controversial, and not all critical realists accepted these ideas (I do). In 2000 his thinking took a spiritual turn, but neither I nor many other critical realists have followed.

7. Bhaskar, *Possibility of Naturalism* 35, 81–83, 90–97; Bhaskar, *Dialectic* 51–52, 173–77, 276–79; Groff 123–31. I think the intended sense of Bhaskar's term "monitoring" is "checking and being aware of," not "scrutiny" or "surveillance."

8. Harré 28, 34–60, 260 (quoting 28 and 35); and see Keat and Urry 32–36; Bhaskar, *Realist Theory of Science* 161–63, 166–68, 194; and Papin.

9. Toulmin provides a historical critique of post-Renaissance thought in terms of its dedication to certainty, systematicity and clean-slate theories of knowledge.

10. The ability to predict was never a good criterion of science anyway. Plenty of sciences do not aim to predict, have no recourse to experimentation and instead focus on explanation, such as evolutionary biology, physiology, anthropology, etc.

11. Bhaskar, *Realist Theory of Science* 16–17, 43, 185–87, 195–99, 249–50; Bhaskar, *Possibility of Naturalism* 21, 57–58; Mohanty 214–25.

12. For a somewhat more detailed analysis, see Nellhaus, "Signs."

13. I have adopted the standard depiction of the Peircean sign, which arranges the elements differently from Bhaskar's triangle.

14. All references to Peirce's *Collected Papers* will be by volume and paragraph number.

15. Peirce identified ten major classes of signs, and occasionally indicated that there are as many as sixty-six, but here the three basic types suffice (as in fact they usually did for Peirce).

16. Peirce, *Collected Papers* 2.292, 4.536, 5.473–93; Bourdieu 468; and see De Lauretis, *Alice Doesn't* 175, 178–79, and De Lauretis, *Technologies of Gender* 39–42.

17. Peirce, *Collected Papers* 4.6, 4.551, 5.354, 5.546; Voloshinov 29, 37–39. Voloshinov may in fact have been Mikhail Bakhtin; at the least, he was a member of Bakhtin's circle. On the compatibility of Voloshinov's (or Bakhtin's) analysis with critical realism, see Bernard-Donals.

18. Cf. Rayner's phenomenological analysis of the discursive, material, and performative dimensions of practice.

19. On the York Cycle, see Twycross, "Places"; Dorrell; Johnston, "York Cycle"; Beadle, *York Plays* 19–39; and Stevens 17, 50–62. On forms of explanation,

see McLennan 58–65; Bhaskar, *Scientific Realism* 131–32, 142–53; Bhaskar, *Possibility of Naturalism* 46, 85, 90–97, 123, 154; Harré 260–61. For fuller analyses of the modes of explanation, see Nellhaus, "Science, History, Theater" and "Signs."

20. Hypothetically, I touch upon economics and gender to differing degrees because that balance reflects the nature of the relationships among communication, economics, and gender. At least at first blush, it appears that gender relations affect communication practices only insofar as they have already been incorporated within economic structures. Thus, e.g., bards may have been male more often than female because males already stood in a better economic position. However, the idea requires further investigation.

2 Orality, Literacy, and Early Theatre

1. See the overview in Wise 1–3, 220–25, and Rozik's thorough critique (*Roots*). Most major theater history textbooks now reject or downplay the theory of theater's ritual origins. Yet it raises its hoary head in, e.g., the Encyclopedia Britannica's article on "Dramatic Literature" (146). The online version was partially corrected after my complaint, but not much: see <http://search.eb.com/eb/article-51065>, <http://search.eb.com/eb/article-51107> and <http://search.eb.com/eb/article-61499>, accessed July 1, 2009. In 2001, Films for the Humanities issued "The Drama of Ancient Greece: From Ritual to Theater." Even a display in Athens's new Acropolis Museum (which opened June 2009) states that "The Athenian cult rituals in honour of Dionysus gradually gave birth to drama and led to the establishment of drama competitions."
2. By "tragedy" I am referring to the performance genre developed in classical Greece, involving a chorus and one to three actors, not to a more generalized category of plays that end sadly.
3. Austin and Vidal-Naquet 53–60, 70–71, 212–15; Hammond 145–46, 157–63, 165–66; J. Fine 104–08, 197–208, 218; Lintott 34–37, 43–47; Jaeger 224–26; Thucydides 43; Aristotle, *Athenian Constitution* 46–53.
4. Aristotle, *Athenian Constitution* 56–59; Hammond 150, 164–65, 179–83; J. Fine 131–34, 210–20; Lintott 48–50.
5. Hammond 180, 182; Finley 150–52; Austin and Vidal-Naquet 100, 121–28; Else 56; Pickard-Cambridge, *Dramatic Festivals* 58–59, 266–68.
6. Scholars differ on whether this occurred under Pisistratus, his son Hipparchus, or even Solon: see Parke 34; Hammond 182–83; J. Fine 221; Else 47; Havelock, *Preface to Plato* 47; Havelock, *Literate Revolution* 181.
7. W. Harris 59; and see Wise 18–19; Havelock, *Preface to Plato* 49n4; Havelock, *Literate Revolution* 180–81, 261–62. Literacy in Athens was more extensive than elsewhere in Greece (W. Harris 65).
8. Havelock, *Literate Revolution* 117, 129n6; Finley 214n39. As William Harris points out, complex writing systems per se are no barrier to widespread literacy, as demonstrated by the near-universal literacy level in

modern Japan (14), although credit for that achievement clearly belongs to the Japanese education system.

9. Havelock, *Literate Revolution* 63–70, 89–90; Ong, *Orality and Literacy* 85–92; W. Harris vii–viii, 45. The dating of the Greek alphabet is disputed: most place it in the first half of the eighth century.
10. Aristotle, *Athenian Constitution* 48; J. Fine 101–4, 200; Pickard-Cambridge, *Dithyramb* 70–71; Else 47; Austin and Vidal-Naquet 52, 56–57; Jaeger 102; W. Harris 61.
11. The following discussion is partly based on Russo's five levels of "regularity" in epic poetry (43–46). However, for my purposes his first two levels (meter and rhythm) can be combined, and the fifth level of regularity (outlook) is defined so broadly that it holds true of almost all verbal art—and other arts as well. Thus my levels of regularity are rhythm, diction, and narrative structure. See Havelock, *Literate Revolution* 283–92 for a similar analysis, using Aristophanes's *Frogs* as his guide. Some theories of oral composition allow the poet very little creativity, but I think it gives plenty of room for individual creativity without contradicting the basic theory about forms of regularity (see Thomas 34–44).
12. Russo 44; Ong, *Orality and Literacy* 33–36; Aristotle, *Poetics* 23; Aristotle, *Rhetoric* 180; Else 61.
13. "Mythic" time reappears in twentieth-century literature and drama. However, the underlying circumstances and causes are drastically different. In Greek tragedy it derived from oral culture, whereas in the twentieth century it developed within a highly literate (and to a major extent, elite) culture in the midst of a new transformation in modes of communication—in this case, radio seems to have played a notable role (see Ong, *Orality and Literacy* 136; McConachie, *American Theatre* 28–38, 48–50, 85–86, 283–85).
14. Curiously, the size (as opposed to the role) of the chorus rose from twelve under Aeschylus to fifteen under Sophocles and Euripides. The reason for this is uncertain; in any case, evidently the chorus disappeared by the late third century. The comic chorus went through a similar decline (Pickard-Cambridge, *Dramatic Festivals* 234). Notably, old comedy did not have restrictions on the number of speaking parts. The number of comic actors probably tightened down to three or four during the fifth century (Pickard-Cambridge, *Dramatic Festivals* 149).
15. The point also holds for syllabaries. It is less clear whether it is true for logographic writing. In a purely logographic script, words simply have two forms, spoken and written. The visual signs represent a whole word or meaning-unit rather than its sounds. However, such writing systems were nearly always replaced by a more phonetic approach—and even that most logographic of scripts, Chinese, incorporates a phonetic element in most of its characters, rendering them to some extent signs of signs. Derrida's criticism (*Of Grammatology* 43–65) that speech too is a system of signs of signs (and thus is a variety of writing) is intelligible only for cultures where

writing is dominant. For most of writing's history, the practical reality was that writing was subsidiary to speech, since writing was used to recall or elicit a vocalization and not read silently. Indeed, many people vocalize to this day. A socially oriented theory must put material practices first.

16. Wise argues that the arbitrary relation between actor and character derives from the relation between letter and phoneme (Wise 62–64, 67–68). I think this analogy is too much of a stretch: the selection of one actor over another is not arbitrary, but motivated—the actor's body, manner, and voice contribute massively to the audience's impression of the character. It also places too much weight on the characteristics of phonetic writing.

17. Possibly it was serious for reasons connected with literacy as well. Comic performance of various sorts existed before tragedy, in wholly oral cultures (see Else 24); it seems reasonable to suspect that the epistemological (and pedagogical) assumptions of ancient satyr plays and farce differ from tragedy. Some aspects of satyr performance seem similar to the "contraries" or "clowns" of Native American cultures.

18. Gellrich, *Idea* 33–35; Allen 33, 37; Stock 315–25; Foucault, *Order of Things* 34–38. "Figural thinking" can also be called a "discourse of patterning": see Reiss, *Discourse of Modernism* 21–107.

19. Italy and elsewhere in Europe seem to have been well ahead of England. See Bäuml, "Medieval Texts"; Ong, "Orality."

20. Davies 160–64; Clanchy, *From Memory* 46–51, 226–34; Bäuml 237–65; Parkes 555–577. On definitions of literacy, see Levine 22–24.

21. Moran, *Growth* 92–122, 179–82. In arriving at my estimate, I considered that the earlier period had roughly one-fourth as many schools in the diocese, but that the city had many more schools than the countryside, as well as people needing to read. My estimate may well be too conservative, especially if reading was taught at home. Clanchy even estimates that maybe half of the population of England could read (*From Memory* 13).

22. Moran, *Growth* 175; Clanchy, *From Memory* 234. Stevens thinks actor literacy is unlikely in part because professional actors were occasionally employed (38–39).

23. Moran, *Growth* 185–210; Moran, *Education* 35–37. However, the extent of this preeminence may be exaggerated by our dependence on bequests as evidence of reading interests: there were religious reasons for singling out devotional works in a will (see K. Harris 163–99).

24. The history and production of the York Cycle is surveyed in many texts; one of the more succinct reviews is by Beadle and King ix–xxvii. City records relating to performances in medieval York are collected in Johnston and Rogerson. On pageant wagons, see Johnston and Dorrell, "Doomsday Pageant" 29–34; and Johnston and Dorrell, "York Mercers" 10–35. On the procession route, see Twycross, "Places" 10–33. The most convincing argument on the York Cycle's processional staging is Dorrell 63–111. See also the survey of theories in Tydeman 104–8; and on medieval staging generally, Kahrl 219–37.

25. Kolve 33–56; Clopper 112–18; Briscoe 152; Stevens 45–49; Beadle 10–11; and see Johnston and Rogerson 1.10–12, 2.697–99. The text is reproduced in facsimile in *The York Play*.
26. Evidence for the abundance of coordinating conjunctions (rather than subordinating ones) is shown by Kinneavy.
27. Beadle points out that the York Cycle employs a narrow vocabulary compared to other writings of the time, such as the works of Chaucer and Langland, presumably to facilitate the audience's rapid understanding, but also providing strong focus on a few select themes ("Verbal Texture" 172–74).
28. On the important of language in the York Cycle generally, see, e.g. Beadle, "Verbal Texture"; King, "Seeing and Hearing"; and Johnston, "His Langage."
29. Sheingorn 173–91. For an analysis of how texts and images interacted in a reading process structured by the relationships between orality and manuscript culture, see Nellhaus, "Mementos."
30. All citations of the York Cycle will be to Beadle, *York Plays*, cited as *York* followed by the play and line numbers. The letter *thorn* is replaced with *th* in quotations.
31. Cf. the regression of causes back to God in Aquinas, summarized in Carré 72–74, 96–97.
32. See Allen 305–6; Stock 47–51; Auerbach 36, 54–57. As Stock observes, "In oral culture a forger was not a person who altered texts; he was a traitor. He betrayed the relationship not between words and things but between men" (60).
33. Stock 64, 71, 90–91, 243–52; Clanchy, *From Memory* 38–39, 70–78, 254–60; Camille, "Seeing and Reading" 33. Musson 112–14 observes the symbolic importance of legal documents.
34. According to this view, rituals merely needed to be enacted properly for sacraments to take effect: sacramental efficacy lay not in the materials or words as such, but in a covenant or pact presented by God setting the conditions of proper performance—a theory modeled on commercial contracts and royal writs.
35. Colish; Courtenay, *Schools* 219–306; Tachau. Gellrich shows that even Ockham sustained a hierarchy of speech over writing, albeit with qualifications (*Discourse* 59, 76–77).
36. Allen discusses some of these issues in connection with the Art of Memory (249–61). See also Stock 91; Gellrich, *Discourse* 126.
37. Twycross and Carpenter, *Masks and Masking*; Twycross and Carpenter, "Masks in Medieval English Theatre"; and see Twycross, "'Apparell Comlye'" 30–49; Davidson, *From Creation* 31; Anglo 27.
38. On nominalism, see Courtenay, *Schools* 216–18; Tachau; and also Courtenay, "Nominalism and Late Medieval Thought," "Nominalism and Late Medieval Religion," and "Late Medieval Nominalism Revisited." For the earlier view of nominalism, see Carré. On universities and theater, see A. Nelson. On York's traditionalism, see Moran, *Growth* 185–220; Moran, *Education* 5; and Vale. However, see Nissé on the Cycle's absorption of

Lollard advocacy for lay understanding of Scriptures; and Beckwith (78–81, 95–111) regarding the issues that Lollardy raised and the Church's counter-reaction as background to the York Cycle's dramaturgy.

39. Tiner 7–13, 44–78; Brawer; King, "Contemporary Cultural Models"; Clopper 10; Beckwith 103–111, 218n57. Nissé notes the Trial plays' "obsessive concern with images of bad government at the expense of more directly sacramental or devotional themes" (428). The plays may also reverberate with the conflict between the aristocracy and Richard II in 1387–88, in which the aristocracy played fast and loose with the legal process, and also possibly the victory of the Yorkists over the Lancastrians in 1461. See also Gellrich, *Discourse* 180–84. The York Cycle's attention to court procedures is additionally interesting in light of the important role that legal oratory played in the development of medieval drama, a case argued by Enders.

40. See Kinneavy. I count sixty-six references to "prophets," "prophecies" and related words in 22 of the 36 extant New Testament plays; prophets are also cited by name.

41. See also Nissé regarding the growth of lay piety in York and the York Cycle's emphasis on lay interpretation as part of civic governance.

42. Stock 104–6; Ginzburg xxiii, 9, 36–39, 51, 57, 62–64, 112, 114, 143 (the quote is from 62). Although Ginzburg's study concerns the late sixteenth century, well after the advent of print, the conditions and relations of communication involved are similar enough to the late-medieval period to make the analogy sound.

43. Tiner, "York Trial Plays," 82, 104, 114–15, 151–87. The unwitting revelation of truth or of God's will plays an important role in Augustine, for instance in the famous "take it and read" scene (177).

44. Twycross, "Apparell Comlye." As Twycross points out, such characters did not necessarily wear contemporary clothing.

45. These essences were more likely conceived in terms of geometric form or image than biological structure. E.g., in the sketchbook of Villard de Honnecourt (ca. 1240), faces, animals, and buildings are drawn over triangles, rectangles, circles, and pentagrams. These shapes seem to be not only drawing aids, but also illuminations of the objects' very natures. See Camille, "Seeing and Reading" 42–43; and Camille, "The Book of Signs" 134–38.

46. Researchers disagree on the extent to which the York Cycle employed the *platea*. Agan implies exuberant usage. Blasting believes that the narrowness of York's streets would have constrained its use significantly. Walsh, drawing his conclusions from the challenges of actually staging some of the pageants, finds that limited space would not have been a major hurdle and that use of the *platea* would have been fairly common.

47. Alexandra Johnston recalls how, during York Cycle performance in Toronto in 1977, the actors who played Jesus ranged broadly in age and appearance. "Yet each portrayed an aspect of Christ's humanity. A profound theological point was made as the many Christs gave us a prismatic sense of Mankind while the essential divinity of the character remained the same.... This

convention, frequently imagined to be cumbersome or distracting, proved to be neither. Instead, it focused the attention of the audience on the character, not the actor" ("York Cycle" 4).
48. Modernized from a Lollard antitheatrical tract called *A Tretise of Miraclis Playinge*, summarized and quoted in Woolf 85–86. The tract's author describes several arguments in favor of mystery and miracle plays, but in order to attack them. Peter Meredith, attempting to gauge how medieval audiences experienced the York Cycle, suggests that the lack of suspense regarding a well-known story may have led spectators not to lose interest in the narrative, but instead to attend to other aspects: "because you know the story and its mode of telling...certain elements catch your attention and the narrative is suspended while your imagination and memory explore the ramifications of the associations. It is at this moment that, for me, typology enters in" (108).
49. Such was the experience of Alexandra Johnston and David Parry at the production of the York Cycle in Toronto in 1977 (Johnston, "York Cycle" 6–8; Parry 19–31). My own experience of watching, directing, and acting in mystery plays has been the same. Scholars involved in reconstructing performance of the York Cycle are quite aware of the limitations of that activity for understanding audience reception (see, e.g., King, "Seeing and Hearing" 163–66), but they are often struck by how well the staging seems to draw modern audiences into a more-or-less medieval mode of response. Post-Renaissance plays seem less likely (though not unable) to elicit such responses when staged outdoors, I think largely because they are founded on performance strategies that are much more akin to modern ones.
50. The process is similar to the emergence of what Marx called "commodity fetishism" from the very structure of capitalist exchange, rather than an ideological superimposition (Marx, *Capital* 163–77, and see 1052–58). The hermeneutics of suspicion concerns itself only with such superimpositions, and doesn't recognize the structural forces behind formations of consciousness. Where it sees a broken stick rising from the water, critical realism finds an appearance of brokenness caused by the water's refraction of light.

3 Embodiment, Agency, and Performance Strategies

1. I discuss these issues in terms of the "primacy of practice" thesis in "From Embodiment."
2. On asymmetry and contextuality in totalities, see Bhaskar, *Dialectic* 127.
3. McConachie, *American Theatre* 23–45; McConachie, "Approaching Performance History" 113–22; and McConachie, "Doing Things" 569–94.
4. For a fuller discussion of the ideas in the previous sections, see Nellhaus, "Embodiment."

5. Cibber 133, 270; *Tatler* no. 89; *Spectator* no. 502; Gildon 38. Citations to *The Tatler* and *The Spectator* will be by issue number.
6. Loftis, *Comedy* 196, 199; Hume 220–31; Peters, *Congreve* 25–30; Ellis 117–23; Hynes; and see Freeman 22–25. My analysis of the dramatic genres relies largely on Brown; but I periodize the changes slightly differently, partly on the basis of J. Smith.
7. On the intimate community in *The Spectator*, see Ketcham 3, 5, 17–18, 51, 63–64, 77.
8. *Tatler* nos. 66, 115, 182; *Spectator* nos. 38, 334, 518; Gildon 25, 41, 51; Victor 8–29, 32–33. See also Roach, "Cavaliere Nicolini" 189–205; and Downer 332–35.
9. References to Locke will be by book, chapter, and paragraph number.
10. Foucault's description of the transformation in theories of the sign summaries the change well (*Order of Things* 54–63).
11. Although a "print" and an "impression" could mean a "wax marking" (as they do in Locke §2.29.3), Locke used these terms interchangeably with "inscription," so that "print" and "impression" often connote the printing press.
12. See Eisenstein, whose discussion also considers the developments in indexing (89–107). Murray Cohen similarly notes that "The alphabet itself was recognized as a conceptual tool in the seventeenth century" (146n29). See also Martin 152–53; Ong, *Ramus* 313–18; Clanchy, *From Memory* 180–82.
13. Ultimately *The Tatler* and *The Spectator* acquired this apparatus themselves: their collected editions included indexes to facilitate their use as a sort of cultural encyclopedia (Bowers 162, 173n29).
14. The opposition is strikingly similar to Saussure's distinction between *langue* and *parole*, a resemblance which is far from coincidental.
15. The concept of the intimate community is broader than Habermas's "intimate sphere," since it includes those not directly related as family or friends. Other sorts of imagined communities also developed, nationhood in particular: see Anderson 32–36, 61–65.
16. On the theory of sentiments, see Ketcham 13, 32, 41–43, 49–50, 53, 63.
17. For an overview, see Holland; Leacroft 89–139; Downer; Roach, "Power's Body."
18. See also Roach, "Cavaliere Nicolini" 204–05; Roach, *Player's Passion* 70–71; and cf. Downer 332–35.
19. "Calculate" is used in a discussion of the correspondence between thought and gesture in *Spectator* no. 518. It echoes the era's attention to measurement and order.
20. See Roach, *Player's Passion* 66–68, 71–73. An example is Charles Le Brun's *Méthode pour apprendre à dessiner les passions*, which appeared in 1702 and was translated into English in 1734.
21. See also Kelly 8, 64–76. Foucault similarly notes that for this epoch, "the human body...serves as a sort of reservoir for models of visibility, and acts as a spontaneous link between what one can see and what one can say" (*Order of Things* 135).

22. On these metaphors see also Neill 10, 17n22. A similar connection is made by Peters, *Congreve* 142. Although the metaphor turns up in earlier texts, it appears to be more common after 1690; and the earlier metaphors often refer to the physical materials of books or the process of reading signs, whereas the later ones generally focus on books' textual nature and the inscribability of the mind and character.
23. See also McConachie's argument that radio shaped the image schemas undergirding American drama in the 1940s and 50s, and that television had likewise affected the plays of the subsequent decades (*American Theatre* 28–38, 48–50, 85–86, 283–85).
24. As with most abstractions, social projection is principally modeled on one image but is supervenient upon many. In this case it probably also depends on fundamental neurology, particularly the "mirror" neurons that cause the brain to simulate others' behavior. If so, it seems likely that both empathic and advisory projection emerge on the basis of an innate proto-empathy generating projection as such.

4 Social Ontology, (Meta)theatricality, and the History of Communication

1. I have adopted the variant spelling "reflexion" in order to emphasize reflexivity.
2. Derrida, "Plato's Pharmacy" 158. See also Derrida's analyses of Rousseau and Saussure in *Of Grammatology*.
3. Allen 151. The original sentence refers to *The Faerie Queene*; Allen then extends his comparison to *Lear* and *Hamlet*.
4. Note, *every* speech act: in some quarters Austin is thought to retain a distinction between performatives and constatives, but that interpretation ignores the burden of the last two lectures, in which Austin dissolves the distinction into an issue of illocutionary force (133–64). "Constatives," one might say, are a species of the performative.
5. Austin famously considered theatrical speech "hollow or void," and therefore "parasitic" upon ordinary speech acts (Austin 22). Derrida's critique in *Limited Inc* is pungent, but as Egginton points out, what renders the actor's speech "hollow" is that it's said in the voice of a character; the character's speech acts and their underlying intentionality are performative for other characters, but not for the audience members, who are the true addressees (17–19).
6. Plays such as *Waiting for Godot* barely evidence individual virtual agency, much less corporate virtual agency. Such examples, however, are decidedly atypical, and aim precisely to question agency.
7. Schechner, *Between Theatre and Anthropology* 36; Schechner "Collective Reflexivity"; Butler, *Bodies that Matter* 2, 12; Butler, "Performative Acts."
8. The link between printing and capitalism in Europe is discussed in Febvre and Martin 37–44, 109–27, 224–44.

9. On willful, possessive, knowledgeable selfhood, see Reiss, *Discourse of Modernism*. I discuss its connection to Jonson in "Self-Possessed Jonson." On Jonson's use of print, see Loewenstein; Murray chaps. 2–5; Helgerson chap. 3; and Newton 31–55.
10. According to Fuzier and Dorsal, at least 56 plays performed 1587–1642 involved a play-within, a rehearsal play or a frame play—almost 9% of the 655 plays published in that period (as listed in the Chadwyck-Healey *English Drama* database), averaging one per year. The figures understate the case, since Fuzier and Dorsal do not indicate when masques, dumbshows and inductions served similar metatheatrical functions, as they do in *The Tempest*, *Hamlet*, and *Bartholomew Fair*, respectively. (An additional eight or so metatheatrical plays were published but not enacted, such as closet dramas; these would add another 1%.) The data in D. Smith and Smith and Lawhon show that at best, only 39 plays-within-plays and framed plays were performed from 1660 to 1799, of the 1227 staged during that period (*English Drama*), about 3%, or slightly over one every four years.
11. On ritual as embodied memory, see Connerton 54, 57–59. I am referring in this discussion strictly to religious rituals, not to rituals in general.
12. Between 1700 and 1777, *The Rehearsal* received no less than 150 performances, and perhaps more than 270, at least of them 65 by David Garrick; *The Critic* was staged over 130 times by the end of the century (D. Smith 259–63; Smith and Lawhon 15).
13. Based on ten-year trailing averages using data gathered in D. Smith, and Smith and Lawhon.
14. Of course in practice an ideology of reason could only go so far: whatever diatribes might be levied against "sensual entertainments" like harlequinades, audiences flocked to see them anyway.
15. As I suggested in chapter 3, it can be shown that empiricism and positivism are themselves products of capitalist print culture. It can also be demonstrated that these philosophies ultimately entail an incoherent, even self-contradictory concept of agency, often resulting in not just an overburdened agency responsible for all things, but also (and even simultaneously!) a denial of agency, an agency that simply leaves things as they are or is wholly the product of forces beyond its control (heredity, environment, society, language, libido...). From that perspective, metatheatricality in the nineteenth century resulted not only from secular social changes, but also from a conceptual fissure *within* the dominant ideologies.
16. See also Newey 87–90, on the use of plays-within-plays (instead of self-presence) to the same end in melodrama.
17. The video was released in December 1997. It won an award for Best Art Direction from MTV in 1998, and was a 1999 Grammy Award nominee for Best Music Video (Short Form). (Michel Gondry, the director, later directed *The Eternal Sunshine of the Spotless Mind*.) Although a music video is not theater, in this instance the video insists on the trope of theater, and a video seems perfect for strict self-presence, since its repetitions and replays are identical.

18. I am considering only the goals and methods that *tend* to characterize community-based performance. Particular instances and projects may operate differently, or be undercut by contradictions in the social circumstances, process, etc.
19. This paragraph draws heavily on Reiss, *Discourse of Modernism* 29–33, 42–51, 55–107.
20. The collapse of being into knowledge of being and the compulsive determination of knowledge by being constitute the epistemic fallacy and the ontic fallacy, respectively. Both are underwritten by the anthropic fallacy, which comprehends being in terms of human being. See Bhaskar, *Realist Theory of Science* 36–45; Bhaskar, *Dialectic* 205.
21. Bhaskar, *Dialectic* 44, 119. This sort of performative contradiction is akin to what Reiss terms the "occultation" of a practice which, however, may emerge as a new basis for meaning (Reiss, *Discourse of Modernism* 96–97, 100–2 and passim). In this instance, experimentation itself is a practice that seemingly undergirds empiricism, yet can be adequately theorized neither by it nor by its subjectifying and linguisticizing opponents, whereas the effort to make experimentation intelligible leads in critical realist directions. On this point see also Crease.

Conclusion: New Media, Old Problems

1. Kenny 310, 313–14; Holland 99–137. Plausibly, scripts published during the classical period and the Renaissance largely served the same purpose, because no other sizable market (e.g., drama classes) would have been likely.
2. A properly crafted emote provides only what might be observed by the audience, just as in the theater; not information about what the character is thinking or feeling.
3. One can debate whether theater is wholly materialist, or instead eschews the materialist/idealist opposition (or at least simplistic forms of it). Given the possibility of theatrical metaphysics by means of metadiscourse, the latter alternative must be taken seriously.
4. Both writers have received critiques from theater theorists. Wilshire finds that Goffman "must see the actor's artistry as a kind of deceit.... And art, specifically cinema and theatre, is merely a copy of what already stands perfectly intelligible 'in itself'" (275, 277). According to Elin Diamond, "Performance and theatre discourse are shunned by Butler with a fastidiousness worthy of J. L. Austin himself.... [For Butler,] performance 'shows' too much; gender identifications in all their precarious ambivalence, their tracery of unconscious disavowal become ossified in performance as seeable 'truth,'" a position Diamond bluntly calls an "animus toward theatre" (33).

Bibliography

Abel, Lionel. *Metatheater: A New View of Dramatic Form.* New York: Hill and Wang, 1963.
Agan, Cami D. "The Platea in the York and Wakefield Cycles: Avenues for Liminality and Salvation." *Studies in Philology* 94 (1997): 344–67.
Agnew, Jean-Christophe. *Worlds Apart: The Market and the Theatre in Anglo-American Thought, 1550–1750.* Cambridge: Cambridge UP, 1986.
Allen, Judson Boyce. *The Ethical Poetic of the Later Middle Ages: A Decorum of Convenient Distinction.* Toronto: U of Toronto P, 1982.
Anderson, Benedict. *Imagined Communities: Reflections on the Origin and Spread of Nationalism.* London: Verso, 1991.
Anglo, Sydney. *Spectacle, Pageantry, and Early Tudor Policy.* Oxford: Clarendon—Oxford UP, 1969.
Archer, Margaret S. *Being Human: The Problem of Agency.* Cambridge: Cambridge UP, 2000.
———. *Culture and Agency: The Place of Culture in Social Theory.* Revised edition. Cambridge: Cambridge UP, 1996.
———. *Realist Social Theory: The Morphogenetic Approach.* Cambridge: Cambridge UP, 1995.
Aristophanes. *The Frogs.* Trans. Richmond Lattimore. New York: NAL, 1962.
Aristotle. *The Athenian Constitution.* Trans. P. J. Rhodes. Harmondsworth: Penguin, 1984.
———. *Poetics.* Trans. Gerald F. Else. Ann Arbor: U of Michigan P, 1967.
———. *Rhetoric. The Rhetoric and the Poetics of Aristotle.* Trans. W. Rhys Roberts. New York: Modern Library, 1984.
Auerbach, Erich. "'Figura.'" *Scenes from the Drama of European Literature.* Trans. Ralph Manheim. Minneapolis: U of Minnesota P, 1984. 11–76.
———. *Mimesis: The Representation of Reality in Western Literature.* Trans. Willard R. Trask. Princeton: Princeton UP, 1953.
Augustine. *Confessions.* Trans. R. S. Pine-Coffin. Harmondsworth: Penguin, 1961.
Auslander, Philip. "Humanoid Boogie: Reflections on Robotic Performance." *Staging Philosophy: Intersections of Theater, Performance, and Philosophy.* Ed. David Krasner and David Saltz. Ann Arbor: U of Michigan P, 2006. 87–103.
———. *Liveness: Performance in a Mediatized Culture.* London: Routledge, 1999.
Austin, J. L. *How to Do Things with Words.* Oxford: Oxford UP, 1962.

Austin, M. M., and Pierre Vidal-Naquet. *Economic and Social History of Ancient Greece: An Introduction*. Trans. M. M. Austin. Berkeley: U of California P, 1977.

Bank, Rosemarie. "The Theatre Historian in the Mirror: Transformation in the Space of Representation." *Journal of Dramatic Theory and Criticism* 3.2 (1989): 219–28.

———. "Time, Space, Timespace, Spacetime: Theatre History in Simultaneous Universes." *Journal of Dramatic Theory and Criticism* 5.2 (1991): 65–84.

Bannet, Eve Tavor. "'Epistolary Commerce' in *The Spectator*." Newman 220–47.

Barish, Jonas. *The Anti-theatrical Prejudice*. Berkeley: U of California P, 1981.

Bäuml, Franz H. "Medieval Texts and the Two Theories of Oral-Formulaic Composition: A Proposal for a Third Theory." *New Literary History* 16 (1984): 31–49.

———. "Varieties and Consequences of Medieval Literacy and Illiteracy." *Speculum* 55 (1980): 237–65.

Beadle, Richard. "The Shipwrights' Craft." Neuss 50–61.

———. "Verbal Texture and Wordplay in the York Cycle." *Early Theatre* 3 (2000): 167–84.

———, ed. *The York Plays*. London: Arnold, 1982.

Beadle, Richard, and Pamela M. King, eds. *York Mystery Plays: A Selection in Modern Spelling*. Oxford: Clarendon—Oxford UP, 1984.

Beckett, Samuel. *Waiting for Godot*. New York: Grove P, 1954.

Beckwith, Sarah. *Signifying God: Social Relation and Symbolic Act in the York Corpus Christi Plays*. Chicago: U of Chicago P, 2001.

Berkeley, George. "A Treatise Concerning the Principles of Human Knowledge." 1710. *The Empiricists*. Garden City: Anchor, 1974.

Bernard-Donals, Michael F. *Mikhail Bakhtin: Between Phenomenology and Marxism*. Cambridge: Cambridge UP, 1994.

Bhaskar, Roy. *Dialectic: The Pulse of Freedom*. London: Verso, 1993.

———. *Plato Etc.: The Problems of Philosophy and Their Resolution*. London: Verso, 1994.

———. *The Possibility of Naturalism: A Philosophical Critique of the Contemporary Human Sciences*. Second edition. New York: Harvester Wheatsheaf, 1989.

———. *A Realist Theory of Science*. Sussex: Harvester P; Atlantic Highlands, NJ: Humanities P, 1978.

———. *Reclaiming Reality: A Critical Introduction to Contemporary Philosophy*. London: Verso, 1989.

———. *Scientific Realism and Human Emancipation*. London: Verso, 1986.

Björk. "Bachelorette." *Volumen*. Dir. Michel Gondry. Videocassette. Elektra Entertainment, 1998.

Blair, Rhonda. "Image and Action: Cognitive Neuroscience and Actor-Training." *Performance and Cognition: Theatre Studies and the Cognitive Turn*. Ed. Bruce McConachie and F. Elizabeth Hart. New York: Routledge, 2006. 167–85.

Blasting, Ralph. "The Pageant Wagon as Iconic Site in the York Cycle." *Early Theatre* 3 (2000): 127–36.

Boal, Augusto. *The Rainbow of Desire: The Boal Method of Theatre and Therapy*. Trans. A. Jackson. London: Routledge, 1995.
Bourdieu, Pierre. *Distinction: A Social Critique of the Judgement of Taste*. Trans. Richard Nice. Cambridge, MA: Harvard UP, 1984.
Bowers, Terence. "Universalizing Sociability: The Spectator, Civic Enfranchisement, and the Rule(s) of the Public Sphere." Newman 150-74.
Brawer, Richard A. "The Characterization of Pilate in the York Cycle Play." *Studies in Philology* 69 (1972): 289-303.
Brecht, Bertolt. *Brecht on Theater*. Trans. John Willett. New York: Hill and Wang, 1964.
———. *Life of Galileo*. Trans. Wolfgang Sauerlander and Ralph Manheim. *Collected Plays*. Ed. Ralph Manheim and John Willett. Vol. 5. New York: Vintage, 1972. 1-98.
Briscoe, Marianne G. "Preaching and Medieval English Drama." Briscoe and Coldewey 150-72.
Briscoe, Marianne G., and John C. Coldewey, eds. *Contexts for Early English Drama*. Bloomington: Indiana UP, 1989.
Brown, Laura. *English Dramatic Form, 1660-1760: An Essay in Generic History*. New Haven: Yale UP, 1981.
Burgh, James. *The Art of Speaking*. Baltimore: "Printed for Samuel Butler, by John W. Butler," 1804.
Burke, Peter. *Popular Culture in Early Modern Europe*. New York: Harper Torchbooks, 1978.
Butler, Judith. *Bodies That Matter: On the Discursive Limits of "Sex."* New York: Routledge, 1993.
———. "Performative Acts and Gender Constitution." *Theater Journal* 40 (1988): 519-31.
Camille, Michael. "The Book of Signs: Writing and Visual Difference in Gothic Manuscript Illumination." *Word and Image* 1 (1985): 133-48.
———. "Seeing and Reading: Some Visual Implications of Medieval Literacy and Illiteracy." *Art History* 8 (1985): 26-49.
Carlson, Marvin. *Theatre Semiotics: Signs of Life*. Bloomington: Indiana UP, 1990.
Carré, Meyrick H. *Realists and Nominalists*. London: Oxford UP, 1946.
Carroll, Noël. "Philosophy and Drama: Performance, Interpretation, and Intentionality." *Staging Philosophy: New Approaches to Theater and Performance*. Ed. David Krasner and David Saltz. Ann Arbor: U of Michigan P, 2006. 104-21.
Caws, Mary Ann, ed. *Manifesto: A Century of Isms*. Lincoln: U of Nebraska P, 2001.
Cibber, Colley. *An Apology for the Life of Colley Cibber*. Ed. B. R. S. Fone. Ann Arbor: U of Michigan P, 1968.
Clanchy, M. T. *From Memory to Written Record, England 1066-1307*. Second edition. Oxford: Blackwell, 1993.
———. "Introduction." *New Approaches to Medieval Communication*. Ed. Marco Mostert. Turnhout: Brepols, 1999. 3-13.

Clopper, Lawrence M. "Lay and Clerical Impact on Civic Religious Drama and Ceremony." Briscoe and Coldewey 102–36 .

Cohen, Murray. *Sensible Words: Linguistic Practice in England, 1640–1785*. Baltimore: Johns Hopkins UP, 1977.

Coldewey, John C. "Some Economic Aspects of the Late Medieval Drama." Briscoe and Coldewey 77–101.

Coleman, Janet. *English Literature in History, 1350–1400: Medieval Readers and Writers*. London: Hutchinson, 1981.

Colish, Marcia L. *The Mirror of Language: A Study in the Medieval Theory of Knowledge*. Revised edition. Lincoln: U of Nebraska P, 1983.

Collier, Richard J. *Poetry and Drama in the York Corpus Christi Play*. Hamden: Archon, 1978.

Congreve, William. *The Complete Plays of William Congreve*. Ed. Herbert Davis. Chicago: U of Chicago P, 1967.

Connerton, Paul. *How Societies Remember*. Cambridge: Cambridge UP, 1989.

Connor, W. R. "City Dionysia and Athenian Democracy." *Classica et Mediaevalia* 40 (1989): 7–31.

Courtenay, William J. "Late Medieval Nominalism Revisited: 1972–1982." *Journal of the History of Ideas* 44 (1983): 159–64.

———. "Nominalism and Late Medieval Religion." *Pursuit of Holiness in Late Medieval and Renaissance Religion*. Ed. Charles Trinkaus and Heiko O. Oberman. Leiden: Brill, 1974. 26–59.

———. "Nominalism and Late Medieval Thought: A Bibliographical Essay." *Theological Studies* 33 (1972): 716–34.

———. *Schools and Scholars in Fourteenth-Century England*. Princeton: Princeton UP, 1987.

Cowan, Brian. "Mr. Spectator and the Coffeehouse Public Sphere." *Eighteenth-Century Studies* 37.3 (2004): 345–66.

Crease, Robert P. *The Play of Nature: Experimentation as Performance*. Bloomington: Indiana UP, 1993.

Davidson, Clifford. *From Creation to Doom: The York Cycle of Mystery Plays*. New York: AMS P, 1984.

———. "The Realism of the York Realist and the York Passion." *Speculum* 50 (1975): 270–83.

Davies, W. J. Frank. *Teaching Reading in Early England*. New York: Barnes & Noble, 1973.

Davis, Tracy C. *Actresses as Working Women: Their Social Identity in Victorian Culture*. London and New York: Routledge, 1991.

———. "Questions for a Feminist Methodology in Theatre History." Postlewait and McConachie 59–81.

De Lauretis, Teresa. *Alice Doesn't: Feminism, Semiotics, Cinema*. Bloomington: Indiana UP, 1984.

———. *Technologies of Gender: Essays on Theory, Film, and Fiction*. Bloomington: Indiana UP, 1987.

Debax, Jean-Paul. "Vices and Doubledeckers: Birth and Survival of the Vice Drama Patters." Laroque 75–87.

Derrida, Jacques. *Limited Inc.* Evanston: Northwestern UP, 1988.

———. *Of Grammatology.* Trans. Gayatri Chakravorti Spivak. Baltimore: Johns Hopkins UP, 1976.

———. "Plato's Pharmacy." *Dissemination.* Trans. Barbara Johnson. Chicago: U of Chicago P, 1981.

Diamond, Elin. "Re: Blau, Butler, Beckett, and the Politics of Seeming." *TDR* 44.4 (2000): 31–43.

Dorrell, Margaret. "Two Studies of the York Corpus Christi Play." *Leeds Studies in English* n.s., 6 (1972): 63–111.

Downer, Alan S. "Nature to Advantage Dressed: Eighteenth-Century Acting." *Restoration Drama: Modern Essays in Criticism.* Ed. John Loftis. New York: Oxford UP, 1966. 328–71.

"Dramatic Literature." *Encyclopædia Britannica Online.* 2002. Encyclopaedia Britannica <http://www.britannica.com/>.

———. *The New Encyclopædia Britannica.* Chicago: Encyclopaedia Britannica, 2002. 143–51.

Edwards, A. S. G., and Derek Pearsall. "The Manuscripts of the Major English Poetic Texts." Griffiths and Pearsall 257–78.

Egginton, William. *How the World Became a Stage: Presence, Theatricality and the Question of Modernity.* Albany: State U of New York P, 2003.

Eisenstein, Elizabeth L. *The Printing Press as an Agent of Change.* Cambridge: Cambridge UP, 1979.

Elam, Kier. *The Semiotics of Theatre and Drama.* London and New York: Methuen, 1980.

Elliott, John R., Jr. "Medieval Acting." Briscoe and Coldewey 238–51.

Ellis, Frank H. *Sentimental Comedy: Theory and Practice.* Cambridge: Cambridge UP, 1991.

Else, Gerald F. *The Origin and Early Form of Greek Tragedy.* New York: Norton, 1965.

Enders, Jody. *Rhetoric and the Origins of Medieval Drama.* Ithaca: Cornell UP, 1992.

Febvre, Lucien Paul Victor, and Henri-Jean Martin. *The Coming of the Book.* Ed. Geoffrey Nowell-Smith and David Wootton. Trans. David Gerard. London: Verso, 1976.

Fine, Arthur. *The Shaky Game: Einstein, Realism and the Quantum Theory.* Second edition. Chicago: U of Chicago P, 1996.

Fine, John V. A. *The Ancient Greeks: A Critical History.* Cambridge, MA: Belknap—Harvard UP, 1983.

Finley, M. I. *The Ancient Economy.* Second edition. Berkeley: U of California P, 1985.

Fish, Stanley. "Authors-Readers: Jonson's Community of the Same." *Representations* 7 (1984): 34–35.

Foucault, Michel. *The Archaeology of Knowledge and the Discourse on Language.* Trans. A. M. S. Smith. New York: Pantheon, 1972.

———. *The History of Sexuality. Volume I: An Introduction.* Trans. Robert Hurley. New York: Vintage, 1978.

Foucault, Michel. *The Order of Things: An Archaeology of the Human Sciences*. New York: Vintage, 1970.
Freeman, Lisa A. *Character's Theater: Genre and Identity on the Eighteenth-Century English Stage*. Philadelphia: U of Pennsylvania P, 2002.
Fulbrook, Mary. *Historical Theory*. London: Routledge, 2002.
Furnish, Shearle. "Play-within-the-Play in the Dramas of the Wakefield Master." *Medieval Perspectives* 14 (1999): 61–69.
Fuzier, Jean, and Jean Dorval. "Appendix: Forms of Metadramatic Insertions in Renaissance English Drama 1580–1642." Laroque 461–68.
Garrison, Mary. "'Send More Socks': On Mentality and the Preservation Context of Medieval Letters." *New Approaches to Medieval Communication*. Ed. Marco Mostert. Turnhout: Brepols, 1999. 69–99.
Gazzo, Michael V. *A Hatful of Rain*. New York: Random House, 1956.
Gellrich, Jesse M. *Discourse and Dominion in the Fourteenth Century: Oral Contexts of Writing in Philosophy, Politics, and Poetry*. Princeton: Princeton UP, 1995.
———. *The Idea of the Book in the Middle Ages: Language Theory, Mythology, and Fiction*. Ithaca: Cornell UP, 1985.
Gildon, Charles. *The Life of Thomas Betterton, the Late Eminent Tragedian*. London: Robert Gosling, 1710.
Ginzburg, Carlo. *The Cheese and the Worms: The Cosmos of a Sixteenth-Century Miller*. Trans. John and Anne Tedeschi. Harmondsworth: Penguin, 1982.
Goodall, Jane. "Transferred Agencies: Performance and the Fear of Automatism." *Theatre Journal* 49.4 (1997): 441–53.
Goody, Jack. *The Domestication of the Savage Mind*. Cambridge: Cambridge UP, 1977.
Graham, Walter. *English Literary Periodicals*. New York: Octagon, 1966.
Griffiths, Jeremy, and Derek Pearsall, eds. *Book-Production and Publishing in Britain, 1375–1475*. Cambridge: Cambridge UP, 1989.
Groff, Ruth. *Critical Realism, Post-positivism, and the Possibility of Knowledge*. London: Routledge, 2004.
Habermas, Jürgen. *The Structural Transformation of the Public Sphere: An Inquiry into a Category of Bourgeois Society*. Trans. Thomas Burger. Cambridge, MA: MIT P, 1989.
Hadas, Moses. *Ancilla to Classical Reading*. Morningside Heights: Columbia UP, 1954.
Hammond, N. G. L. *A History of Greece to 322 BC*. Third edition. Oxford: Clarendon—Oxford UP, 1986.
Harré, Rom. *The Principles of Scientific Thinking*. Chicago: U of Chicago P, 1970.
Harré, Rom, and E. H. Madden. *Causal Powers: A Theory of Natural Necessity*. Totowa: Rowman and Littlefield, 1975.
Harré, Rom, and Paul F. Secord. *The Explanation of Social Behaviour*. Oxford: Blackwell, 1972.
Harris, Kate. "Patrons, Buyers and Book Owners: The Evidence for Ownership, and the Rôle of Book Owners in Book Production and the Book Trade." Griffiths and Pearsall 163–99.

Harris, William V. *Ancient Literacy*. Cambridge, MA: Harvard UP, 1989.
Hart, F. Elizabeth. "The Epistemology of Cognitive Literary Studies." *Philosophy and Literature* 25 (2001): 314–34.
Havelock, Eric A. *The Literate Revolution in Greece and Its Cultural Consequences*. Princeton: Princeton UP, 1982.
———. "Oral Composition in the Oedipus Tyrannus of Sophocles." *New Literary History* 16 (1984): 175–97.
———. *Preface to Plato*. Cambridge, MA: Belknap—Harvard UP, 1963.
Hawkes, Terence. *Structuralism and Semiotics*. Berkeley: U of California P, 1977.
Hays, Michael. "Theater History and Practice: An Alternative View of Drama." *New German Critique* 12 (1977): 85–97.
Helgerson, Richard. *Self-crowned Laureates: Spenser, Jonson, Milton, and the Literary System*. Berkeley: U of California P, 1983.
Hey, David. *Yorkshire from AD 1000*. London: Longman, 1986.
Holland, Peter. *The Ornament of Action: Text and Performance in Restoration Comedy*. Cambridge: Cambridge UP, 1979.
Homan, Richard L. "Ritual Aspects of the York Cycle." *Theatre Journal* 33 (1981): 303–15.
Hornby, Richard. *Drama, Metadrama, and Perception*. Lewisburg: Bucknell UP, 1986.
Hubert, Judd D. *Metatheater: The Example of Shakespeare*. Lincoln: U of Nebraska P, 1991.
Hudson, Anne. "Lollard Book Production." Griffiths and Pearsall 125–42.
Hume, Robert D. *The Rakish Stage: Studies in English Drama, 1660–1800*. Carbondale: Southern Illinois UP, 1983.
Hynes, Peter. "Richard Steele and the Genealogy of Sentimental Drama: A Reading of *The Conscious Lovers*." *Papers on Language and Literature* 40.2 (2004): 142–66.
Jaeger, Werner. *Paideia: The Ideals of Greek Culture*. Vol. 1. Trans. Gilbert Highet. Second edition. New York: Oxford UP, 1945.
Johnson, Mark. *The Body in the Mind: The Bodily Basis of Meaning, Imagination, and Reason*. Chicago: U of Chicago P, 1987.
Johnston, Alexandra F. "'His Langage Is Lorne': The Silent Centre of the York Cycle." *Early Theatre* 3 (2000): 185–95.
———. "The York Cycle, 1977." *U of Toronto Quarterly* 48 (1978): 1–9.
Johnston, Alexandra F., and Margaret Dorrell. "The Doomsday Pageant of the York Mercers, 1433." *Leeds Studies in English* n.s., 5 (1971): 29–34.
———. "The York Mercers and Their Pageant of Doomsday." *Leeds Studies in English* n.s., 6 (1972): 10–35.
Johnston, Alexandra F., and Margaret Rogerson [née Dorrell], eds. *Records of Early English Drama: York*. Toronto: U of Toronto P, 1979.
Jonson, Ben. *Timber, or Discoveries. Ben Jonson*. Ed. C. H. Herford and Percy Simpson. Oxford: Clarendon—Oxford UP, 1925–52.
Justice, Alan D. "Trade Symbolism in the York Cycle." *Theatre Journal* 31 (1979): 47–58.

Kahrl, Stanley J. "Medieval Staging and Performance." Briscoe and Coldewey 219–37.

Keat, Russell, and John Urry. *Social Science as Theory*. Second edition. London: Routledge, 1982.

Kelly, Vera Veronica. "Embodied and Inane: Literature on the Perceptual Threshold, 1689–1743." Unpublished thesis. Cornell, 1987.

Kenny, Shirley Strum. "The Publication of Plays." *The London Theatre World, 1660–1800*. Ed. Robert D. Hume. Carbondale: Southern Illinois UP, 1980. 309–36.

Kerckhove, Derrick de. "A Theory of Greek Tragedy." *Sub-Stance* 29 (1981): 23–36.

Kernan, Alvin. *Printing Technology, Letters and Samuel Johnson*. Princeton: Princeton UP, 1987.

Ketcham, Michael G. *Transparent Designs: Reading, Performance, and Form in the "Spectator" Papers*. Athens: U of Georgia P, 1985.

Kimmelman, Burt. "The Trope of Reading in the Fourteenth Century." *Reading and Literacy in the Middle Ages and Renaissance*. Ed. Ian Frederick Moulton. Turnhout: Brepols, 2004. 25–44.

King, Pamela. "Contemporary Models for the Trial Plays in the York Cycle." *Drama and Community: People and Plays in Medieval Europe*. Ed. Alan Hindley. Turnhout: Brepols, 1999. 200–16.

———. "Seeing and Hearing." *Early Theatre* 3 (2000): 155–66.

Kinneavy, Gerald Byron. *A Concordance to the York Plays*. Intro. Richard Beadle. New York: Garland, 1986.

Kobialka, Michal. "Inbetweenness: Spatial Folds in Theatre Historiography." *Journal of Dramatic Theory and Criticism* 5.2 (1991): 85–100.

———. "Theatre History: The Quest for Instabilities." *Journal of Dramatic Theory and Criticism* 3.2 (1989): 239–52.

Kolve, V. A. *The Play Called Corpus Christi*. Stanford: Stanford UP, 1966.

Kruger, Loren. *The National Stage: Theatre and Cultural Legitimation in England, France, and America*. Chicago: U of Chicago P, 1992.

Kuhn, Thomas S. *The Structure of Scientific Revolutions*. Second edition. Chicago: U of Chicago P, 1970.

L'Estrange, Roger. *Fables of Aesop, and Other Eminent Mythologists: With Morals and Reflexions*. London: R. Ware, 1692.

Laclau, Ernesto, and Chatal Mouffe. *Hegemony and Socialist Strategy: Towards a Radical Democratic Politics*. London: Verso, 1985.

Lakoff, George. *Women, Fire, and Dangerous Things: What Categories Reveal about the Mind*. Chicago: U of Chicago P, 1987.

Lakoff, George, and Mark Johnson. *Metaphors We Live By*. Chicago: U of Chicago P, 1980.

———. *Philosophy in the Flesh: The Embodied Mind and its Challenge to Western Thought*. New York: Basic, 1999.

Laroque, François, ed. *The Show Within: Dramatic and Other Insets: English Renaissance Drama (1550–1642): Proceedings of the International Conference Held in

Montpellier, 22–25 Novembre 1990. Publications de U Paul-Valéry—Montpellier III, Centre d'études et de recherches Élisabéthaines, 1992.
Leacroft, Richard. *The Development of the English Playhouse*. London: Methuen, 1988.
Leggatt, Alexander. *Ben Jonson: His Vision and His Art*. London: Methuen, 1981.
Levine, Kenneth. *The Social Context of Literacy*. London: Routledge, 1986.
Ley, Graham. "Performance and Performatives." *Journal of Dramatic Theory and Criticism* 8.1 (1998): 5–18.
Lintott, A. W. *Violence, Civil Strife and Revolution in the Classical City*. London: Croom Helm, 1982.
Locke, John. *An Essay Concerning Human Understanding*. Ed. P. H. Nidditch. Oxford: Clarendon—Oxford UP, 1975.
Loewenstein, Joseph. "The Script in the Marketplace." *Representations* 12 (1985): 101–14.
Loftis, John C. *Comedy and Society from Congreve to Fielding*. Stanford: Stanford UP, 1959.
———. *Steele at Drury Lane*. Berkeley: U of California P, 1952.
Lovell, Terry. *Pictures of Reality: Aesthetics, Politics and Pleasure*. London: BFI, 1980.
Lutterbie, John. "Neuroscience and Creativity in the Rehearsal Process." *Performance and Cognition: Theatre Studies and the Cognitive Turn*. Ed. Bruce McConachie and F. Elizabeth Hart. New York: Routledge, 2006. 149–66.
Mackie, Erin Skye. "Being Too Positive about the Public Sphere." Newman 81–104.
Martin, Henri-Jean. *The History and Power of Writing*. Trans. Lydia G. Cochrane. Chicago: U of Chicago P, 1994.
Marx, Karl. *Capital: A Critique of Political Economy*. Intro. Ernest Mandel. Trans. Ben Fawkes. New York: Vintage, 1976.
———. *Grundrisse: Foundations of the Critique of Political Economy*. Trans. Martin Nicolaus. New York: Vintage, 1973.
Marx, Karl, and Friedrich Engels. *The Marx-Engels Reader*. Ed. Robert C. Tucker. Second edition. New York: Norton, 1978.
McCarty, T. L. *Language, Literacy, and Power in Schooling*. Mahwah: Erlbaum, 2005.
McConachie, Bruce. *American Theatre in the Culture of the Cold War: Producing and Contesting Containment, 1947–1962*. Iowa City: U of Iowa P, 2003.
———. "Approaching Performance History Through Cognitive Psychology." *Assaph* 10 (1994): 113–22.
———. "Doing Things with Image Schemas: The Cognitive Turn in Theatre Studies and the Problem of Experience for Historians." *Theatre Journal* 53 (2001): 569–94.
———. "Metaphors We Act By: Kinesthetics, Cognitive Psychology, and Historical Structures." *Journal of Dramatic Theory and Criticism* 7.2 (1993): 23–45.
———. "Reading Context into Performance: Theatrical Formations and Social History." *Journal of Dramatic Theory and Criticism* 3.2 (1989): 229–37.

McConachie, Bruce. "Towards a Postpositivist Theatre History." *Theatre Journal* 37 (1985): 465–86.

———. "Using the Concept of Cultural Hegemony to Write Theatre History." Postlewait and McConachie 37–58.

McLennan, Gregor. *Marxism and the Methodologies of History*. London: Verso, 1981.

McLuhan, Marshall. *The Gutenberg Galaxy: The Making of Typographic Man*. Toronto: U of Toronto P, 1962.

Meale, Carol M. "Patrons, Buyers and Owners: Book Production and Social Status." Griffiths and Pearsall 201–38.

Mehl, Dieter . "Forms and Functions of the Play Within a Play." *Renaissance Drama* o.s. 8 (1965): 41–61.

Meredith, Peter. "The Fifteenth-Century Audience of the York Corpus Christi Play: Records and Speculation." *"Divers Toyes Mengled": Essays on Medieval and Renaissance Culture/Etudes sur la culture européenne au Moyen Age et à la Renaissance*. Ed. Michel Bitot with Roberta Mullini and Peter Happé. Tours: Publication de l'Université Francois Rabelais, 1996. 101–11.

Mills, David. "Characterization in the English Mystery Cycles." *Medieval English Theatre* 5 (1983): 5–17.

Mohanty, Satya P. *Literary Theory and the Claims of History: Postmodernism, Objectivity, Multicultural Politics*. Ithaca: Cornell UP, 1997.

Moran, Joann H. *Education and Learning in the City of York, 1300–1560*. York: U of York, Borthwick Institute of Historical Research, 1979.

———. *The Growth of English Schooling, 1340–1548: Learning, Literacy, and Laicization in Pre-Reformation York Diocese*. Princeton: Princeton UP, 1985.

Munson, William F. "Audience and Meaning in Two Medieval Dramatic Realisms." *The Drama of the Middle Ages: Comparative and Critical Essays*. Ed. Clifford Davidson, C. J. Gianakaris, and John H. Stroupe. New York: AMS P, 1982. 183–206.

Murray, Timothy. *Theatrical Legitimation: Allegories of Genius in Seventeenth-Century England and France*. New York: Oxford UP, 1987.

Musson, Anthony. "Law and Text: Legal Authority and Judicial Accessibility in the Late Middle Ages." *The Uses of Script and Print, 1300–1700*. Ed. Julia Crick and Alexandra Walsham. Cambridge: Cambridge UP, 2004. 95–115.

Neill, Michael. "Horned Beasts and China Oranges: Reading the Signs in the Country Wife." *Eighteenth Century Life* 12 (1988): 3–17.

Nellhaus, Tobin. "Critical Realism and Performance Strategies." *Staging Philosophy: New Approaches to Theater and Performance*. Ed. David Krasner and David Saltz. Ann Arbor: U of Michigan P, 2006. 57–84.

———. "From Embodiment to Agency: Cognitive Science, Critical Realism, the Framework of Communication." *Journal of Critical Realism* 3.1 (2004): 103–32.

———. "Mementos of Things to Come: Orality, Literacy and Typology in the Biblia Pauperum." *Printing the Written Word: the Social History of Books, c. 1450–1520*. Ed. Sandra Hindman. Ithaca: Cornell UP, 1991. 292–321.

———. "Science, History, Theater: Theorizing in Two Alternatives to Positivism." *Theatre Journal* 45 (1993): 505–27.

———. "Self-possessed Jonson: Reason, Will, Ownership, Power." *Journal of Dramatic Theory and Criticism* 8.1 (1993): 5–17.

Nelson, Alan H. "Contexts for Early English Drama: The Universities." Briscoe and Coldewey 137–49.

Nelson, Robert J. *Play Within a Play: The Dramatist's Conception of His Art: Shakespeare to Anouilh.* New Haven: Yale UP, 1958.

Neuss, Paula, ed. *Aspects of Early English Drama.* Cambridge: Brewer, 1983.

Newey, Katherine. "Melodrama and Metatheatre: Theatricality in the Nineteenth Century Theatre." *Journal of Dramatic Theory and Criticism* 11.2 (1997): 85–100.

Newman, Donald J., ed. *The Spectator: Emerging Discourses.* Newark: U of Deleware P, 2005.

Newton, Richard C. "Jonson and the (Re)-invention of the Book." *Classic and Cavalier: Essays on Jonson and the Sons of Ben.* Ed. Claude J. Summers and Ted-Larry Pebworth. Pittsburgh: U of Pittsburgh P, 1982. 31–55.

Nissé, Ruth. "Staged Interpretations: Civic Rhetoric and Lollard Politics in the York Plays." *Journal of Medieval and Early Modern Studies* 28.2 (1998): 427–52.

Norris, Christopher. *Against Relativism: Philosophy of Science, Deconstruction and Critical Theory.* Oxford: Blackwell, 1997.

———. *Quantum Theory and the Flight from Realism: Philosophical Responses to Quantum Mechanics.* London: Routledge, 2000.

Ong, Walter J. *Orality and Literacy: The Technologizing of the Word.* London: Methuen, 1982.

———. "Orality, Literacy, and Medieval Textualization." *New Literary History* 16 (1984): 1–12.

———. *Ramus, Method and the Decay of Dialogue.* Cambridge, MA: Harvard UP, 1958.

Orme, Nicholas. *English Schools in the Middle Ages.* London: Methuen, 1973.

Papin, Liliane. "This Is Not a Universe: Metaphor, Language, and Representation." *PMLA* 107 (1992): 1253–65.

Parke, H. W. *Festivals of the Athenians.* Ithaca: Cornell UP, 1977.

Parkes, Malcolm. "The Literacy of the Laity." *The Medieval World.* Ed. David Daiches and Anthony K. Thorsby. London: Aldus, 1973. 555–77. Vol. 2 of *Literature and Western Civilization.*

Parry, David. "The York Mystery Cycle at Toronto, 1977." *Medieval English Theatre* 1 (1979): 19–31.

Pearsall, Derek. "Introduction." Griffiths and Pearsall 1–10.

Peirce, Charles S. *Collected Papers.* Ed. Charles Hartshorne and Paul Weiss. 8 vols. Cambridge, MA: Belknap—Harvard UP, 1960–66.

———. *The Essential Peirce: Selected Philosophical Writings.* Bloomington: Indiana UP, 1998.

Peters, Julie Stone. *Congreve, the Drama, and the Printed Word.* Stanford: Stanford UP, 1990.

Peters, Julie Stone. *Theatre of the Book, 1480–1880: Print, Text, and Performance in Europe*. Oxford; New York: Oxford UP, 2000.
Pickard-Cambridge, Arthur Wallace. *Dithyramb Tragedy and Comedy*. Rev. T. B. L. Webster. Second edition. London: Clarendon—Oxford UP, 1962.
———. *The Dramatic Festivals of Athens*. Rev. John Gould and D. M. Lewis. Second edition. London: Clarendon—Oxford UP, 1968.
Pickering, Frederick P. *Literature and Art in the Middle Ages*. Coral Gables: U of Miami P, 1970.
Polly, Greg. "A Leviathan of Letters." Newman 105–28.
Postlewait, Thomas, and Bruce McConachie, eds. *Interpreting the Theatrical Past: Essays in the Historiography of Performance*. Iowa City: U of Iowa P, 1989.
Rader, Margaret. "Context in Written Language: The Case of Imaginative Fiction." *Spoken and Written Language: Exploring Orality and Literacy*. Ed. Deborah Tannen. Norwood: Ablex, 1982. 185–98.
Rastall, Richard. "'Alle Hefne Makyth Melody.'" Neuss 1–12.
———. "Music in the Cycle Plays." Briscoe and Coldewey 192–218.
Rayner, Alice. *To Act, to Do, to Perform: Drama and the Phenomenology of Action*. Ann Arbor: U of Michigan P, 1994.
Reiss, Timothy J. *The Discourse of Modernism*. Ithaca: Cornell UP, 1982.
———. *Tragedy and Truth*. New Haven: Yale UP, 1980.
Riggs, David. *Ben Jonson: A Life*. Cambridge, MA: Harvard UP, 1989.
Roach, Joseph R. "Cavaliere Nicolini: London's First Opera Star." *Educational Theatre Journal* 28 (1976): 189–205.
———. *The Player's Passion: Studies in the Science of Acting*. Newark: U of Delaware P, 1985.
———. "Power's Body: The Inscription of Morality as Style." Postlewait and McConachie 99–118.
Robinson, J. W. "The Art of the York Realist." *Modern Philology* 40 (1963): 241–51.
Romilly, Jacqueline de. *Time in Greek Tragedy*. Ithaca: Cornell UP, 1968.
Rozik, Eli. *The Roots of Theatre: Rethinking Ritual and Other Theories of Origin*. Iowa City: U of Iowa P, 2002.
———. "Theatre at One of its Borderlines: Reflections on *Suz/o/suz* by La Fura dels Baus." *Theatre Annual* 49 (1996): 92–104.
Russo, Joseph. "How, and What, Does Homer Communicate? The Medium and Message of Homeric Verse." *Communication Arts in the Ancient World*. Ed. Eric A. Havelock. New York: Hastings, 1978. 39–52.
Saenger, Paul. "Silent Reading: Its Impact on Late Medieval Script and Society." *Viator* 13 (1982): 369–413.
Saltz, David Z. "Editorial Comment: Performance and Cognition." *Theatre Journal* 59 (2007): 547–51.
Saussure, Ferdinand de. *Course in General Linguistics*. LaSalle: Open Court, 1986.
Schechner, Richard. *Between Theater and Anthropology*. Philadelphia: U of Pennsylvania P, 1985.
———. "Collective Reflexivity: Restoration of Behavior." *A Crack in the Mirror: Reflexive Perspectives in Anthropology*. Ed. Jay Ruby. Philadelphia: U of Pennsylvania P, 1982. 39–81.

Schumacher, Claude, ed. *Naturalism and Symbolism in European Theatre, 1850–1918.* Cambridge: Cambridge UP, 1996.

Schwartz, Joel D. "Human Action and Political Action in Oedipus Tyrannos." *Greek Tragedy and Political Theory.* Ed. J. Peter Cuban. Berkeley: U of California P, 1986. 183–209.

Sheingorn, Pamela. "The Visual Language of Drama: Principles of Composition." Briscoe and Coldewey 173–91.

Shelley, Percy Bysshe. "A Defense of Poetry." *Critical Theory Since Plato.* Ed. Hazard Adams. New York: Harcourt, 1971. 499–513.

Shklovsky, Viktor. "Sterne's Tristram Shandy: Stylistic Commentary." *Russian Formalist Criticism: Four Essays.* Ed. Lee T. Lemon and Marion J. Reis. Lincoln: U of Nebraska P, 1965. 25–57.

Simons, Herbert D., and Sandra Murphy. "Spoken Language Strategies and Reading Acquisition." *The Social Construction of Literacy.* Ed. Jenny Cook-Gumperz. Cambridge: Cambridge UP, 1986. 185–206.

Smith, Dane Farnsworth. *Plays about the Theatre in England, from the Rehearsal in 1671 to the Licensing Act in 1737.* London: Oxford UP, 1936.

Smith, Dane Farnsworth, and M. L. Lawhon. *Plays about the Theatre in England, 1737–1800: Or, the Self-conscious Stage from Foote to Sheridan.* Lewisburg: Bucknell UP, 1979.

Smith, John Harrington. "Shadwell, the Ladies, and the Change in Comedy." *Restoration Drama: Modern Essays in Criticism.* Ed. John Loftis. New York: Oxford UP, 1966. 236–52.

The Spectator. Ed. Donald F. Bond. Oxford: Clarendon—Oxford UP, 1965.

States, Bert O. *Great Reckonings in Little Rooms: on the Phenomenology of Theater.* Berkeley: U of California P, 1985.

Steele, Richard. *The Conscious Lovers. The Plays of Richard Steele.* Ed. Shirley Strum Kenny. Oxford: Clarendon—Oxford UP, 1971.

Stevens, Martin. *Four Middle English Mystery Cycles: Textual, Contextual, and Critical Interpretations.* Princeton: Princeton UP, 1987.

Stock, Brian. *The Implications of Literacy: Written Language and Models of Interpretation in the Eleventh and Twelfth Centuries.* Princeton: Princeton UP, 1983.

Straub, Kristina. *Sexual Suspects: Eighteenth-Century Players and Sexual Ideology.* Princeton: Princeton UP, 1992.

Street, Brian V. *Literacy in Theory and Practice.* Cambridge: Cambridge UP, 1984.

Tachau, Katherine H. *Vision and Certitude in the Age of Ockham: Optics, Epistemology, and the Foundations of Semantics, 1250–1345.* Leiden: Brill, 1988.

The Tatler. Ed. Donald F. Bond. Oxford: Clarendon—Oxford UP, 1987.

Thomas, Rosalind. *Literacy and Orality in Ancient Greece.* Cambridge: Cambridge UP, 1992.

Thucydides. *The Peloponnesian War.* Trans. Rex Warner. Harmondsworth: Penguin, 1954.

Tillott, P. M., ed. *A History of Yorkshire: The City of York, the Victoria History of the Counties of England.* London: Oxford UP, 1961.

Tiner, Elza Cheryl. "'Inventio,' 'Dispositio,' and 'Elocutio' in the York Trial Plays." Unpublished thesis. U of Toronto, 1987.
Tomashevsky, Boris. "Thematics." *Russian Formalist Criticism: Four Essays*. Ed. Lee T. Lemon and Marion J. Reis. Lincoln: U of Nebraska P, 1965.
Toulmin, Stephen. *Cosmopolis: The Hidden Agenda of Modernity*. New York: Free P, 1990.
Twycross, Meg. "'Apparell Comlye.'" Neuss 30–49.
———. "'Places to Hear the Play': Pageant Stations at York, 1398–1572." *REED Newsletter* 2 (1978): 10–33.
Twycross, Meg, and Sarah Carpenter. *Masks and Masking in Medieval and Early Tudor England*. Aldershot: Ashgate, 2002.
———. "Masks in Medieval English Theatre." *Medieval English Theatre* 3 (1981): 7–44, 69–113.
Tydeman, William. *English Medieval Theatre, 1400–1500*. London: Routledge, 1986.
Vale, M. G. A. *Piety, Charity, and Literacy among the Yorkshire Gentry, 1370–1480*. York: St. Anthony's P, 1976.
Vance, Eugene. *Mervelous Signals: Poetics and Sign Theory in the Middle Ages*. Lincoln: U of Nebraska P, 1986.
Veltrusky, Jiří. "Contribution to the Semiotics of Acting." *Sound, Sign and Meaning: Quinquagenary of the Prague Linguistic Circle*. Ed. Ladislav Matejka. Ann Arbor: Michigan Slavic Contributions, 1976. 553–606.
Vernant, Jean-Pierre, and Pierre Vidal-Naquet, *Myth and Tragedy in Ancient Greece*. Trans. Janet Lloyd. New York: Zone, 1988.
Victor, Benjamin. *Memoirs of the Life of Barton Booth, Esq*. London: John Watts, 1733.
Voloshinov, V. N. *Marxism and the Philosophy of Language*. Trans. Ladislav Matejka and I. R. Titunik. Cambridge, MA: Harvard UP, 1973.
Walsh, Martin. "High Places and Travelling Scenes: Some Observations on the Staging of the York Cycle." *Early Theatre* 3 (2000): 137–54.
Weimann, Robert. *Shakespeare and the Popular Tradition in the Theater: Studies in the Social Dimension of Dramatic Form and Function*. Ed. Robert Schwartz. Baltimore: Johns Hopkins UP, 1978.
Wiles, David. "Shakespeare and the Medieval Idea of the Play." Laroque 65–74.
Williams, Raymond. *Keywords: A Vocabulary of Culture and Society*. Second edition. New York: Oxford UP, 1983.
———. *Problems in Materialism and Culture*. London: Verso, 1980.
Wilshire, Bruce. *Role Playing and Identity: The Limits of Theatre as Metaphor*. Bloomington: Indiana UP, 1982.
Wise, Jennifer. *Dionysus Writes: The Invention of Theatre in Ancient Greece*. Ithaca: Cornell UP, 1998.
Woolf, Rosemary. *The English Mystery Plays*. Berkeley: U of California P, 1972.
Worthen, William B. *Print and the Poetics of Modern Drama*. New York: Cambridge UP, 2005.
Wright, Erik Olin. *Class, Crisis and the State*. London: Verso, 1978.
Yates, Frances A. *The Art of Memory*. Chicago: U of Chicago P, 1966.

The York Play: A Facsimile of British Library MS Additional 35290, Together with a Facsimile of the "Ordo Paginarum" Section of the A/Y Memorandum Book. Intro. Richard Beadle and Peter Meredith. Leeds: U of Leeds, School of English, 1983.

Zola, Émile. "Naturalism in the Theatre" [excerpts]. *The Theory of the Modern Stage.* Ed. Eric Bentley. Harmondsworth: Penguin, 1968. 351–72.

INDEX

Abel, Lionel, 145, 146, 166
absence, 26, 105, 162, 164, 171, 173, 178
access to a mode of communication, *see* communication
actors and acting, 15, 16, 26, 35, 65, 66, 68, 71, 76, 90, 93, 102, 105, 108–10, 123, 124, 127, 136, 139, 140, 144, 146, 152, 155, 157, 159, 161, 169–73, 175–9, 185–8, 190, 191, 194–7, 202, 203, 205, 206, 208, 210
actors' "points," 108, 124, 127
Addison, Joseph, 113, 118, 121, 124, 125, 128–31
administrative institutions, 15, 70, 72, 73, 85, 86–7, 111
Aeschylus, 58, 66, 68, 202
  The Oresteia, 64, 172
aesthetic realism, 69–70, 84, 85, 87, 96, 134, 135, 160
  see also naturalism; verisimilitude
aesthetics, *see* art and artistry
affiliations and disaffiliations, 192–3
agential level of society, *see* agents and agency; social ontology
agents and agency, 14–16, 20, 28, 29, 41–51, 55, 57, 66, 93–5, 100–5, 108, 109, 130, 136, 138–41, 143, 145–7, 149–51, 153–62, 166–70, 172–81, 185–93, 196, 198, 208, 209
  corporate agents and agency, 20, 48, 49, 150, 153, 156, 167, 170, 172, 173, 174, 186, 188, 208
  see also social ontology; virtual agents

allegorical characters, 1, 69, 83, 111, 148
  see also personifications
allegory, 15, 68, 69, 81, 83, 87, 89, 91, 111, 123, 138, 148, 165
  see also figural thinking
alphabet, 60–2, 66, 68, 78, 79, 114–15, 183, 202, 207
analogy, 15, 20, 30, 35, 36, 38, 49, 68, 77, 80–3, 89, 93, 100, 105–7, 114, 115, 125, 127, 148, 151
  see also metaphors
Anderson, Benedict, 118, 164
anthropocentrism, 25, 28, 34, 39, 40, 47, 117, 122, 125, 129, 132, 165, 171, 173, 175, 179
anthropomorphism, 81, 100, 101, 153
antitheatricalism, 17, 147, 194–7, 206
Archer, Margaret S., 41–3
Aristophanes, 64
Aristotle, 1, 24, 35, 64, 111
art and artistry, 1, 4, 11, 13, 19, 24, 34, 48, 49, 50, 55, 57, 60, 61, 64, 68, 75, 82, 84, 85, 87, 89, 96, 108, 123, 132, 134, 135, 140, 144–7, 149, 151, 160, 174, 176, 177, 186, 187, 189, 190, 193, 194, 197, 210
  see also aesthetic realism
Art of Memory, 63, 80–2, 111, 112
Artaud, Antonin, 166
artisans, 58, 59, 60, 62, 67, 70
Athens, 14, 15, 58, 63, 66, 67, 93, 99, 109
  see also Greece
audiences and audience experience, 3, 4, 7, 12, 13, 17, 35, 43, 44, 50, 52, 54, 62–4, 66, 71, 75, 76, 82, 84,

audiences and audience experience—
Continued
85, 87, 89–92, 94, 101, 102, 107–10, 116, 121, 122, 136–40, 144, 147, 149, 151–3, 155, 156, 159–62, 169–72, 175, 176, 178, 180, 186, 187, 189–96, 203, 204, 206, 208, 209, 210
see also stage/audience relationship; theatrical performance
Augustine, 79, 88, 111, 205
Auslander, Philip, 7, 16, 50, 184–9
Austin, J. L., 151, 208, 210
authority and authorization, 10, 43, 53, 72, 79, 81, 85, 111, 116, 165, 166, 171, 195
authors and authorship, 7, 73, 78, 112, 128, 129, 147, 165–6, 170, 171, 173, 175, 177, 195

Beckett, Samuel, 166
  Waiting for Godot, 175
behavior, 5, 20, 23, 26, 44, 45, 90, 102, 104, 109–10, 119–20, 124, 138, 153, 158–60, 170, 171, 173, 175, 180, 208
behavior manuals, 109, 110, 125–7
Berkeley, George, 23, 25
Bhaskar, Roy, 24, 26–8, 31, 34, 36, 41, 100, 101, 200
Bible, 15, 44, 68, 69, 72–4, 76, 78, 80, 81, 86, 87, 91, 93, 111, 112, 148, 163
Biblia pauperum, 75, 81
Björk, 175
Blair, Rhonda, 12
blank paper metaphor, 128–9
  see also writing metaphors and models
Boal, Augusto, 161, 177, 180, 187
book culture, 116, 118, 133, 134
Book of Nature, 69, 77, 92, 112
  see also writing metaphors and models
books, 15, 72, 73, 76–7, 81, 85, 87, 92, 93, 111, 114, 116–18, 126, 129, 146, 163, 165, 175, 176, 208
Bourdieu, Pierre, 39, 43, 55, 105
Brecht, Bertolt, 1, 134–5, 176–7, 179, 180, 187, 198

Bush, George W., 33
business, 72, 73, 86, 87, 118, 150
Butler, Judith, 13, 158–9, 160, 196, 210

capitalism, 1, 25, 27, 47, 50, 55, 103, 143, 144, 155, 164, 165, 169, 173, 206, 208, 209
Carroll, Noël, 152, 188
Castelvetro, Lodovico, 164
casting, 108, 152, 173, 191
The Castle of Perseverance, 69, 75
catalogs, 52, 114, 125, 126
categorization, 29, 30, 38, 46, 47, 98, 100, 114, 189
causal powers, 5, 13, 14, 19, 20, 22, 23, 25–31, 33, 40, 44, 49, 50, 66, 68, 70, 93, 94, 98, 130, 131, 135, 157, 159, 163, 194, 202, 204, 206, 208
  see also criteria of reality; critical realism; generative mechanisms
causality, 3, 4, 8, 20, 22, 23, 26, 34, 61, 64, 65, 100, 105, 156, 179
certainty, 11, 20, 29, 31, 34, 164, 178, 197, 200
change, 1, 4, 5, 8, 14, 15–16, 21, 22–4, 26, 28, 32, 33, 42, 48, 51, 52, 55, 57, 63, 67, 70, 87, 96, 106, 109, 112, 117, 118, 131, 135, 139, 146, 149, 156, 159, 163, 167–9, 172, 174, 183, 191, 198, 209
characters and characterization, 1, 16, 35, 40, 45, 65–9, 75, 82, 83, 88–90, 92, 101, 102, 105, 107–10, 121–2, 124, 125, 127–30, 133, 139–40, 144–9, 152–7, 161, 162, 167, 170–7, 186, 188, 190–3, 196, 203, 205–6, 208, 210
  see also virtual agents
Chaucer, Geoffrey, 70, 78
  The Canterbury Tales, 75, 92
Church, 70, 72, 74, 78, 80, 85, 87, 93, 164, 205
Cibber, Colley, 108, 121
City Dionysia, 59, 60, 66, 67, 169
civic functions, 45, 59, 60, 67, 86, 205
civil society, 96, 109, 130

cognition, 4, 7–10, 15, 16, 19, 25, 50, 96–100, 106, 109, 119, 123, 130, 139, 160, 162
    see also thought
cognitive science, 15, 95–8, 101, 105, 107, 110, 160
comedy, 35, 57, 59, 67, 121, 122, 138, 141, 147, 187, 193, 202
commodities and commodification, 54, 155, 165, 188, 206
communication
    changes and revolutions in, 2, 15, 16, 51, 72, 73, 87, 106, 118, 163–9, 174, 181, 183
    cycle, 52, 74–7, 112; consumption, 52, 76–7, 104, 116–18, 180, 187 (*see also* reception); distribution, 52, 75–6, 117, 118, 188; exchange, 2, 52, 75–6, 117; preservation, 15, 52, 54, 63, 64, 69, 76, 77, 80–1, 112, 114; production, 2, 45, 52, 54, 74–7, 104, 106, 112, 117, 151
    as discourse, 161, 162, 167; *see also* discourses
    as embodied practices, 2, 15, 35, 51, 94, 95, 104, 106, 117, 130, 139, 151, 161, 162, 167, 189, 192
    framework, 54–5, 68–70, 74, 77, 87, 93, 94, 106, 112, 113, 120, 130, 133, 135, 139, 140, 143, 146–7, 149, 163, 167, 169, 174, 183, 194, 195, 197
    means and forces of, 2, 9, 10, 46, 51, 52, 93, 96, 106, 112, 117, 119, 151, 183
    modes of, 2, 3, 6, 8, 10, 14, 15, 51–5, 57, 61, 74, 93, 106, 112, 151, 163, 166, 168, 181, 183, 202
    social relations of, 9, 10, 46, 51, 52, 54, 71, 77, 140, 205; access, 53, 54, 71, 87; deployment, 54, 71–2, 77, 87; permeation, 54, 71, 73–4, 87; utilization, 53, 54, 62, 71–3, 77, 79, 86, 87, 112, 113, 117, 163 (*see also* directivity; validation)
    as social structure, 14–16, 35, 51, 71, 107, 139, 163, 166, 168, 172, 183, 189, 190
    theories of, 2, 6–10, 51–2
communitas, 192
communities, 46–8
    discursive, 54, 119, 165, 192
    imagined, 47, 117–20, 130, 134
    intimate and benevolent, 110, 118, 121, 122
community-based theatre, 177, 180, 210
computers, 6, 135, 184
Congreve, William, 129
containment (image schema), 98–100, 103, 106, 135, 136, 137, 139, 140, 174, 179
contracts, 15, 62, 79, 80, 86, 147, 164, 204
conventional signs, *see* semiology; semiotics; symbols
conventions, 3, 35, 111, 152, 158, 165, 175, 193, 196, 206
costumes, 82–3, 90, 122, 140
crisis in representation, 163–6, 169, 178
criteria of reality, 23, 25, 34, 47, 113, 132, 134, 156, 158, 171, 174
The Critic (Richard Brinsley Sheridan), 169
critical realism, 2, 11–14, 17, 24–51, 54, 67, 94, 97, 137, 162, 189, 190, 194, 197
    epistemological position, 29–32
    ontological position, 24–9
    philosophical critiques, 34–5
    theory of signs, 35–40; *see also* semiotics
    see also causal powers; generative mechanisms; ontology; realism; social ontology
culture, 1, 6, 7, 9, 15, 23, 29–33, 43–4, 53, 57, 98, 101, 105–7, 130, 153, 161, 163, 189, 191, 198
    see also under specific cultures

dance, 46, 47, 124, 127, 150, 188–9
Davis, Tracy, 12
deconstruction, 3, 8, 13, 179, 186

democracy, 14, 59–60, 62, 66–7, 169, 190–1
deployment of a mode communication, *see* communication
Derrida, Jacques, 4, 8, 145–6, 160, 202–3, 208
Descartes, René, 31, 96, 125, 178
dialogism, 14, 40, 52, 148, 161, 177, 192
dictionaries, 115
digital technologies, 7, 187, 188
Dionysus, 59, 67, 201
directivity (aspect of communication), 54, 86, 113–14, 126, 128, 156
see also communication
discourses, 9, 14–16, 20–3, 28, 40, 43–55, 80, 81, 93, 102, 104, 107, 109, 130, 136, 140–1, 145–6, 149–62, 164–7, 170, 172, 174–6, 178–80, 193, 196–8
see also discursive strategies; epistemes; social ontology
discursive level of society, *see* discourses
discursive strategies, 2, 9, 10, 46, 47, 51–3, 68, 70, 77, 84, 89, 93–4, 104, 107–9, 112, 118–20, 143, 158, 164–5
see also discourses; performance strategies
domains, *see* ontology
doubling
in medieval and Renaissance discourse, 88, 148, 149, 158, 164, 165
in theatre ontology, *see* theatrical performance
drama, 13, 16, 21, 57, 106, 107, 120, 131, 140, 152–3, 155–7, 170, 184, 186, 192
see also theatrical performance

eclecticism, 3–5, 10–11, 135, 199
economics, 1, 14, 15, 26, 43, 49–55, 58–60, 62, 67, 68, 103, 104, 106, 118, 123, 130, 172, 187, 190, 191, 194, 195, 201
see also modes of production, economic

education, 8, 52, 54, 62, 63, 70–3, 79, 130, 163, 203
Egginton, William, 146, 208
electronic media, 2, 7, 16–17, 51, 168, 183, 185
embodiment, 2, 12, 15, 28, 42, 48, 57, 94, 95–8, 100, 101, 104–6, 111, 115, 120, 139, 140, 147, 159, 169, 176, 186, 189–91, 193, 195, 197, 198, 209
emergence, *see* ontology
empiricism, 5, 16, 19, 21, 23, 85, 95–7, 112–13, 116–17, 123, 125, 131–3, 125, 171, 173, 179, 209, 210
see also positivism
Enlightenment, 16, 111–13
epistemes, 20–2, 107, 164
see also discursive strategies
epistemic fallacy, 23, 25, 160, 179, 199, 210
epistemology, 3, 25, 28, 29, 34, 40, 80, 103, 104, 110–11, 113, 120, 132, 168, 169, 171, 178, 196, 199, 203
error, 24–5, 31, 101, 198
see also fallibilism
ethics, 5, 11, 32–4, 92
Euripides, 64, 93, 169, 202
The Bacchae, 172
evidence, 5, 11, 20, 21, 25, 31, 54, 72, 73, 76, 79, 80, 86, 99, 111, 163
exemplary characters, 121–2, 130
explanatory analysis, 4–6, 13, 20, 22, 31, 34, 44–8, 54, 100, 148, 200
expressionism, 131, 138, 140

fallibilism, 5, 31, 32, 34, 101, 180, 197
Feast of Corpus Christi, 88, 92
fictions, 37, 66, 92, 108, 128, 153–5, 177, 188, 196
figural thinking, 69, 70, 77–84, 258, 178
see also allegory; similitudes; typology
figure and fulfillment, *see* typology
film, 57, 138, 184, 186–7, 192
flip sides, 99, 131, 137
Foucault, Michel, 4, 20–2, 107

Freud, Sigmund, 137

gender, 26, 50–1, 53–4, 67, 116–17, 136, 172, 190, 201, 210
generative mechanisms, 25, 26, 30, 41, 47, 67, 68, 77, 105, 120, 163
    see also causal powers; critical realism
genre, 16, 19, 99, 107–9, 131, 134, 138, 140, 141, 145, 173, 185, 189, 190
    see also styles
gesture, 16, 108, 110, 116, 118, 120, 121, 123–30, 171
The Glass Menagerie (Tennessee Williams), 26
Goffman, Erving, 13, 196, 210
Greece, 58–63, 67, 69, 93, 168, 173, 194, 201
    see also Athens
groups, see agents and agency; social groups
guilds, craft and mercantile, 45, 70, 71, 74, 82, 86, 89, 91, 92

Habermas, Jürgen, 119–20, 207
habit, 39, 46, 48, 127
habitus, 39, 46, 48, 105
Handke, Peter, 166, 176, 179
handwriting, 14, 51, 53, 57, 69, 114, 163
    see also manuscript culture
A Hatful of Rain (Michael V. Gazzo), 135–8, 191
Hauptmann, Gerhard, 131
hegemony, 47, 63, 106, 135
historiography, 1–4, 12–15, 19, 20, 23–4, 35, 49–51, 55, 90, 197
Homer, 60, 61, 65
Hubert, Judd, 145

Ibsen, Henrik, 131
    Peer Gynt, 175
icons (type of sign), 15, 20, 30, 35, 36, 38, 46, 47, 94, 97, 99, 105, 151, 157, 158, 160, 180, 191, 193
    see also image schemas; models; semiotics
idealism, 36, 87, 89, 178, 179, 194–7, 210

identity, 33, 46–8, 102–4, 133, 144, 175, 192–3
    see also self
ideology, 7, 9, 33, 46, 52, 54, 104, 106, 144, 171, 187, 195, 206, 209
illusionism, see naturalism; verisimilitude
image schemas, 15–16, 46, 47, 96–108, 110, 111, 113, 115, 117–20, 122, 127, 129–31, 134–40, 153, 163, 197, 208
    see also containment; embodiment; icons; path
images, 2, 7, 20, 29, 30, 37, 44–7, 63, 64, 66, 69, 76, 78–82, 87–9, 95–100, 102, 103, 105, 106, 111, 112, 125, 133, 136, 146, 148, 152, 153, 157, 158, 162, 167, 184, 185, 187, 204, 205, 208
imagined communities, see communities
imitation, 195–6
Incarnation, 88, 92
indexes (reference tool), 52, 114, 207
indexes (type of sign), 36, 38, 39, 43, 46, 47, 94, 94, 136, 151, 157, 158, 192, 193
    see also semiotics
individualism, 15, 19, 40, 47, 103, 104, 111, 116–17, 120, 132, 137, 138, 145, 146, 169, 172, 185–6
individuality, 65, 66, 90, 102, 103, 110, 132, 133, 138, 160, 169, 173
    see also interiority; self; subjectivity
individuals (persons), 14, 20, 29, 47–9, 134, 150, 151, 153, 167, 170, 173, 188, 208
    see also agents and agency
inner speech, 40, 46, 48, 79
instrumentalism, 4–6
intellectual labor, see mental and manual labor
intentionality, 26–9, 42–8, 50–2, 100, 101, 150, 165, 166, 176, 186, 188, 189, 208
    see also agents and agency; reasons as causes for action

interests, 9, 10, 43–6, 48, 52, 59, 150, 153
interiority, 65, 97, 101–3, 109, 119, 121, 125, 127, 128, 132, 133, 136–9, 169, 171, 173
　see also individuality; psychology; self; subjectivity
irrealism, 23, 135, 195–7

Johnson, Mark, 96–8, 100, 102, 139, 199
Jonson, Ben, 16, 147–9, 163–5, 196
　The Alchemist, 147
　Bartholomew Fair, 144, 147, 149, 165, 174, 196, 209
　Epicoene, 147, 149, 166
　The Staple of News, 149, 180
　Volpone, 147, 148
journalistic print culture, 109, 117, 119, 133, 134, 166, 169, 192
　see also journals; print and print culture
journals, 16, 119, 122, 124, 134
　see also journalistic print culture; periodicals
judgmental rationality, 32, 137
　see also critical realism

Kant, Immanuel, 24
knowledge, 8, 11, 13, 15, 16, 20–5, 29–32, 34, 38, 42, 60, 63, 67, 73, 93, 95, 97, 99, 100, 110–11, 113–15, 117, 120, 135, 139, 160, 164–6, 169, 173, 178–80, 184, 197, 198, 200, 210
　see also models
Kuhn, Thomas, 20, 22

Lakoff, George, 96–102, 136, 139, 199
Latin, 69, 71, 80
law, 15, 53, 54, 61, 62, 71–3, 78, 79, 85–8, 111, 163, 169, 204, 205
letters (alphabetic), 79, 114–15, 127–8, 130, 203
　~s (epistolary), 53, 72, 119–20, 124, ?6, 128
　　?2, 114

linearity, 16, 20, 21, 26, 65, 113–15, 120, 123, 127, 164
　see also textual space
linguistic fallacy, 160
　see also epistemic fallacy
literacy, 7–9, 14–15, 54, 57, 58, 60–73, 87, 168, 169, 183, 201–2, 203
　see also literate culture
literal meaning, 80, 86–9, 99, 148, 163, 176
literal viewing, 111, 123
literate culture, 44, 66, 68, 72, 81, 87, 91, 169
Locke, John, 35, 112–15, 117, 125, 127–30, 207
locus and *platea* staging, 75, 89–90, 205
　see also performance space
logic, 7–8, 10, 20, 22, 23, 26, 30, 31, 49, 77, 93, 97, 100, 105–7, 179
　see also reasoning
Lollards, 72, 73, 84, 205
Lutterbie, John, 12

manuscript culture, 14, 53, 65, 68, 70–3, 76, 80, 81, 91, 111, 114, 163, 164, 195
manuscripts, 8, 73–4, 76–7, 163
Marat/Sade (Peter Weiss), 177
Marx, Karl, 24, 55, 206
marxism, 1, 12, 40, 106
masks, 82, 89, 90, 169, 178
mass culture, 116, 118, 165, 187–8
materialism, 6, 54, 87, 194, 200, 210
materiality, 8–10, 26, 33–5, 43–52, 77, 79, 88, 93, 94, 96, 102, 106, 112, 125, 140, 150–1, 157, 179, 190, 194–7
McConachie, Bruce, 12, 106, 135–7, 139, 208
McLuhan, Marshall, 6
means of communication, *see* communication
media, 183–9
medieval culture, 15, 68–93, 103, 111, 112, 133, 134, 146, 148, 164, 171

melodrama, 47, 109, 133, 138, 144, 209
memory, 15, 63, 76, 77, 79–83, 111, 112, 169
mental and manual labor, 55, 73, 105, 177, 195, 197
merchants, 14, 15, 45, 58–60, 62, 67, 70, 73, 86, 108, 117, 164, 169
metadiscourse, 154–5, 157, 189, 193, 210
  see also theatrical performance
metaphors, 8, 9, 15, 87, 95–103, 105–7, 120, 128–31, 135, 139, 140, 189, 193
  see also analogy; image schemas; see also under specific metaphors and image schemas
metatheatricality, 16, 92, 143–9, 164–8, 170, 172–8, 193, 209
  see also plays-within-plays
mimesis, 16, 89, 148, 155, 159, 160
mirror neurons, 190, 208
models
  in knowledge, 5, 15, 20, 30, 35, 38, 96, 100, 204
  of knowledge (as similar to writing), 47, 79–80, 93, 104, 113, 115, 130
  see also icons; image schemas; writing metaphors and models
modes of communication, see communication
modes of production, economic, 51, 52, 54, 55
  see also economics
Mohanty, Satya P., 32, 199
moral claims, 32–3, 90, 100
moral types, 82–3, 88, 103, 125, 139, 157, 191
moral worth, 103, 109, 121, 133, 172
morality plays, 69, 91, 173
mystery cycles, 44, 69, 83, 86, 91, 92, 173

narrative, 64–5, 104, 153, 156, 202
naturalism (aesthetic approach), 70, 84, 90, 111, 131–2, 134–5, 138, 155–6, 158, 160, 176
  see also aesthetic realism; verisimilitude

newspapers, 96, 118, 120
  see also journalistic print culture; journals; periodicals
noh, 68
nominalism, 36, 80, 84–5
Norris, Christopher, 32

objectivism, 11, 19, 132
objectivity, 7, 9, 10, 20, 21, 23, 24, 32, 132–4
Ockham, William of, 84, 204
Ong, Walter J., 6, 113–14
ontic fallacy, 179
ontological shift, see theatrical performance
ontology, 3, 27, 34–5, 51, 103, 120, 146, 149, 155, 168, 171, 178, 186, 187
  domains, 27–8, 40–2
  emergence, 10, 13–14, 26–9, 34, 41–4, 47, 49, 52, 61, 68, 94, 96–7, 100, 106, 106, 111, 115, 138–9, 143, 152, 156, 162, 166, 171, 172, 179, 189, 193, 206, 208
  monovalence, 3, 23, 28, 34, 146, 160, 174, 176, 177, 188, 196
  in positivism and social constructionism, 20, 25, 34, 35, 132, 135, 173–4, 179, 180, 186, 188
  scientific vs philosophical, 27
  stratification in, 12, 13, 26–8, 34, 40, 42, 43, 45, 50, 106, 153, 156, 160, 177, 179, 188, 189, 196, 198
  see also causal powers; causality; criteria of reality; critical realism; generative mechanisms; social ontology; theatrical performance
oral communication and culture, 7–8, 14–15, 43, 46, 48, 52–4, 57, 60–8, 71–82, 87, 89–91, 111–14, 116–17, 119, 128, 133, 160, 163, 166, 168–9, 180, 183, 184, 194, 195, 202–3, 204

pageants, 44–5, 74–5, 89
  see also York Corpus Christi Cycle

paideia, 60, 67
paradigms, 20–2, 30, 32, 49, 114, 120, 135, 152
  see also models
path (image schema), 96–7, 99, 113, 137
Peirce, Charles S., *see* semiotics
perception, 3, 5, 13, 14, 21, 23, 25, 29–30, 34, 35, 37–9, 97, 99, 100, 120, 135, 137, 144, 175, 177–9, 188
performance, generalized idea of, 2, 7, 12, 13, 17, 68, 151, 153, 154, 158–9, 162, 166–7, 184–5
performance art, 188
performance space, 44, 75–6, 89–90, 107, 108, 129–30, 136–7, 146, 153, 157, 171, 190–1
  see also stage/audience relationship
performance strategies, 2, 15–16, 46, 47, 51–3, 57, 75, 77, 90, 91, 93, 94, 104, 105, 107–10, 118, 120, 122, 123, 125, 130, 131, 137–41, 143, 144, 146, 148, 149, 158, 165, 168, 176–80, 196–7, 206
performatives (speech acts), 73, 151, 154, 159–62, 176, 208
performativity, 158–60, 167
periodicals, 15–16, 96, 109, 116, 118–23, 130
  see also journalistic print culture; journals; newspapers
permeation of a mode of communication, *see* communication
personifications, 69, 81, 111, 133
  see also allegorical characters
perspective (artistic device), 108, 123, 137
perspective switches, 28, 99, 131, 134, 138, 140
Peters, Julie Stone, 2–6
phenomenology, 39, 44–6
philosophy of science, 19, 20, 24
  see also critical realism; positivism; science; social constructionism
onocentrism, 8, 145–6, 194
  ⟨ra⟩tratus, 58–60, 67
  ⟨a⟩nd platonism, 77, 84, 89, 145, ⟨19⟩6–7, 200

plays-within-plays, 144–6, 149, 165, 167–78, 180, 196
  see also metatheatricality
plot, 65–7, 104, 129, 144, 156
politics, 9, 22, 32–5, 58–60, 62, 66–7, 85, 86, 106, 135, 172, 187
positivism, 1, 5, 13, 19–21, 23–6, 31, 32, 34–5, 50, 96, 132–5, 158, 175, 186, 199, 200, 209
  see also empiricism
postmodernism, 20, 23, 32, 33, 94, 175, 180, 183, 186
post-structuralism, 3, 36–7, 158
power, sociopolitical, 1, 5, 8–9, 12, 21–3, 33, 46–9, 52, 54, 55, 58–60, 70, 85, 166
print and print culture, 2, 3, 6, 10, 16, 52, 63, 72, 104, 109–18, 120, 122, 123, 129, 130, 132–5, 137–8, 147, 163–5, 168, 171, 183, 209
  see also journalistic print culture
print capitalism, 143, 164, 169, 173
projection (advisory and empathic), 102, 136–9, 191–2, 208
prophecy, 80, 85–6, 89, 91
Protestants, 163
psychological realism, 134, 135, 138
psychology, 15, 16, 40, 48, 84, 90, 96, 103, 104, 109, 110, 117, 121, 134, 137–8, 146, 173, 191
  see also interiority; self
public and private spheres, 16, 116, 119, 124, 130, 134, 161, 170–2
puppetry, 155, 188

rationality, *see* reason
realism (philosophy), 24
  embodied, 24, 97
  medieval, 84, 89, 134
  platonic, 84, 196
  postpositivist, 24, 32
  see also critical realism; irrealism; ontology
reason, 7–9, 10, 32, 133, 170–1
reasoning, 8–10, 73–4, 97–100

reasons as causes for action, 26, 28, 29, 41, 44–5, 50, 167
  see also intentionality
reception, 52, 76, 104, 159
  see also communication
recording media, 184–8
reflexivity, 16, 28, 29, 99, 101, 104, 138, 145, 148, 150, 154, 160–3, 165, 167–8, 171–2, 176, 177–9, 186, 193, 199
The Rehearsal (George Villiers, Duke of Buckingham), 169, 209
relative autonomy, 27, 54, 106
relativism, 5, 8, 9, 11, 20, 23, 32, 132, 133, 179, 191, 197
  see also social constructionism
religion, 14, 58, 59, 66, 70, 72–4, 79, 82, 84, 85, 87, 168, 169, 173, 178, 194
rhapsodic performance, 60, 62, 64
ritual, 14, 57–9, 66, 68, 79–81, 86–7, 89, 153, 159, 168–9, 172–3, 201, 204, 209
roleplay games, 188
Romanticism and Romantics, 131–3, 138, 179, 194
royal entries, 85, 148
Rozik, Eli, 12, 160

Sanskrit theatre, 68
Saussure, Ferdinand de, *see* semiology
Schechner, Richard, 158
schools, *see* education
science, 20–2, 24, 31–3, 95, 132, 179, 200
scribes, 61, 62, 72, 195
script, dramatic, 57, 75, 76, 108, 149, 152–4, 157, 177, 184–6, 193, 210
  see also theatrical performance
scriptive level, *see* theatrical performance
scripts (forms of writing), 61–2, 202
  see also alphabet
Scriptures, 73, 75, 80, 82, 86, 87, 91, 194
seating, *see* performance space

self
  concepts of, 15, 16, 47, 100, 101, 103, 104, 109, 125, 130, 136, 138, 160, 167, 191, 192
  performance of, 116, 144, 146, 167, 173
  sense of, 101–2, 104, 137, 191
  as sign, 40, 104
  see also agents and agency; identity; individuality; interiority; psychology; reflexivity
semiology, Saussure's theory of, 6, 35–40, 42, 55, 112–13, 123, 145, 146, 207
semiosis, 12, 14, 41, 43, 46–8, 51, 52, 93–4, 160, 175
semiotic chain, 77–80, 82, 112
semiotics, Peirce's theory of, 14, 15, 36–41, 55, 97, 104, 127, 136, 151, 152, 157–8, 180, 193, 200
  interpretant, 37–9, 41, 52, 127, 151, 152
  object, 36–9, 41
  representamen, 37–8, 46
  see also icons; indexes (type of sign); symbols
sentimental response and sentimental drama, 15, 16, 108–10, 118, 120–2, 125, 128–31, 133, 138, 172
Shakespeare, William, 122, 148, 168
  Hamlet, 144, 149, 166, 174, 180
  King Lear, 148
  A Midsummer Night's Dream, 171
Shelley, Percy Bysshe, 55
signs, *see* icons; indexes (type of sign); semiology; semiotics; symbols
silent reading, 8, 73, 76–9, 104, 116, 118–20, 171, 203
similitudes, 15, 21, 68–70, 80–1, 83, 85, 89–90, 92–3, 134, 148, 164, 171, 173, 178
  see also allegory; figural thinking; typology
Six Characters in Search of an Author (Luigi Pirandello), 168, 175
skepticism, 11, 25, 31

social constructionism, 1, 6, 8–11, 13, 19–25, 29, 31–5, 38, 50, 52, 160, 196–7
  see also relativism
social groups, 20, 21, 50, 53, 71, 102, 105, 150
  see also agents and agency
social ontology, 14, 41–50, 54, 55, 102–3, 141, 149–51, 153–62, 180, 186–8, 190–1, 193, 196, 198
  structures/agents/discourses model, 14, 44–51, 55, 94, 102–3, 130, 141, 149–51, 153–8, 162, 166, 167, 176–8, 186, 189–93, 198
  see also agents and agency; critical realism; discourses; social structures
social relations, 9, 10, 45–7, 50–5, 71, 77, 85, 87, 102, 103, 108, 140, 149, 150, 153, 155, 157, 159–62, 164, 165, 172, 192
  see also social ontology; social structures
social relations of communication, see communication
social structures, 14, 25, 41–6, 48–51, 54, 58, 62, 70, 93, 106–7, 130, 139–40, 146, 149–51, 156–7, 161, 172, 190, 192
  see also agents; discourses; social ontology
Solon, 58, 62
Sophocles, 65, 202
  Oedipus Tyrannos, 65, 169
space of social performance, 115–16, 119, 122, 124, 127, 129, 133, 134, 170, 171
spatialization, see textual space
The Spectator, 16, 96, 109–10, 118–21, 124–5, 171, 207
spectators, see audiences and audience experience
speech, see oral communication and culture
 ch acts, see performatives
  see performance space

stage/audience relationship, 45, 107, 129–30, 155–7, 190
  see also theatrical performance
stage settings, 15, 123, 136
Steele, Richard, 16, 96, 108–10, 116, 121–4, 126–31, 171
  The Conscious Lovers, 16, 96, 109, 120–30
stratification, see ontology
Strindberg, August, 131
structural level of society, see social structures
structures/agents/discourses, see social ontology
structures, social, see social structures
styles, 1, 5, 22, 70, 93, 94, 107, 131, 138, 140, 141, 143, 146, 166
  see also genre
subjectivity, 10, 13, 20, 23, 27, 40, 41, 47, 99, 103, 104, 132, 137–9, 157, 174, 179, 210
  see also identity; individuality; interiority; psychology; self
subtexts, 127–9
symbolism, 45, 68, 73, 76–83, 86, 88, 90, 92, 111, 112, 123, 125, 134, 148, 204
symbolist drama, 131–4, 138, 140
symbols (type of sign), 36, 38–9, 46–7, 97, 151, 157–9, 193
  see also semiotics

The Tatler, 16, 109–10, 118–20, 207
technological determinism, 3, 6–9, 11, 51, 57, 114, 184
technology, 7–10, 15–16, 21, 32, 52, 96, 114, 117–18, 184–5, 187
television, 3, 7, 54, 57, 138, 184, 208
testimony, 54, 79
textual memory, 80–1
textual space, 113–15, 123, 127, 130, 133, 134
textuality, 79–82, 93, 111, 116, 128–30, 133, 163, 171, 208
  see also textual space; writing metaphors and models

theatre space, *see* performance space
theatrical performance
   doubling of social ontology, 66, 154–8, 161, 162, 177, 178, 186, 187, 190, 193, 196
   as a model of society and agency, 16, 139, 155, 156, 158, 161, 167, 168, 176, 180, 186
   ontological shift, 154–5, 162, 167, 178, 193
   as social reflexivity, 160–3, 167, 172, 193
   theatre/drama/script ontology, 152–62, 167, 174–8, 180, 186, 188, 193
   see also metatheatricality; social ontology; stage/audience relationship; virtual agents
Thespis, 58, 59, 62, 67
thought, 2, 6, 7, 15, 21, 51, 63, 95–9, 111, 113, 115, 117, 130, 164, 171, 189
   see also cognition
Three Sisters (Anton Chekhov), 156
time, concepts of, 65, 85, 88–9, 96, 127, 134, 202
totalities, 28–9, 41, 53, 68, 93, 101, 105, 106, 162, 189
tragedy (Greek), 14, 57–68, 169, 201, 203
tragic chorus, 59, 65–6, 68, 168–9, 202
tragoidia, 59, 62, 67–8
truth, 5, 9, 11, 21, 32–3, 35, 79, 81, 86, 111, 122, 132, 138, 164–5, 178, 180, 184, 196, 198, 205, 210
Turner, Victor, 192
typology, 69, 75, 80, 83, 85, 86, 88, 148

utilization of a mode of communication, *see* communication

validation (aspect of communication), 79–80, 86, 111, 129, 164, 165
   see also communication
Veltrusky, Jiří, 152
verisimilitude, 16, 84, 96, 111, 123, 132, 147, 156, 160, 173, 178, 180

   see also aesthetic realism; naturalism
virtual agents, 40, 153–8, 161, 162, 167, 172, 177, 186–9, 192, 193, 196, 208
   see also characters and characterization
visuality, 63, 76, 111, 113, 120, 123–4, 128, 130
Voloshinov, V. N., 40, 43, 200

Wilde, Oscar, 190, 197
Wilshire, Bruce, 160, 210
Wittgenstein, Ludwig, 131
Worthen, William B., 6–7
writing, *see* alphabet; communication; handwriting; literacy; manuscript culture; manuscripts; print; print culture; scripts; silent reading; textuality; visuality
writing metaphors and models
   handwriting or printing, 113, 120, 207
   letters (alphabetic), 114–15, 127
   text, 47, 53, 69, 79–80, 93–4, 120, 127–30, 160
   see also blank paper metaphor; Book of Nature; models

York (city), 15, 44, 70–2, 74, 83–6, 205
York Corpus Christi Cycle, 15, 44–5, 69, 70, 74–7, 80–8, 90, 148, 178, 191, 204, 205
   Abraham, 69, 83
   The Building of the Ark, 77–8, 82
   The Entry into Jerusalem, 80, 83, 86, 88, 148
   The Expulsion, 82
   The Last Supper, 82
   Noah's Flood, 77, 83
   The Supper at Emmaus, 91–2
   Trial plays, 74, 85, 88, 205
York Realist, 69, 74, 84–5

Zola, Émile, 131–2

GPSR Compliance
The European Union's (EU) General Product Safety Regulation (GPSR) is a set of rules that requires consumer products to be safe and our obligations to ensure this.

If you have any concerns about our products, you can contact us on

ProductSafety@springernature.com

In case Publisher is established outside the EU, the EU authorized representative is:

Springer Nature Customer Service Center GmbH
Europaplatz 3
69115 Heidelberg, Germany

www.ingramcontent.com/pod-product-compliance
Lightning Source LLC
LaVergne TN
LVHW041955060526
838200LV00002B/19